FORD
POLICE CARS

1932-1997

Edwin J. Sanow

Motorbooks International
Publishers & Wholesalers ®

Dedication
This book is dedicated to Cindy Jo, my wife and best friend.

First published in 1997 by Motorbooks International Publishers & Wholesalers, 729 Prospect Avenue, PO Box 1, Osceola, WI 54020 USA

Motorbooks International books are also available at discounts in bulk quantity for industrial or sales-promotional use. For details write to Special Sales Manager at the Publisher's address

Library of Congress Cataloging-in-Publication Data

Sanow, Edwin J.
    Ford police cars, 1932-1997 / Edwin J. Sanow.
        p. cm.
    Includes index.
    ISBN 0-7603-0372-X (paperback : alk. paper)
    1. Police vehicles--History. 2. Police vehicles--History--Pictorial works. 3. Ford automobile--History. 4. Ford automobile--History--Pictorial works.
    HV7936.V4S362   1997
    629.2'088'3632--dc21   97-15953

On the front cover: This 1985 CHP Ford Mustang has a 302ci HO V-8 engine. It is owned by John Bujosa of Spokane, Washington. Bujosa is the president of Emergency Vehicle Owners and Operators Association.—*Greg Field*

On the back cover: In 1931, the Michigan State Police used the 4-cylinder Model A (left). By 1936 they patrolled in V-8 powered Tudor sedans (right).—*Michigan State Police*
Bottom: For the first time in many decades, the Michigan State Police selected this 1997 Crown Vic as their patrol vehicle. Note the traditional hood mounted STOP sign. —*Matt Campbell*

Printed in the United States of America

CONTENTS

Acknowledgments

This book on Ford and Mercury police cars covers everything from the 1930 CHP Ford, to the 1958 NYPD 361-ci Custom, to the 1969 Indiana State Police 428-ci Mercury Monterey, to the 1982 CHP 5.0L Mustang, to the 1997 Michigan State Police 4.6L SOHC Crown Victoria. A book that spans this much history is made possible only by the help of hundreds of police car enthusiasts on both sides of the badge. They contributed police car photos, flyers, magazine articles, owners manuals, shop manuals, official testing results, original police car sales literature, and experiences with Ford police cars.

Thank you one and all for the time and effort that went into making this book the complete and accurate history of Ford and Mercury police cars. A list of contributors, both police departments and individuals, is in the appendix. We sincerely hope no one has been overlooked. Some enthusiasts went above and beyond the call of duty to Ford police cars. We would like to give them special thanks here for their efforts and for their support of the police car–collecting hobby.

Special thanks goes to Bob Bondurant, world-famous race car driver, police pursuit driving instructor, and Ford Motor Company spokesman. Bondurant runs the Bob Bondurant School of High Performance Driving in Phoenix, Arizona, and, in fact, taught the author in the first police pursuit instructor's class at Firebird Raceway. Bondurant took time from his busy training and speaking schedule to write the foreword.

Special thanks goes to the two guest authors, Bill Hattersley for his coverage of the Washington State Patrol and Matt Campbell for his review of all the Special Service package Mustangs. Police departments in the South, such as the Georgia State Patrol, South Carolina Highway Patrol, North Carolina Highway Patrol, Florida Highway Patrol, and Alabama Highway Patrol are typically considered as Ford strongholds. As it turned out, the state police in Bill Hattersley's home state, the Washington State Patrol, have actually been Ford's most loyal major police agency. Matt Campbell was likewise close to home in his coverage of the 1982 to 1993 Mustangs. He has owned a 1990 Missouri State Highway Patrol Mustang and has made the police car show circuit with the fully marked Mustang.

Special thanks goes to five police car photo collectors who shared their huge collections with all of us. Menlo Park, California, Police Communications Officer Darryl Lindsay is the West Coast representative for the Police Car Owners of America (PCOOA). Lindsay is the host of the annual Ripon, California, police car show that rivals the PCOOA Nationals. Lindsay also provided half the original police car literature, by year, for this book. Sparta, Illinois, Police Officer Dave Dotson is the Midwest representative for the Emergency Vehicle Owners and Operators Association (EVOOA). Dotson was the host of the first PCOOA Nationals in Sparta, Illinois, and the host of the first EVOOA Nationals in St. Louis, Missouri. Chicago Police Officer Greg Reynolds is extremely active in the Chicago area promoting the police car hobby by everything from parades to Blues Brothers re-enactments. Agent Ned Schwartz gives a New England perspective to the book. His photos of New York police cars balances the coverage from the West Coast and Midwest. Bill Hattersley is a writer and professional photographer. The quality of his photos shows it!

Each of these photo collections number in the thousands, and photo swapping among enthusiasts is quite informal. As a result, the identity of the original photographer is sometimes lost or mixed. The photo credits in this book indicate the photo came from the "collection" of the contributor. However, the work of two other photographers is known to be a part of these collections. With this in mind, a special thanks for uncredited photos goes to Glenn Sokolofsky and Jay Weinstein.

Special thanks goes to Bob Johnson and D. J. Smith. Both are Ford employees and both own collectible cars. Both are members of the PCOOA. In fact, Johnson is the Michigan state representative and the hard-working host of the sixth annual PCOOA National Convention, which included tours of the Henry Ford Museum in Dearborn and the St. Thomas, Ontario, assembly plant where Crown Vics are built. Bob Johnson provided technical information on the Ford-Edsel series of big-blocks. D. J. Smith provided technical information to make sense of the 351 Cleveland, 351 Windsor, 400 Cleveland, and 351 Modified engines used in the 1970s. Smith also provided the other half of the original factory police literature, by year, used in this book.

Special thanks goes to John Bellah, a corporal with the California State University, Long Beach, Police where he serves as an investigator. Bellah provided both information and contacts for our joint efforts, *Dodge, Plymouth & Chrysler Police Car, 1956–1978* and *Dodge, Plymouth & Chrysler Police Cars, 1979–1994*. That support carried over to this book on Ford and Mercury police cars.

Special thanks goes to Donna Rogers and Tricia Walsh-McGlone, editors at *Law Enforcement Technology*, and Bruce Cameron, editorial director at *Law and Order*. Rogers allowed me to start formal coverage of the influential Michigan State Police vehicle tests, arranged for me to attend Bill Scott's exclusive Tactical Driving School at Summit Point, West Virginia, and arranged for me to be the first to test the exciting new 1992-1/2 4.6L Crown Vic on Ford's Proving Ground. Cameron assigned me to cover the Los Angeles County Sheriff vehicle tests and arranged for me to attend Bob Bondurant's famous School of High Performance Driving, which is absolute Ford heaven.

Special thanks goes to Sheriff B. L. "Butch" Pritchett of the Benton County, Indiana, Sheriff's Office. He has given me the authority to act on behalf of his office in areas where law enforcement connections were absolutely necessary. Pritchett has actively supported my writing over the past 15 years. Under his colors, I have tested every police package vehicle in the recent past including the very last of the Special Service package Mustangs.

Special thanks goes to Indiana State Police Sergeant Jerry Parker, Iowa State Patrol Trooper Robert Parks, and Missouri State Highway Patrol Captain Clarence Greeno. These men provided a large number of photos, both from private collections and departmental archives, showing police cars from the agencies with whom they proudly serve.

Special thanks goes to Chris Watson who owns a 1970 CHP Mercury Monterey. The 1970 Monterey was the first Ford or Mercury Enforcement-Class vehicle used by the California Highway Patrol since the early 1950s. Watson provided CHP archive photos and a complete CHP motor pool log of the 428-ci pursuit car.

Special thanks goes to Cindy Sanow, who served as typist, editor, proofreader, photographer, and travel planner. Even though she was raised in a family of Chrysler enthusiasts, the motivation to cover Ford and Mercury police cars came from her. Cindy, thanks again and again.

Foreword

By Bob Bondurant, Owner,

Bob Bondurant School of High Performance Driving

My experience with the police vehicles designed and built by Ford Motor Company began in 1983. My driving school had entered into a sponsorship relationship with Ford and I was glad to see police cars integrated into my fleet. Ford has always felt that "Quality is Job #1," and this shows throughout the product line. Ford's police vehicles are no exception.

For many years I have witnessed various aspects of police work; the most important aspect, from my point of view, is driving. Because police officers spend most of their time in their police vehicles, the driving techniques they possess are of vital importance to their safety and well-being.

During the 1980s, the Bondurant School was chosen to train all of the hired police cadets from both Santa Rosa Valley and Napa Valley, California, Police Departments. My instructors taught a one-day police course that covered the following areas: brief ground school; slalom course; accident avoidance simulator; handling oval; skid car (understeer with front wheel slides, oversteer with rear wheel slides); forward and reverse 180s and 360s; precision maneuvers course in both drive and reverse gears; stress test through the precision maneuvers course with distractions including windshield wipers going and both the radio and sirens blaring; chase scenarios around the handling oval, driven in both clockwise and counter-clockwise directions (officers in pursuits of my driving instructors).

This police course was invaluable to both of these police departments. We gave their "rookies" the opportunity to role-play in many scenarios that they would eventually encounter while on patrol. I feel that these officers gained valuable insights into the high performance techniques associated with driving. Police officers who understand the logic behind weight transfer, threshold braking, panic stops, and proper corning techniques and are able to perform these techniques have saved numerous lives over the years, many of which have been their fellow police officers.

Practice makes perfect. This applies to everyone, but especially to police officers. When an officer is assigned to a particular vehicle, he or she should find a large empty parking lot to test out the limitations of that vehicle. How far does it take to stop the vehicle at varying speeds? What is the acceleration rate of the vehicle? How does the vehicle handle and turn corners at varying speeds? Each officer should understand and remember these limitations, especially in pressure situations. The first concern and bottom line should always be safety.

Through my hands-on experience with Ford police vehicles, I have learned that these cars are built with quality and can withstand an extreme amount of wear and tear. For the past 14 years, I have had Ford police cars as an integral part of my fleet. We run these vehicles hard, day in and day out. When I say hard, I mean above and beyond the call of duty. We have put our police cars through every type of situation that you can imagine. I stand behind these vehicles because they are proven safe, and when driven correctly will "help catch the bad guys."

For the past 30 years, the Bondurant School has trained and graduated over 65,000 students, including housewives, racers, celebrities, teenagers, professionals, and police officers. These graduates continue to apply the car control techniques learned here in their everyday driving. Weekly, we receive phone calls and letters that credit our instruction with helping to prevent potentially fatal accidents. The roadways on which we drive are no longer friendly. Each individual must learn additional driving techniques in order to avoid accidents. People want to feel safe and in control of their vehicles and my school helps them to achieve this confidence.

I am honored to have been asked by Edwin Sanow to write the foreword for this book. The information contained herein is invaluable.

I wish all of you safe journeys on the roadways.

All the best!

—Bob Bondurant

Introduction

Police officers have been driving Fords as long as there have been Fords. Ford, along with Chevrolet and Plymouth, made up the Low-Priced Three. For years, cops did not really have a strong preference among the three makes. All that changed in 1932 with the release of Ford's flathead V-8. Ford would be the only low-priced car with a V-8 for more than two decades. As a result, Ford absolutely dominated the police market in the 1930s, 1940s, and 1950s.

In the late 1940s, Ford became the first automaker to develop a special combination of parts specifically designed for the severe duty associated with police work. They were the first to put all these parts together in one ordering package called the police package. The police package was also developed by Chevrolet and Plymouth in the mid-1950s. Chevrolet and Plymouth also released V-8 engines in the mid-1950s, but it was too late. The Ford flathead V-8, then the Ford police package, extended the Ford police car dominance well into the 1960s. In fact, Ford was America's Number One Police Car from 1932 until 1969, when Plymouth wrested the title away.

In the 1950s and 1960s, Ford did not produce a 3,800-pound, 122-inch wheelbase police car. This disqualified them from bidding on the prestigious state contracts, like the California Highway Patrol. Mercury did have such a car, but was underbid by Dodge every year except 1970. While Ford was not the number one choice of high-profile state police and highway patrol agencies in the 1950s and 1960s, they were the number one choice of cities and counties from coast to coast. Dodge got the glory, but Ford got the sales volume.

In the 1960s and 1970s, the technology of Ford police cars kept pace with that from Chevrolet and Plymouth. Ford and Mercury police engines were not the most powerful, but they always got the job done. Ford was not the first one out with front disc brakes. That was Dodge. However, they were the first one out with four-wheel discs. No, not the 1992 Crown Vic, but the 1976 LTD.

Ford was a pioneer in the use of a four-speed automatic overdrive transmission with its 1980 California police cars. Ford was not the first with a front-drive police car. That was the Mopar K-car. However, they were the first out with a widely accepted, high-performance, front-drive police car, the 1990 Taurus. Of course, Ford was the first automaker to use an overhead-cam engine in a full-size police car, the 1992-1/2 Crown Vic.

Starting in the late 1970s, and with the exception of some state police contracts captured by Mercury, Ford and Chevrolet were distant competitors to Dodge and Plymouth. Nothing, it seemed, ran like a 440-ci V-8 Mopar. Then the "Great Downsizing" of the mid- to late 1970s obsoleted all the long wheelbase cars and all the big-block V-8s. All of the automakers were forced to start over in the police car market. Fuel economy, exhaust emissions, and midsize cars were the top concerns.

From this era of extremely poor police car performance came Ford's most influential police car, the 1982 5.0L HO Mustang. Close behind was the whip-quick 1984 fuel-injected 302-ci HO midsize LTD, also built on the Mustang's Fox-platform. These were clearly the fastest police cars on the road at a time when no full-size police sedan of any make could even reach 120 miles per hour. The Special Service package Mustang literally changed forever the concept of a police pursuit car.

The 1980s were a period of transition. The full-size Crown Victoria held its own as the Dodge Diplomat and Plymouth Gran Fury slowly lost dominance and the Chevrolet Caprice slowly gained it. The Diplomat and Gran Fury were dropped after 1989, and the Caprice was at its peak only to be dropped after 1996. This leaves us where we were 65 years ago: Ford, with no real competition.

Welcome to the complete account of Ford and Mercury police cars. You will find that nearly all the great Ford engines were, at one time or another, police car engines: the flathead V-8, the 312-ci V-8, the 390-ci and 428-ci Ford-Edsel block, the 289-ci and 302-ci small-block, the 351-ci Windsor and 351-ci Cleveland, the 429-ci and 460-ci 385-series big-block and, of course, the 4.6L SOHC "modular" V-8. We have included the history of the Special Service package Mustang from the 1979 CHP Special Purpose Vehicle Study to the last police Mustang in 1993. We have experiences from Ford's most loyal major police department, the Washington State Patrol. Pay attention. The book closes with a Ford cop car quiz!

Chapter One

1932-1949

The Flathead V-8 Years

"If it's cylinders they want, we'll give them cylinders." That was Henry Ford's famous response to the 1929 announcement of the Chevrolet Six. The result was one of the most famous engines in automotive history, the Ford flathead V-8.

Henry Ford founded the Ford Motor Company on June 16, 1903. Ford's first production automobile was the 1903 Model A. (Another, more famous, Model A would be introduced in 1928.) The 1903 Model A was powered by a 100-ci, two-cylinder engine that produced 8 horsepower. It had a two-speed planetary transmission with a chain drive delivering power to the differential. The 1,250-pound two-seater had a top speed of 30 miles per hour.

By 1904, Ford was producing a four-cylinder–powered Model B. The 24-horsepower, 318-ci In-line Four pushed the Model B to speeds of 40 miles per hour.

In 1906, Ford's Model K got a 405-ci In-line Six that cranked out 40 horsepower. Top speeds reached 60 miles per hour.

In 1908, Ford moved his car building efforts from Detroit to Highland Park, Michigan. It was here that Ford introduced the moving assembly line for which he is legendary. Ford continued to produce the Model K, N, R, and S until the Model T was introduced in October 1908.

The 1909 Model T was powered by a 177-ci, In-line Four rated at 22 horsepower. It had a removable L-head cylinderhead, which was quite novel for its time. The compression ratio was 4.5:1.

The Model T continued to be improved each year. While the In-line Four was greatly improved in terms of durability, the displacement remained at 177-ci and the horsepower never exceeded 22.5 horsepower. The Model T production ended in May 1927. Roughly 15 million Model Ts were produced.

In December 1927, Ford introduced his second Model A. The 1928 Model A was much more complex than the Model T and had many technical advances. The 200-ci, L-head In-line Four used a water pump instead of a thermo-syphon. The new engine still only had a 4.2:1 compression ratio, but it used a 2-bbl Holley carburetor.

This was good for 40 horsepower and top speeds of 65 miles per hour. The Model T's planetary transmission was replaced with a three-speed sliding gear unit. The Model A had four-wheel mechanical brakes and double-action hydraulic shocks.

Up to this point, archrival Chevrolet had been using an overhead-valve (OHV), 171-ci In-line Four rated at 35 horsepower. In 1929, however, Chevrolet introduced its soon-to-be-famous "Stovebolt Six." This was an overhead-valve, 194-ci In-line, six-cylinder with a 5:1 compression and 46 horsepower. Chevrolet lured potential Ford customers with an advertising campaign that bragged, "A Six for the Price of a Four."

Since the horseless carriage, the Ford has been used as a police car. However, up to the late 1920s, the police did not have a clear and strong preference for the make of police car. A wide variety of marques were used. Due to the lower price, most police cars were retail versions of either the Ford or the Chevrolet. In 1924, for example, Ford outsold Chevrolet by more than eight to one. In 1928, the Plymouth was introduced as an entry level car line. For the next four

This 1922 Ford Model T was used by the West Virginia State Police. It was powered by a 177-ci flathead Four with a 4:1 compression ratio and 20-horsepower. *A. W. Robinson*

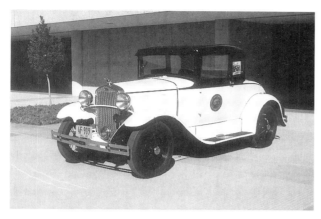

A 1930 California Highway Patrol Ford Model A. Its 200-ci Four produced 40 horsepower. Note the single red light bolted to the bumper. *Darryl Lindsay*

decades, these three—Ford, Chevrolet and Plymouth—were known as the Low-Priced Three.

Contrary to popular belief, the release of the Chevy Six in 1929 did not drive Henry Ford to develop his V-8. He began the V-8 design work in 1928. Ford wanted a V-8 engine that the typical Ford buyer could afford. Cadillac had been building V-8s since 1914. Other expensive cars at the time had V-12 and V-16 engines; however, none of these were affordable.

In 1928, Ford engineers Ray Laird, Ray Ensinger, Carl Schultz, and Don Sullivan began their top secret work on the flathead V-8 in a secluded lab at Greenfield Village in Dearborn. Most V-8s at the time had a two-piece engine block and crankcase. Henry Ford wanted a one-piece engine block. The casting and machining of a one-piece V-8 block became one of the toughest engineering and production challenges ever to be faced by Ford Motor Company.

Henry Ford also had some other ideas about the new V-8 that hampered the design. He wanted to use the old thermo-syphon cooling system used on the Model T engine, instead of the water pump used on the Model A engine. The engineers tried this but the V-8 simply produced too much heat. The flathead V-8, in fact, ended up with two water pumps: one per bank. Ford also wanted to avoid the use of an oil pump like the Chevy Stovebolt Six. This didn't work either.

One of the early working prototypes of the flathead V-8 displaced 299-ci. This was a shoe-horn fit into the Model A. Since Ford wanted the same car to have either a Four or a V-8, Ford engineers had to shrink the flathead by 3 inches. They reduced the bore diameter and bore spacing to result in a totally new engine.

All of the V-8 engine testing was done in Model A cars on the road. No testing took place on engine dynamometers for fear of being seen by people outside the core groups. Henry Ford's hallmark was extreme secrecy. The Ford-style of product development was a small team of people working in seclusion under relatively

In 1931, the Michigan State Police used the four-cylinder Model A, left. By 1936, right, they patrolled in V-8-powered Tudor sedans. *MSHP*

"If it's cylinders they want, we'll give them cylinders," were the immortal words of Henry Ford. The result was this flathead V-8 in 1932. Note the cooling hoses for each bank of cylinders. This is a 1937 engine.

Spartan conditions and under the direct, close, personal supervision of Henry Ford himself. The Model A with the 65 horsepower, 221-ci flathead V-8 was very fast for the time and for the price range. With 4.33 rear gears, these cars hit speeds of 85 miles per hour.

The first V-8-powered Model 18 rolled off the River Rouge assembly line on March 9, 1932. The L-head V-8 powered cars hit the showrooms on March 31, 1932, amid much fanfare and media hype. The use of a V-8 was not new; however, a V-8 at Ford prices was an automotive milestone.

Ford made automotive history with mass production of a low-priced, one-piece, 90-degree V-8 engine block. Ford could now answer Chevrolet with a V-8 for the price of a Six. The Ford V-8 had 25 more horsepower than the Model A four-cylinder. It also had 5 horsepower more than Chevrolet's best engine. At

$460, the Ford with a V-8 was $35 less than a Chevy with a Six.

The Ford L-head V-8 got the name "flathead" because the cylinder heads appeared to be flat slabs of cast iron. Instead of the overhead-valve design, which requires a valve cover on top of the head, the flathead V-8 has its valves in the block, alongside the cylinders. Overhead-cam engines have both the camshaft and valves in the head. On the Ford V-8, the cam was in the block and activated the valves via tappets. The flathead V-8 cylinder heads contained only the intake and exhaust ports, combustion chamber, and water passages.

The new Ford V-8 used a Ford-designed Detroit-Lubricator 1-bbl carb, had a compression ratio of 5.5:1 and used aluminum pistons. The 221-ci engine produced 65 horsepower.

History has recorded that the flathead V-8 was put into production too hastily. It was underdeveloped from an engineering viewpoint and the one-piece engine block was much too complex for existing casting processes. The result was piston failures, bearing failures, ignition coil breakdowns, block cracking, and overheating. Changes in production took place as often as daily to solve these issues.

With its valve-in-block design and a one-piece block crankcase, the new V-8 was a nightmare to cast. The block involved many sand cores and these would shift during the casting process. The scrap rate was as high as 50 percent. The biggest problem was that the exhaust ports were designed to go through the water jackets of the block. These were loose cores and it took Ford production engineers quite a while to develop fixtures to hold these cores in place. That solved the problem.

The early flathead V-8 also used a lot of oil, which eventually led to piston failures. The rod and crank bearings could not take the pounding of the V-8.

This Ford V-8 may have been the only engine in history where the motoring public filled the role as proving

An 1937 Oklahoma Highway Patrol Ford. This was the year Ford released a smaller V-8 to compete with the Chevy Six. The Fords used by the cops had the bigger 85-horsepower V-8.

This beautiful 1938 Ford Fordor bears the markings of the Huntington County, Indiana, Sheriff's Department. It is powered by a 221-ci V-8. *Sheriff Rod Jackson*

The Florida Highway Patrol has always been a Ford stronghold. Here's a 1940 Tudor with an 85-horsepower flathead V-8. *Greg Reynolds*

Check out the combination siren and red light on this 1942 Ohio State Highway Patrol Ford Tudor. For 1942, the flathead V-8 was rated at 96 horsepower. *John Yeaw*

ground drivers. Incredibly, customers put up with the breakdowns and the overheating long enough for Ford to fix the problem. And they did eventually get all the bugs worked out. In the meantime, Ford gave its dealers pistons for free and reimbursed them for the labor to install the pistons.

The Ford V-8 had an immediate and profound effect on law enforcement. Ford had the only V-8 of the Low-Priced Three. This made Ford the clear police car of choice from the early 1930s through the mid-1950s. Even though Chevrolet and Plymouth introduced V-8s in the mid- and late 1950s, Ford had enough brand loyalty among cops to maintain a dominant position until the mid-1960s.

The sheer power of the V-8 in a low-priced car made Ford an obvious early choice among cops. However, the long-term popularity of the Ford V-8 was due to both power and its durability at higher speeds.

Chevrolet's Stovebolt Six was almost as powerful as the Ford V-8; however, it was reliable only at low engine speeds. At higher speeds, the Chevy Six, which lacked a pressurized oil system, would turn a bearing, throw a rod, or lose a timing chain. Low speed engine durability made the Stovebolt Six a great taxi engine but a lousy police pursuit engine. The Ford V-8, however, had both the power and high-speed stamina to become legendary among cops.

The Ford V-8's ability to reliably cruise at high speeds also caught the attention of bad guys looking for a getaway car. Both Clyde Barrow, of Bonnie and Clyde fame, and John Dillinger wrote to Henry Ford, praising him for the power and reliability of the Ford V-8, even if their business with the Ford wasn't "strictly legal." Both gangsters specifically stole Fords for their dirty work.

On May 16, 1934, one of America's most notorious criminals took time from his busy bank-robbing schedule to thank Henry Ford in a note:

Hello Old Pal:

Arrived here at 10 A.M. today. Would like to drop in and see you. You have a wonderful car. Been driving it for three weeks. It's a treat to drive one. Your slogan should be, "Drive a Ford and watch the other cars fall behind you." I can make any other car take a Ford's dust.

Bye-bye,

John Dillinger:

In 1933, the flathead V-8 was bumped to 75 horsepower thanks to aluminum cylinder heads and an increase in compression to 6.3:1. It was bumped again to 85 horsepower in 1934 after a switch to the Stromberg 2-bbl carb. This was the last model year for the In-line Four.

In 1937, Ford introduced a smaller V-8 to compete with the Chevy Six, rather than develop an In-line Six of his own. The 136-ci, 2-bbl flathead V-8 produced 60 horsepower compared to the Chevy OHV Six at 216-ci and 85 horsepower. The little Ford V-8 did not perform like a V-8 and was dropped after 1940. It was replaced in 1941 with a 226-ci In-line Six with 90 horsepower. At the time, Ford's Six produced as much power and actually more torque than its V-8. This was a preview to the problems of the future. The flathead and overhead-valve Sixes from all makes would steadily close the performance gap with the flathead Ford V-8.

Also in 1937, Ford redesigned the aluminum heads, moving the water inlets and both water pumps to the front of the engine. The power remained at 85 horsepower, with the rest of the drivetrain including a three-speed stick and 4.33 rear gears.

In 1939, Ford adopted Lockheed hydraulic brakes. This was a significant technical development and a desperately needed feature. Chevrolet had

The California Highway Patrol used this 1947 Mercury two-door as its Enforcement-Class vehicle. It was powered by a 100-horsepower, 239-ci V-8. *Darryl Lindsay*

A 1948 Ford on-duty with the Los Angeles Police Department. Note the fender-mounted, mechanical "growler" siren. *LAPD*

A 1949 NYPD Ford working the 109th Precinct in Flushing. The roof-mounted light says it all. Dallas and Omaha also used Fords. *Ned Schwartz*

introduced hydraulic brakes in 1936. Plymouth used hydraulic brakes since its debut in 1928.

In 1941, output from the 221-ci V-8 was pushed up again, this time to 90 horsepower. The Chandler-Groves 2-bbl, used as an option to the Stromberg 2-bbl, was now replaced with a Ford 2-bbl. An equal horsepower rating with Ford's own flathead In-line Six would just not do. In 1942, the V-8 was increased in power to 96 horsepower. The 226-ci Six still held a significant torque advantage. Production of Ford cars was halted in February 1942. Ford's massive River Rouge assembly plant produced everything from Jeeps to B-24 bombers.

The last major change to the Ford flathead V-8 took place in 1946. The engine was bored out to 239 ci, the compression was bumped to 6.8:1, and a Holley 2-bbl carb was used. The result was 100 horsepower. These sweeping changes cause us to be suspicious of the 1942 V-8 rating of 96 horsepower.

In 1949, Ford totally redesigned its Ford-series and Custom-series cars. The chassis was a wishbone-type. Longitudinal rear springs replaced the old transverse springs. A three-speed stick with synchronizers for second and third gears was standard. A three-speed with automatic overdrive became optional. The 0.70:1 overdrive cut in at 27 miles per hour and cut out at 21 miles per hour. The rear axle was 3.73:1 for the stick car and 4.10:1 with overdrive.

The 100-horsepower Ford V-8 with the new overdrive trans became the "hot ticket" for cops all across the United States. Chevrolet's top drivetrain was a 90-horsepower OHV Six, three-speed stick and 4.11 gears. The best from Plymouth was a 97-horsepower L-head Six, three-speed stick and 3.73, 3.90, or 4.10:1 rear gears.

The North Carolina Highway Patrol used Ford police cars in 1941. The Ohio State Highway Patrol used Fords in 1942. In 1946, the Delaware State Police used Fords. In 1947, the California Highway Patrol used Mercurys. In 1948, the Los Angeles Police and Iowa State Patrol prowled in Fords. In 1949, Fords were used by the North Carolina Highway Patrol, Michigan State Police, California Highway Patrol, Indiana State Police, Arkansas State Police, Dallas Police, Omaha Police, and the New York City Police.

The 1949 Ford used by the Michigan State Police was the first totally new car produced by Ford since World War II. An automatic overdrive was optional for the three-speed stick. *MSP*

The Kentucky State Police patrolled in 1949 Fords. Note the red light mounted on each fender. The California Highway Patrol and Arkansas State Police also drove Fords. *Monty McCord*

Chapter Two

1950-1953
The Ford Police Package

From the era of the horseless carriage until the 1950s, police officers drove retail cars. The cars may have had bigger brakes or better cooling systems as a part of a towing package or other suspension option, but it was not a police package car.

By the mid-1940s, Ford offered heavy-duty components developed for towing, export use, various forms of racing, and for police use.

Of all the beefed-up parts, the heavy-duty brakes were the first components commonly referred to as "police" items. Eventually, a number of commonly ordered, heavy-duty components were put together in one ordering package, called the "Police Package."

Of all the automakers, Ford was the first to develop a police package. This makes sense since Ford dominated the police market with its flathead V-8 retail cars. The police package was a specially developed group of heavy-duty suspension, brake, drivetrain, cooling, and interior components designed to withstand extreme abuse.

Not even officials at Ford's Fleet Sales Department are certain exactly when the first police parts were developed, nor when the police package was first formalized.

Without question, the formal Ford police package was available for 1950. The full package could have been available in 1949.

In comparison, Chevrolet introduced the long lead time police package in 1955 and the short lead time police package in 1956. In 1956, Dodge released its formal police package, followed by Plymouth in 1957.

From all automakers, the police package was designed to improve the drivetrain and suspension durability and reliability. To a lesser degree, the police package improved braking power, cornering performance, and high-speed stability. The police package did not make the car more powerful, but it did make the car more durable. Again, the police package had nothing to do with horsepower, torque, acceleration, or top speed. The police package was available with the most sluggish, fuel-miserly Six and with the most powerful, multiple-carbureted V-8 as well.

Just because a police department uses a retail car for police work does not make that car a police car. A police car is defined as any car that comes from the factory with the engineered police package. No police package, no police car. The car is a retail car instead.

A perfectly restored 1950 Los Angeles Police Ford. Many of the 1950 Ford police cars used the 239-ci flathead V-8.

By 1950, Ford put together a number of heavy-duty suspension, interior, and engine components in one package called the Police Package. This LAPD car has it.

This 1950 Ford Deluxe was used to chase gangsters in the Windy City. These cars used both the 226-ci Six and the 239-ci V-8. *Greg Reynolds*

Many car enthusiasts are shocked, or even disappointed, to discover that the police car seldom was equipped with the largest displacement, highest compression, or most carbureted engines. They are even more amazed to find the same engine used in mom and pop's grocery-getter was also used in the fearsome black-and-white that cruised the streets and highways in search of violators. The police engine was not more powerful, but the police drivetrain was much more reliable. Plus, the police car handled much better at higher speeds.

While the police package did not necessarily mean larger engines, it did give the automakers a chance to cross over traditional car lines when it came to engine selection. As early as 1950, Ford-marque police cars were available with Mercury-marque engines. That never happened with retail cars.

The use of a Mercury engine in a Ford police car emphasizes that police package cars are an entirely different breed than retail cars. The powertrains were frequently different. This can become quite confusing for someone familiar with retail powertrains for the same model and year!

Sometimes a police package car would get an optional engine a year earlier than the retail car. In other cases, the police package cars would not include an engine until a year after the retail car got it. In yet other cases, the police package car would still have access to an engine after it had been discontinued for retail cars.

Interestingly, the use of an engine that was supposed to be "exclusive" to another model or car line was common practice among police package cars. Ford police package sedans used engines "restricted" to the Thunderbird. Ford-marque police package sedans used engines "restricted" to Mercury-marque cars. All the police carmakers did this. Chevrolet police sedans used Corvette-only engines. Mopar police sedans used engines that were only available for the Chrysler 300 or Imperial. Police package cars play by a different set of engine and drivetrain option rules than retail cars.

In the late 1940s, the six-cylinder engines from Chevrolet and Plymouth were starting to close the performance and high-speed durability gap with Ford's 239-ci flathead V-8. This was only a minor concern in the retail business. However, it was a big problem if Ford was going to hold onto the prestigious police car market.

At the time, Ford had an overhead-valve V-8 planned for the 1952, but it was still under development. However, Ford did have an easy solution for police package cars ONLY: The company made a larger displacement Mercury-marque flathead V-8 available. In 1950, the Ford-marque 239-ci V-8 was rated at 100 horsepower. The Mercury-marque 255-ci V-8 was rated at 110 horsepower. This was the first use of a special "Law Enforcement" engine in Ford police cars. The 255-ci Mercury engine was a long-stroke version of the 239-ci flathead Ford V-8.

Marque	Ford	Mercury
Engine	239 ci, V-8	255 ci, V-8
Bore	3.19	3.19
Stroke	3.75	4.00
Comp	6.8	6.8
Carb	2-bbl	2-bbl
Hp	100	110

The 255-ci V-8 had been in the Mercury line since 1949. The 255-ci Law Enforcement engine was never available in retail Ford cars. The Mercury 255-ci V-8 was the top gun in Ford police cars until the 256-ci overhead-valve engine was introduced in 1954.

The San Francisco Police Department used Ford police cars in 1950, right, and 1951. Note the variety of roof- and fender-mounted lights, spotlights sirens, and speakers. *Darryl Lindsay*

15

Red lights? This 1951 New Jersey State Police Ford has them: roof-mounted, continuous-burn red spotlight and two big grille lights. *John Martin*

For its retail cars, Mercury used exactly the same 100-horsepower, 239-ci V-8 as Ford from 1946 through 1948. During this time, the largest engine from Mercury was also the largest engine from Ford.

In 1949, the 239-ci V-8 was stroked by a quarter inch to now displace 255-ci. With no other major changes to the engine, the horsepower was bumped from 100 to 110 horsepower. The 255-ci Merc mill was rated at 110 horsepower in 1949 and 1950. In 1951, it was re-rated at 112 horsepower. In 1952 and 1953, the horsepower was increased to 125 thanks to an increase in compression from 6.8 to 7.2.

Ford was careful not to make the use of a Mercury engine widely known. The larger engine was one of the Mercury's main selling points to retail customers. Mercury wanted the engine to be exclusive. For its part, Ford did not want its retail customers demanding to have the bigger engine either. To say the engine was "police-only" seemed to work. In fact, with rare occasion, all the car companies have been extremely successful in giving cops what they wanted while also protecting the brand distinction among their retail cars.

Fleet officials called this 110-horsepower 255-ci V-8 a "special highway patrol engine." The 1950 Ford police car literature also avoided the word Mercury. Instead, the 110-horsepower, 255-ci V-8 is called a "Ford V-8 H.P. Special," in contrast to the "Ford 100 H.P. V-8" and the "Ford 95 H.P. Six." The flyer makes it clear that this 110 horsepower engine is "Special for Police Cars Only." Other literature calls the 255-ci engine the "Law Enforcement V-8." The 1952 and 1953 police literature identifies the 255-ci Mercury engine only as "125 H.P. Interceptor," in contrast to the 110 H.P. Strato-Star Ford V-8 and the 101 H.P. Mileage Maker Ford Six. This low-profile use of a Mercury engine in a Ford police car continued for a number of years. While Mercury cars were

not significant players in the police car market until the late 1960s, Mercury engines had a starring role from the beginning of the police package.

The 1950 police package for either the Fordor or Tudor included a 13-leaf rear suspension, heavy-duty front springs, and heavy-duty "aircraft-type" shock absorbers. It also included "24-hour Duty" special heavy-duty front and rear seats with non-sag seat springs, heavy-duty seat frames, and heavy-duty vinyl plastic upholstery. The police package floormats were reinforced at the critical wear spots beneath the clutch, brake, and accelerator pedals.

To provide for heavy electrical loads, including the new-fangled two-way police radios, the 1950 police package also included a 60-amp generator and a 130-amp battery. The engine oil pan with a removable "clean-out" plate provides access to the oil pump screen. The Ford police cars came standard with 6.00x16 four-ply tires on 4.5-inch rims. Special Order tires up to the 6.70x15 six-ply on 5.0-inch wheels were available.

In 1951, the 255-ci Ford Law Enforcement engine from Mercury was bumped up from 110 horsepower to 112 horsepower. The two-speed Fordomatic automatic transmission first became an option. This was a torque-converter–based transmission with a three-speed automatic planetary geartrain, and single-stage, three-element, hydraulic torque converter.

The Fordomatic was considered a two-speed trans because the automatic intermediate gear was used only for starting. The Mercury version of this same transmission was the Merc-O-Matic, also introduced this year.

The 1951 Fordomatic was in response to Chevrolet's 1950 introduction of the two-speed Powerglide. Chevrolet teamed a more powerful 105-horsepower, 235-ci Six to its Powerglide. The only change in the Ford drivetrain with the automatic was a

In 1951, the two-speed Fordomatic automatic transmission was an option. This Fair Oaks, Illinois, Police Ford Deluxe, like most police cars, used the three-speed stick. Note the V-8 emblem on the fender. *Greg Reynolds*

Check out this 1951 Colorado State Patrol Ford with the missing right front turn signal light. *Darryl Lindsay*

A 1952 Los Angeles Police Department Ford Mainline. This was the first year for Ford's first overhead-valve engine, the 215-ci Six, but this squad has a V-8. *Darryl Lindsay*

reduction in gear ratio from 3.73 to 3.31. Plymouth did not have its Powerflite trans available until 1954.

Bragging rights aside, the availability of an automatic transmission made no difference whatsoever to cops. For both low maintenance and low initial price reasons, most police cars had manual transmissions long after most retail cars had automatic transmissions. In 1952, for example, over 32 percent of the Fords had the Fordomatic trans. While it was offered on the police package cars, less than 1 percent of police departments specified this $170 option on their $1,530 four-door Mainline. Over 20 percent of the Fords were equipped with the $102 overdrive. For cops, that was money well spent.

This thinking extended all the way into the 1980s! Most Special Service Mustangs were ordered with manual transmissions because they were less expensive outright and less costly to maintain. A clutch is easier to fix than an automatic transmission.

In 1952, Ford released its first overhead-valve engine, the 215-ci Six. Compared to the old 226-ci Six, the completely redesigned 215-ci Six had a much larger bore and a much shorter stroke. Even though the displacement dropped from 226 ci to 215 ci, the horsepower increased from 95 horsepower to 101 horsepower. This is due to the higher compression, bore and stroke change, and the use of overhead-valves. The Ford Six got an overhead-valvetrain two years before the Ford V-8.

Less piston travel on the new Six reduced the internal friction losses from 48 horsepower to just 31 horsepower. The change to overhead-valves resulted in a stronger and stiffer block. Boring the block for the valve chambers weakened the old L-head engine. The new engine had so much less cylinder distortion at speed, that one of the piston oil rings would be eliminated. Again, less friction.

To keep pace, in 1952, the 239-ci flathead V-8 was boosted from 100 horsepower to 110 horsepower thanks to an increase to 7.2:1 compression. For 1952, the 255-ci Ford Law Enforcement engine was also increased in compression from 6.8 to 7.2. The result was a huge jump in output from 112 horsepower to 125 horsepower. This was called the Interceptor V-8. The Interceptor V-8 was much more powerful than the 110 horsepower, 239-ci Ford V-8, which was struggling to stay ahead of the 101 horsepower, 215-ci Ford Six. The police package was available on both the Mainline and the more upscale Customline.

By 1952, the Chevy 216-ci Stovebolt Six had almost closed the performance gap with the Ford 239-ci V-8:

Car/Engine	Chevy Six	Ford V-8
0–60 mph	20.46 sec	20.47 sec
Top Speed	80.93 mph	86.70 mph

While the overhead-valve Chevy Six was closing the gap on the flathead Ford V-8, the new overhead-valve Ford Six had indeed overtaken the flathead V-8.

Motor Trend tested two 1952 Fords. One was powered by the brand-new overhead-valve Six. The other was powered by the old flathead V-8. The agenda was quite clear: Prove that the overhead-valve Six was just as powerful as the flathead V-8 and push Ford into replacing the aging flathead V-8 with an overhead-valve V-8.

The magazine found the OHV Six had quicker acceleration, both the OHV Six and the flathead V-8 produced the same top speeds, and the V-8 got better gas mileage at low speeds, but the OHV Six was more economical at high speeds.

Engine, ci	215, Six	239, V-8
Valvetrain	overhead	flathead
Carb	Holley 1-bbl	Ford 2-bbl
Compression	7.0:1	7.2:1
Horsepower	101 @3,500	110 @3,800
Torque	185 @1,500	194 @2,000
Trans	3-speed overdrive	3-speed overdrive
Axle ratio	3.90:1	3.90:1
Test weight, lb	3,370	3,530
0–60 mph, sec	19.45	20.47
1/4-mile ET, sec	21.27	21.35
Top speed, mph	86.3	86.7

A 1953 Florida Highway Patrol Ford Mainline. This was the last year for the in-block valve, flathead V-8. The 255-ci engine was now rated at 125 horsepower. *John Yeaw*

This 1953 Nevada Highway Patrol Ford police car is based on the Mainline series. It packs a V-8. *Darryl Lindsay*

This 1953 Nevada Highway Patrol Ford uses a three-speed stick with an automatic overdrive transmission. *Darryl Lindsay*

Except for styling changes, and in spite of the pressure from Chevrolet and the press, the 1953 Ford police cars were mostly a carryover from the 1952 banner year. All changes were on hold while Ford devoted full time to the upcoming overhead-valve V-8. To turn up the heat in 1953, Chevrolet released a brand-new 235-ci Six with aluminum pistons, fully pressurized oil system, 7:1 compression, and 108 horsepower.

For 1953, the Ford powertrains were the 101-horsepower, 215-ci Ford OHV Six, the 110-horsepower, 239-ci Ford flathead V-8, and the 125-horsepower, 255-ci Mercury "Interceptor" flathead V-8. The three-speed stick, Overdrive, and Fordomatic transmissions were available. The police package was once again built around the Mainline and the Customline models.

The flathead V-8 was more than 20 years old. For the record, over the years the flathead V-8 had grown in displacement from 221 ci to 239 ci (Ford) and 255 ci (Mercury). The compression had been inched up from 5.5:1 to 7.2:1. It had increased in power from 65 horsepower to 110 horsepower (Ford) and 125 horsepower (Mercury). However, it simply needed overhead-valves to remain competitive. Ford had actually been working on such an engine since 1949 for use in the 1952 Lincoln. The OHV V-8 reached the Ford police cars in 1954.

The 114-inch wheelbase 1950 Ford was used by the Indiana State Police, Arkansas State Police, Iowa State Patrol, Nebraska State Patrol, Delaware State Police, Pennsylvania State Police, Kentucky State Police, Colorado State Patrol, Nassau County, New York Police, Los Angeles Police, Chicago Police, Dallas Police, Omaha Police, and San Francisco Police. The big police car news in 1950, however, was the New York City Police purchase of 430 Ford police cars. At the time, this was one of the largest fleet orders ever placed by any police department.

Agencies using the Ford police car in 1951 included the New Jersey State Police, Colorado State Patrol, Arizona Highway Patrol, Indiana State Police, Wisconsin State Patrol, Iowa State Patrol, Washington State Patrol, and San Francisco Police.

Ford police cars and retail cars alike were stretched an inch to a wheelbase of 115 inches for 1952. Police departments that used the longer Ford included the Los Angeles County Sheriff, Iowa State Patrol, Los Angeles Police, Oregon State Police, Nebraska State Patrol, Colorado State Patrol, California Highway Patrol, and Missouri State Highway Patrol. In 1953, Fords were used by the Nevada Highway Patrol; Arkansas State Police; Milwaukee, Wisconsin, Police; Florida Highway Patrol; New Hampshire State Police; and the Georgia State Patrol.

The Los Altos, California, Police used six-cylinder-powered Fords in 1953. The Milwaukee, Wisconsin, Police also used Fords.

This 1951 Ford carries quite a bit of gear for the Missouri State Highway Patrol, including a .351 Winchester rifle and 12-gauge shotgun.

This 115-inch wheelbase Ford Mainline was used by the New Hampshire State Police. Its 215-ci OHV Six is as fast as the 239-ci flat-head V-8.

Ford Police Drivetrains, 1950 and 1951

226-ci Ford Six	L-Head	1-bbl	95 hp
239-ci Ford V-8	L-Head	2-bbl	100 hp
255-ci Mercury V-8	L-Head	2-bbl	110 hp, 112 hp

trans/axle:	3-speed stick with 3.73 or 4.10 axle
	3-speed overdrive with 4.10 axle
	2-speed Fordomatic with 3.31 or 3.54 (1951 only)

Ford Police Drivetrains, 1952 and 1953

215-ci Ford Six	OHV	1-bbl	101 hp
239-ci Ford V-8	L-Head	2-bbl	110 hp
255-ci Mercury V-8	L-Head	2-bbl	125 hp

trans/axle:	3-speed stick with 3.90 or 4.10 axle
	3-speed overdrive with 3.90 or 4.10 axle
	2-speed Fordomatic with 3.31 or 3.54 axle

Chapter Three

1954

The Overhead-Valve V-8

The 1954 model year was Ford's most significant one since the introduction of the flathead V-8 in 1932. In 1954, Fords got the overhead-valve V-8 engine.

With the exception of the release of the flathead V-8 and the introduction of the 1982 Special Service package Mustang, the 1954 overhead-valve engine was the biggest news in Ford police car history. In perspective, this was much bigger news than the development of the single overhead-cam (SOHC) 4.6L "modular" V-8 for 1992.

Ford had controlled the police market for decades with the sheer power of the flathead V-8. However, in the early 1950s, the overhead-valve In-line Sixes from everyone, including Ford, were catching the Ford's flathead V-8 in terms of performance. Ford also knew that both Chevrolet and Plymouth had overhead-valve V-8 engines under development.

Ford's answer was the Y-block, overhead-valve V-8. All else equal, the overhead-valve V-8 engine held an 18 percent horsepower advantage over the flathead V-8. The Y-block came in two versions for Ford police cars. One was the 130-horsepower, 239-ci Ford-marque V-8. The other was the 160-horsepower, 256-ci Mercury-marque V-8. Future Y-blocks would displace 272, 292, and 312 cubic inches. In 1954, the 115-horsepower, 223-ci I-block, In-line Six was the standard police car engine.

The Lincoln got its overhead-valve engine in 1952. This 318-ci, 2-bbl mill produced 160 horsepower. The 1953, higher compression, 4-bbl version generated 205 horsepower. These were never used in police package cars.

The overhead-valve V-8 was totally new: new block; new heads; new crank, rods, and pistons; new valvetrain; and new intake and exhaust manifolds. The gear drive used in the L-head cam was replaced with a chain drive. Both new Ford police overhead-valve V-8 engines had a "power charge" intake manifold, "twin tornado" combustion chambers "power stroke" con rods, and a "super structure" crank. Ford also emphasized their short-stroke piston travel, free-turning valves, and 7.5:1 high-compression ratio.

The Y-block V-8 had a chain-driven camshaft, a single water pump, full-flow oil filtration, and rotating valves that lowered valve temperatures. The block used the "deep-skirt" design to stiffen the block and allow future increases in compression. The deep-skirt design led to the name Y-block.

The OHV V-8 block was much simpler to cast than the flathead. The flathead V-8 required 29 sand cores to cast the engine block. The OHV V-8 required only 14 cores.

The larger bore allowed both larger intake and larger exhaust valves compared to the flathead V-8. The OHV head itself was much stiffer than the flathead unit. The flathead V-8 needed 24 bolts to secure the head to the block. The OHV V-8 only needed 10 head bolts.

The new V-8 engine was heavily promoted as being "low friction" compared to the old flathead. With the flathead, friction stole 30 percent of the horsepower it produced. With the overhead-valve engine, just 18 percent of the power was lost due to friction. Most of the improvement was due to the shorter piston stroke. The example used in 1954 was this: The piston on the flathead V-8 moved up and down in the cylinder a distance of 21 miles for 100 miles on the road. The piston on the overhead-valve V-8 traveled 21 miles for 129 miles on the road. Less piston travel means less friction and less wear.

This 1954 Customline was used by the Grant's Pass, Oregon, Police. Note the window-mounted radar and fender-mounted red light and siren. *Darryl Lindsay*

The Chicago Police used the V-8-powered Mainline in 1954. This was the first year for a 4-bbl Ford or Mercury police engine. *Greg Reynolds*

The bore and stroke of both engines clearly tell the story. The old 239-ci flathead had a 3.19-inch bore and 3.75-inch stroke. The new 239-ci overhead-valve V-8 had a 3.50-inch bore and a 3.10-inch stroke. Both engines had the same displacement and compression ratio. The overhead-valve version had a 20-horsepower and 18-foot-pound of torque advantage.

Nostalgia has a way of obscuring the facts. The Ford flathead V-8 had more power than the competition, but it also had serious design problems. The biggest problem was keeping the L-head engine from overheating. It had two water pumps, two thermostats, and four main radiator hoses. If any one of these failed, the engine overheated.

The exhaust passages ran sideways through each bank of the block, putting an extra load on the cooling system. In comparison, the OHV engine pumps the exhaust gas directly out of the head putting less heat in the block.

Unlike the on-the-job development of the flathead V-8, Ford was taking no chances on the durability of its new OHV V-8.

In 1954, Ford introduced its first overhead-valve V-8, the so-called Y-block. All else equal, the overhead-valve engine was 18 percent more powerful than the flathead engine. *Ford Division*

More than 400 experimental engines went into the development of the OHV V-8. The testing and evaluation included more than 160,000 hours on the dynamometer. The engines were installed in cars that logged more than 2.5 million miles. When the OHV V-8 was released for production, it was right. All the bugs had been worked out long before the first police officer or retail customer got behind the wheel.

The I-block Six was also new for 1954. It was proclaimed in the Ford police car flyer to be "the only completely modern Six in the industry." It, too, boasted high (7.2:1) compression. For 1954, the old 215-ci Six was bored and stroked to now displace 223 ci. The horsepower was boosted from 101 horsepower to 115 horsepower.

All of the police engines could be bolted to a three-speed stick, three-speed overdrive stick, or the Fordomatic two-speed automatic. The use of an automatic trans for police work was still extremely rare in 1954.

In 1954, the police package was available on the 115.5-inch wheelbase Ford Mainline and Ford Customline models. For 1954, these cars got a new "double-drop" frame, new ball-joint front suspension, new variable rate rear leaf springs with up to seven leaves, new dual-servo brakes, and new steering linkage.

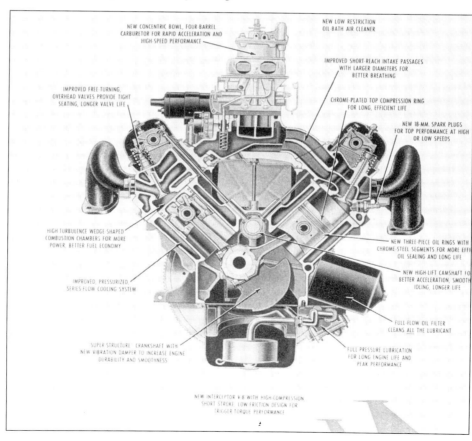

Other technical breakthroughs for Ford in 1954 included the first use of a ball joint front suspension. This replaced the kingpin and spindle front suspension design used on both Ford and Mercury police cars through 1953. This change also allowed the engine to sit lower in the chassis for better handling. The number of points needing lubrication on the front suspension was dropped from 16 to just 4.

This was the first year for power steering and power brakes as an option. These were introduced on the 1953 Mercury retail car. The Fords got Master Guide power steering in June 1953. Since most police fleet contracts are filled early in the model year, the first likely appearance of power steering in Ford police cars was 1954. This was also the first year for a 4-bbl carburetor on any Ford police car. This Holley 4-bbl was available only on the Mercury Law Enforcement V-8 used by Ford.

The 1954 Ford police car powered by the 130-horsepower, 239-ci OHV V-8 and three-speed stick reached 60 miles per hour in 16 seconds. This compares to 19 seconds for the 1953 Ford with the 239-ci flathead. The 1954 Ford with the 239-ci mill and two-speed Fordomatic hit 60 miles per hour in 18.5 seconds. The top speed for the 239-ci-powered Ford was 96 miles per hour.

The 1953 Mercury powered by the 125-horsepower 255-ci flathead V-8 had a 0-to-80-miles-per-hour time of 52 seconds. The 1954 Mercury with the 160 horsepower, 256-ci overhead-valve V-8 reached 80 miles per hour in just 34 seconds. With the Merc-O-Matic automatic transmission, the big Merc reached 60 miles per hour in 18 seconds compared to 21 seconds in 1953.

The 1954 model year for Ford was a banner year

The 1954 Ford with a 239-ci, 2-bbl V-8 rated at 130 horsepower reached 60 miles per hour in 16 seconds. This unit was used by the Sacramento, California, Police. *Darryl Lindsay*

because of the overhead-valve engine. Police departments using Fords in 1954 included the Indiana State Police, Tennessee Highway Patrol, South Carolina Highway Patrol, New Mexico State Police, Louisiana State Police, Nevada Highway Patrol, Iowa State Patrol, Sacramento Police, Chicago Police, Alaska State Troopers, North Carolina Highway Patrol, Pennsylvania State Police, and the Missouri State Highway Patrol.

The 1954 Ford with the new 130-horsepower overhead-valve V-8 had a top speed of 96 miles per hour. Here's a Tennessee Highway Patrol cruiser. *John Yeaw*

Note the V-8 fender emblem on this 1954 Mainline used by the Grant's Pass, Oregon, police. This is a mechanical "growler" siren. *Darryl Lindsay*

With the exception of the 1932 flathead V-8 and the 1982 severe ser- vice Mustang, the 1954 introduction of its overhead-valve V-8 was the biggest news in Ford police car history. A Louisiana State Police Mainline is shown. *John Yeaw*

The overhead-valve V-8 used in this 1954 South Carolina Highway Patrol cruiser was originally developed for the 1952 Lincoln. *John Yeaw*

In addition to the Indiana State Police (shown), other agencies using the 1954 included the Nevada Highway Patrol, Missouri State Highway Patrol, and the Alaska state troop- ers. *Jerry Parker*

1954 Engine Comparison

Engine	ci	horsepower	hp/ci
Mercury OHV V-8	256	160	.625
Ford OHV V-8	239	130	.544
Ford L-Head V-8 ('53)	239	110	.459
Chevy OHV I-6 (auto)	235	125	.531
Chevy OHV I-6 (stick)	235	115	.488
Ford OHV I-6	223	115	.516
Plymouth OHV I-6	218	100	.459

Police Drivetrains for 1954

Layout	ci/liter	carburetor	comp	horsepower
I-6	223	1-bbl	7.2	115
V-8	239	2-bbl	7.2	130
V-8	256	4-bbl	7.5	160

Trans/rear gear: 3.90, 4.10 with 3-speed and overdrive
3.31, 3.54 with Fordomatic

Chapter Four

1955-1957
The 272-ci, 292-ci, and 312-ci Y-Block

In 1955, Ford introduced the 272-ci Ford Y-block and the 292-ci Mercury and Thunderbird Y-block for use in Ford police cars. The 272-ci engine had the same bore as the 1954 256-ci, but had a longer stroke. The 292-ci Y-block, in turn, was a bored and stroked version of the 256-ci mill. The 272-ci and 292-ci shared the same stroke, with the larger engine having a larger bore. The 272-ci, 2-bbl "Ford Y-block" V-8 produced 162 horsepower. This exactly equaled the much-heralded 265-ci, 2-bbl Chevy small-block. The 292-ci, 4-bbl "Interceptor" V-8 was rated at 188 horsepower. This out-powered the Chevy 265-ci, 4-bbl "Plus Power" V-8 at 180 horsepower. The 182 horsepower, 4-bbl version of the 272-ci Ford Y-block was not used as a police engine.

While often confused as such, this early-release 292-ci Interceptor engine was not one of the Thunderbird engines. The engines were, however, very close. The 188-horsepower Interceptor had a 7.6 to 1 compression. The two Thunderbird engines had an 8.1 to 1 compression and 193 horsepower and an 8.5 to 1 compression and 198 horsepower. Compression ratio is the only difference between the Interceptor and Thunderbird versions. Both the 292-ci-powered police car and the Thunderbird used dual exhausts.

New for 1955 engines was the wedge cylinder design, high-lift cam, and "power charge" intake manifold. Ford police engines were advertised as having "trigger torque performance." The optional transmission was the "Speed-Trigger" Fordomatic. Again, Ford hyped the high-efficiency design of its deep-block, short stroke, low-friction V-8.

Ford still used a 6-volt electrical system. The police package included up to a 60-amp generator or up to a 95-amp alternator, and up to a 136-amp "power punch" battery.

A combination fuel pump and vacuum pump ensured positive windshield wiper operation. In models without this system, the vacuum-operated wipers simply stopped working at wide-open throttle or other low-vacuum operating conditions. The dual-purpose pump came as standard equipment on police cars with the 292-ci V-8 and with the Fordomatic or Overdrive.

In 1955, Ford police cars like this Auburn, California, Police unit were available with the 272-ci Ford Y-block or the 292-ci Mercury Y-block. *Darryl Lindsay*

Some state laws also required positive windshield wiper operation.

In 1955, the 223-ci I-block Six received a compression boost from 7.2 to 7.6 to 1. This was good for a 5 horsepower increase to 120 horsepower.

In 1954, depending on the engine and transmission, Ford had a total of four different axle ratios available. For 1955, this was increased to eleven different ratios from 3.30 to 4.27 to 1.

The 1955 Fords were totally redesigned. Compared to the 1954 Fords, the 1955 models were longer, lower, and wider. This trend would continue throughout the 1950s. The 1955 police package was based on the Mainline and Customline sedans. However, the two-door Ranch Wagon and four-door Country Sedan station wagons were also available with the police gear.

In 1955, the top trim level for the full-size Ford sedan was the Fairlane-series. For the first time, the Crown Victoria name was used to describe the absolute top-of-the-line within the upscale Fairlane series.

In 1956, the 312-ci "Thunderbird" V-8 was introduced in Ford police cars like this Chicago Police cruiser. *Greg Reynolds*

car. Introduced in October 1954, the Thunderbird rapidly established a reputation for excitement and performance. For the next decade, the top Ford police engines all had some tie to the Thunderbird. This was clearly and boldly advertised—as opposed to the Mercury heritage that was downplayed. The facts are, the Thunderbird and Mercury shared engines that were not generally available on any Ford except the police cars.

Motor Trend tested a 1955 Ford four-door Customline powered by a 162-horsepower, 272-ci, 2-bbl V-8 teamed with a two-speed Fordomatic trans and 3.31 rear gears.

0–60 mph	14.5 sec
1/4 mi ET	19.4 sec
1/4 mi Speed	74 mph
Top Speed	95 mph
60 mph Braking	178 feet
Fuel Economy, Actual	13.4 mpg

In the middle of the model year, Chevrolet introduced a Plus Power Package for its 265-ci V-8. With a 4-bbl carb and dual exhaust, the small-block reached 180 horsepower. Late in the model year Ford responded with a new HO (high output) engine for police work. The term "HO" has been used for the hottest Ford engines ever since. The new engine was the Thunderbird version of the 292-ci V-8 rated at 205 horsepower.

In the mid-1950s, using a "Thunderbird" engine in a Ford police car meant the same as using a "Corvette" engine in a mid-1990s Chevrolet police

New for 1956 was the 312-ci Y-block V-8. This was developed primarily as a high-output engine for the Thunderbird. All versions of the 312-ci engine had a 4-bbl carb and dual exhaust. The compression ratio and the resulting horsepower varied by the transmission used with the 312-ci engine. The 312-ci engine

In 1956, more than 70 percent of the state troopers in the United States drove Fords like this New Jersey State Police unit.

The Reno, Nevada, Police used 1956 Fairlanes to respond to brawls among gamblers. *Darryl Lindsay*

The 312-ci V-8 used in this 1956 Reno, Nevada, Police patrol car was a slightly bore and stroked version of the 292-ci V-8. *Darryl Lindsay*

The Y-8 emblem on the fender of this 1956 ex-California city cruiser gave notice it was powered by a Y-block V-8. *John Bellah*

was yet another example of an engine exclusive to the Thunderbird and Mercury ending up in a Ford police sedan.

The 312-ci V-8 was a bored and stroked version of the 292-ci Y-block. The bore was only .05 inch larger and the stroke was only .10 inches longer. However, that was all it took. The 312-ci V-8 is legendary among Ford fans.

Ford billed its brand-new, 215-horsepower "Interceptor Y-8" as the successor to the V-8. The die-cast fender emblems that showed the engine size had the "8" sitting on top of a "Y." The 312-ci engine was advertised as another Ford first, as revolutionary as the first V-8 in 1932. The "Y-8" term came from the cross-section of the engine layout: twin cylinder banks 90 degrees apart and a deep-skirt block. In spite of the marketing hype, the term "Y-8" never caught on. By 1957, Ford was back to using the term "V-8."

To equate the police engines to the more familiar retail engine terms, the "Special Police Y-8" was exactly the same engine as the 292-ci "Thunderbird" V-8. The "Interceptor Y-8" was exactly the same engine in all regards as the 312-ci "Thunderbird Special" V-8. At 215 horsepower, the new 312-ci, 4-bbl Ford police engine outperformed Chevy's 265-ci, 4-bbl "power pack" V-8 now rated at 205 horsepower.

For 1956, compression ratios were increased from 7.5 and 7.6 to one to 8.0 and 8.4 to one. This resulted in an average increase of 15 horsepower across-the-board. Part of this increase was the switch to "turbo-wedge" shaped combustion chambers.

Also for 1956, Ford teamed a separate V-8 engine with the Fordomatic cars from the engine used with the three-speed stick and three-speed Overdrive. Cars using the I-block Six were not affected. To make up for some of the losses in the automatic trans, the compression ratio for the V-8 Fordomatic cars was 0.4:1 higher than the manual trans V-8 cars. This resulted in a 2 to 5 horsepower advantage, giving the Fordomatic cars acceleration performance closer to the manual trans cars.

In 1956, Ford converted from a 6-volt electrical system to a 12-volt system. This did, indeed, provide faster starts, better high rpm ignition reliability and the ability to handle more power accessories. The upside of this change was a greatly improved electrical system. The downside was that police departments had to buy new 12V radios, emergency lights, spotlights, and other electrical accessories. And they had to throw away their excess inventory of 6V repair and replacement parts. The conversion from 6V to 12V was a big enough problem for some agencies; Ford made the 6V system OPTIONAL at extra cost. This gave police departments one more year of use with 6V emergency gear and one more year to use up their inventory of 6V replacement parts.

For 1956, the Ford police package was again based on the Mainline and Customline models, in both Tudor and Fordor versions. The two-door and four-door Ranch

In 1956, the electrical system powering this Wisconsin sheriff's department unit was upgraded to 12 volts. A 6-volt system remained an option. *Greg Reynolds*

In 1957, the 312-ci V-8 was available with twin Holley 4-bbl carbs producing 270 horsepower. This was the only year for dual quads. This Indiana State Police Ford Custom has the single 4-bbl engine.

In addition to the Michigan State Police (shown), police agencies using the 1957 Ford included the New York City Police, Dallas Police, and Kansas City, Missouri, Police. *MSP*

Wagon and Country Sedan station wagons were also available in police trim.

The 1956 model year emphasized safety. New for 1956 was a steering wheel with a deeply recessed center hub, padded dash, padded visors, newly designed, double-grip door latches, and seat belts. That's right, seat belts were offered by Ford for the first time in 1956. They became standard in all cars in 1964.

The V-8-powered, upscale Fairlane retail car had rear bumpers with slots in each end for the exit of the dual exhaust pipes. The Fairlane was not available with a police package. The tailpipes from the dual exhaust police engines exited below the bumper. As a midyear release, in time for Daytona's Speed Week in February, Ford police cars were available with a 225-horsepower version of the 312-ci Interceptor V-8. This 4-bbl, dual-

In 1957, Ford introduced a longer wheelbase chassis. Note the pusher bar on this Chicago Park District Ford Custom. *Greg Reynolds*

The 1957 Ford police cars like this Los Angeles Police Department unit had a new ball joint front suspension and modified rear leaf springs. *LAPD*

exhaust, HO engine was restricted to the Fordomatic transmission.

In 1956, over 70 percent of all state police and highway patrol squad cars were made by Ford.

In 1957, in the middle of a horsepower race between Ford, General Motors, and Chrysler Corporation, Ford upped the power of its police engines again. The star of the lineup was the 312-ci Y-block, now rated at 245 horsepower with the single Holley 4-bbl and 270 horsepower with twin Holley 4-bbls. For the first time, all engines were available with all transmissions. The axle was beefed up to take the 336 pounds-feet of torque.

The 270-horsepower "Ford Interceptor 312 Super V-8" was the first, last, and only Ford police engine to use dual 4-bbl carbs. Ford also reached new limits with compression ratios. The 9.7:1 ratio used with both versions of the 312-ci engine was the first time this high of a ratio was used on a Ford police package engine.

A "racing kit" was available for retail cars with this dual-quad, 312-ci engine. This boosted the compression from 9.7 to 10.0:1 and the horsepower from 270 to 285. This was not available with the police package.

Perhaps a more famous variation of the 312-ci V-8 was the "Thunderbird Special Supercharged V-8." This 8.5:1 engine used a single Holley 4-bbl teamed with a Paxton centrifugal supercharger. The result was 300 horsepower in street trim and 340 horsepower in the NASCAR version. The supercharged 312-ci engine was a response to Chevrolet's solid lifter fuel-injected 283-ci V-8 that produced 283 horsepower. One big difference existed between the Ford and Chevy approach to police cars. The fuel-injected 283-ci was available on Chevrolet's police package sedans. The supercharged 312-ci was not available on Ford's police package cars. This was also the "last hurrah" for the 312-ci engine. It would be replaced in 1958 with one of the FE-block series of engines.

For 1957, the names "Mainline" and "Customline" were replaced with "Custom" and "Custom 500." This Santa Cruz, California, Sheriffs unit is powered by a Thunderbird 312-ci Special V-8. *John Yeaw*

For 1957 the names Mainline and Customline were replaced with Custom and Custom 300.

The full-size Fords were completely restyled for 1957 and divided into different wheelbase lengths. The Custom series had a 116-inch wheelbase. This was a half inch longer than the 1956 models. The police package was available only for the Custom series, which included the base trim level Custom and the upscale Custom 300.

The Fairlane series now had a longer, 118-inch wheelbase. This may be a little confusing for those who remember the Fairlane as a compact car from the 1960s. The Ford police package was not available for either the Fairlane or Fairlane 500.

The 1957 Custom was 3 inches longer overall and 5 inches lower than the 1956 model. To help in lowering the cars, 14-inch wheels were used for the first time. The police sedans came with only one tire and wheel combination: 7.50x14 4-ply on 14x5 wheels. Neither 15-inch wheels nor 6-ply tires were available.

In 1957, Ford introduced a totally new chassis. This included a new four-way ball joint front suspension, outboard-mounted rear leaf springs and a deep-offset rear axle. Other first-time advancements included finned or ribbed brake drums, a manual throttle control, and up to a 100-amp alternator. In 1956, Ford offered a total of 11 axle ratios for its police package vehicles. For 1957, this number was reduced to five, with a choice from 3.10 to 4.11 to 1.

Police departments that used 1955 Fords included the Los Angeles County Sheriff, New York State Police, Montana Highway Patrol, Dallas Police, San Francisco Police, Iowa State Patrol, New Jersey State Police, and the Missouri State Highway Patrol. In 1956, Fords were used by the New Jersey State Police; Reno, Nevada, Police; Los Angeles County Sheriff; Florida Highway Patrol; Alaska State Troopers; Colorado State Patrol; Kansas City, Missouri, Police; Missouri State Highway Patrol; and Nebraska State Patrol. The 1957 Fords were nearly as popular as the 1954 Fords. Those using the 1957 Fords

A sharp V-8-powered 1956 Missouri State Highway Patrol Ford. Emergency equipment included spotlight, roof light, and deck light. Note the whip antenna.

included Los Angeles Police; Los Angeles County Sheriff; New York State Police; New York City Police; Iowa State Patrol; Dallas Police; Kansas City, Missouri, Police; Alaska State Troopers; Massachusetts State Police; Michigan State Police; and Indiana State Police.

Police Drivetrains for 1955

Layout	ci/liter	carburetor	comp	horsepower
I-6	223	1-bbl	7.5	120
V-8	272	2-bbl	7.6	162
V-8	292	4-bbl	7.6	188
V-8 HO	292	4-bbl	n/a	205

transmission: 3-speed, Overdrive, Fordomatic
axles: 3.30, 3.31, 3.54, 3.55, 3.73, 3.78, 3.89, 3.92, 4.09, 4.11, 4.27

Police Drivetrains for 1956

Layout	ci	carburetor	comp	horsepower	exhaust	transmission
I-6	223	1-bbl	8.0	137	single	all
Y-8	272	2-bbl	8.0	173	single	stick
Y-8	272	2-bbl	8.4	176	single	auto
Y-8	292	4-bbl	8.0	200	dual	stick
Y-8	292	4-bbl	8.4	202	dual	auto
Y-8	312	4-bbl	8.0	210	dual	stick
Y-8	312	4-bbl	8.4	215	dual	auto
Y-8 HO	312	4-bbl	n/a	225	dual	auto

transmissions: 3-speed, Overdrive, Fordomatic
axles: 3.22, 3.31, 3.54, 3.55, 3.73, 3.78, 3.89, 3.92, 4.09, 4.11, 4.27

Police Drivetrains for 1957

Layout	ci	carburetor	comp	horsepower	exhaust
I-6	223	1-bbl	8.6	144	single
V-8	272	2-bbl	8.6	190	single
V-8	292	2-bbl	9.1	212	single
V-8	312	4-bbl	9.7	245	dual
V-8	312	8-bbl	9.7	270	dual

transmission: 3-speed stick, 3-speed Overdrive, 2-speed Fordomatic
axles: 3.10, 3.56, 3.70, 3.89, 4.11

Chapter Five

1958-1960
The Ford-Edsel Big-Blocks

For 1958, the Ford police package was based on the Custom 300 model in both two-door and four-door sedans and the two-door Ranch Wagon and four-door County Sedan station wagons. These cars all had a 116-inch wheelbase. The 118-inch wheelbase Fairlane-series was not available with the police package.

For 1958, the Fords were restyled slightly to include a fake hood scoop and honeycomb grille adapted from the Thunderbird. New for 1958 was the FE-series of big-block engines (FE stands for Ford-Edsel). The Ford police cars got 332-ci, 352-ci, and 361-ci versions. Future police FE-blocks included the famous 390-ci in 1961 and the potent 428-ci in 1966. For the first time ever a Ford-marque police engine produced over 300 horsepower with the 303-horsepower, 361-ci, 4-bbl V-8. At the time, achieving 300 horsepower was a huge selling point. Chevrolet first reached 300 horsepower with its 315-horsepower, 348-ci, 6-bbl V-8 in 1958. Plymouth first got to this lofty level with its 305-horsepower, 350-ci, 8-bbl V-8 in 1958.

The Ford big-block V-8s fall into one of two categories. First is the FE-series, which included the 332-ci, 352-ci, 360-ci, 361-ci, 390-ci, 391-ci, 406-ci, 460-ci, 427-ci, and 428-ci V-8 engines. These engines all have 4.63-inch bore centers. The other big-blocks are the 385-series, which include the 429-ci and 460-ci police engines. These have 4.90-inch bore centers.

The FE-series was introduced in 1958. The 385-series was introduced in 1969. These engines used the deep-skirt design, which was started with the 1955 Y-block.

The two 332-ci V-8s were called "Interceptor" engines while the 352-ci and 361-ci V-8s were called "Police Interceptor" engines. The Police Interceptor V-8 engines were said to have "split-second response, lightning acceleration, and pavement pounding performance." Compression on the 300-horsepower, 352-ci, 4-bbl was 10.2 to 1 while the squish on the 303-horsepower, 361-ci, 4-bbl was 10.5 to 1.

This was the only year for the 361-ci V-8 in a police car. Little mention is made of this 361-ci engine in the retail literature. However, the popular 390-ci V-8 introduced in 1961 was simply a stroked 361-ci V-8. The 352-ci and 361-ci engines used single 4-bbl carbs. The days of

multiple carburetion in Ford-marque police cars were over. Mercury police cars, however, were still available with triple 2-bbl carbs.

Compared to the 292-ci Y-block, the 332-ci FE-block had the same stroke but a larger bore. The 352-ci FE-block had the same bore as the 332-ci but a longer stroke. The 352-ci and 361-ci engines differed only by a .05-inch larger bore on the bigger V-8.

In 1958, the three-speed Cruise-O-Matic automatic transmission was introduced to law enforcement. This was in response to the three-speed TorqueFlite released in 1957 by Chrysler for its Dodge and Plymouth police cars. Chevrolet retained its two-speed Powerglide until the three-speed TurboHydraMatic in 1966! The two-speed Fordomatic was still used.

The three-speed Cruise-O-Matic was the same unit as the Fordomatic except the Cruise-O-Matic had three forward speeds. It had two selectable drive ranges. One was for first, second, and third gear full-power starts. The other was for more gradual acceleration starting off in second gear. A 2.69 to 1 rear gear was used, available for the maximum fuel economy, while the Fordomatic retained its 3.10 rear gearing. The gas-saving 2.69 rear axle that was teamed with the Cruise-O-Matic was claimed to increase fuel economy by 15 percent.

Like the integrated traction control built into the automatic transmissions from the 1990s, the 1958

New for 1958 was the Ford-Edsel series of big-block engines. The FE-series included the 361-ci V-8 powering this Indiana State Police Ford Custom. *Jerry Parker*

A 1958 Mercury Monterey used by a California Sheriff's Department. This could have had a 400-horsepower, 430-ci V-8. *Darryl Lindsay*

A 1958 Edsel Ranger used by the Milwaukee deputy fire chief. Edsels were never available with a police package. *Chuck Madderom*

Cruise-O-Matic could take off in second gear for "gentle, sure-footed, intermediate starts on wet, icy, or loose surfaces."

The Fordomatic was a $180 option while the Cruise-O-Matic was a $197 option. The three-speed Cruise-O-Matic was only available with the 332-ci, 352-ci, and 361-ci FE-block engines. The two-speed Fordomatic used 3.56 gears with the I-block Six, 3.10 gears with the 292-ci Y-block V-8, and 2.91 gears with the FE-block V-8s. The three-speed Cruise-O-Matic came only with 2.69 rear gears. This substantially lowered the acceleration; however, it greatly increased the top end and fuel economy.

Ford was proud of the research and development that went into the 1958 FE-block V-8 and three-speed Cruise-O-Matic. Here is what the police flyer said:

In the most extensive road test ever given a new car before its introduction, the 58 Ford was driven around the world to prove its masterful performance and roadability under the most rugged conditions imaginable. Powered by the great 58 Interceptor V-8 with new Cruise-O-Matic Drive, Ford conquered the steep winding roads of the Swiss Alps with easy grace . . . swept like a breeze through the rugged terrain of the Balkans . . . penetrated the great deserts and jungles of southeast Asia . . . to complete the greatest car test ever known. Here's dramatic proof that the 58 Ford delivers its own brand of high performance with real economy that's made to order for police duty.

The secret of Ford's world proved and approved stamina and dependability is the great 58 Inner Ford—the new, tougher, more silent, solid and secure body and chassis, plus the mighty new 1958 Ford engines with power and performance to spare whether climbing mountains or challenging blistering 100-plus degree heat. More than this has never been required of any police car, even in round-the-clock duty under the most demanding conditions.

Ford's built to take it, and take it longer with less maintenance. No wonder more police cars are Fords than all other makes combined!

For years Ford has been the leader in safety engineering, and again in 58, safety is the keynote of this safest and most comfortable of all Fords! Lifeguard Steering Wheel, Safety-Type Seat Anchorage and Lifeguard Double-Grip Door Locks are standard equipment on all 1958 Ford models. New easier-handling Magic-Circle Steering means greater maneuverability, greater handling ease, greater safety in traffic. Ford's Giant-Grip Double-Sealed Brakes are designed for quick, safe stopping and minimum maintenance. The entire body and chassis construction of the sturdy new Inner Ford is designed to ride smoother, more solid and secure—and give greater passenger protection with Lifeguard Design throughout . . . further good reasons why over 70% of all state police cars sold are Fords.

Magic-Circle steering referred to the new-for-1958 recirculating ball steering gear instead of the traditional worm and roller. The result was less steering effort whether driving or parking.

In 1958, Ford remained the United States' best-selling police car.

In 1958, the Mercury police package was based on the 122-inch wheelbase two-door and four-door Monterey sedan. This 4,100-pound cruiser easily met the requirements for state police and highway patrol use. The standard engine was the 312-horsepower, 383-ci, 4-bbl. One optional police engine was the 360-horsepower, 430-ci, 4-bbl normally restricted to the Montclair. This was the first year for Mercury's massive 430-ci V-8. The 430-ci was a stroked version of the 383-ci big-block.

The 430-ci police mill came in two versions. One was the 360-horsepower, 4-bbl while the other was the 400-horsepower, 6-bbl. That's right, three two-barrel carbs. This was the first year for triple deuce induction

The 1958 Edsel was an upscale car aimed at Chrysler and Oldsmobile buyers. Troopers would drive 1958 Fords and 1958 Chevys (left two), while the police brass used the Edsel (right two) as a staff car. *Robert Parks*

For 1959, the full-size Ford like this Nashville, Tennessee, Police unit, was bumped up an inch to a 118-inch wheelbase. Every inch added to high-speed stability. *Dave Dotson*

on any Mercury police car. This also marked the first time any Ford or Mercury police car was powered by a 400-horsepower engine.

This was not Mercury's first use of multiple carburetion. In 1956, the 312-ci Y-block was available with twin 4-bbl carbs in the M-260 package producing 260 horsepower. In 1957, the M-335 power package included dual quads on a 368-ci V-8, resulting in 335 horsepower. The 1958 model year was the last for multiple carburetion, either dual quads or triple deuces on a Ford or Mercury police engine.

The 400-horsepower Super Marauder 430-ci was only available with the Merc-O-Matic automatic. A 2.91 rear gear was used with this power team. The

For 1959, the Equa-Lock limited slip differential was introduced on Ford police cars like this Santa Clara County, California, Sheriff's Fairlane. *Darryl Lindsay*

312-horsepower, 383-ci V-8 used 2.69 rear gears with the Merc-O-Matic and 3.56 gears with either the three-speed or Overdrive.

In 1958, FoMoCo introduced its Edsel car line. The 118-inch wheelbase Edsel Ranger and Pacer were powered by the 303-horsepower, 361-ci, 4-bbl V-8. The 124-inch wheelbase Edsel Corsair and Citation were powered by the 345-horsepower, 410-ci, 4-bbl V-8. The Edsel was produced from July 1957 to November 1959 and is arguably the biggest marketing disaster in the history of automobiles.

The Edsel was aimed at the Chrysler New Yorker and Oldsmobile 98 market. The Edsel was never intended to be used as a police car and a police package was never available for any model or vintage of Edsel. The Edsel was, however, used by an occasional police chief or county sheriff. These were all simply retail cars used for police work. Edsel never made a police package car.

In 1959, a new series called the Galaxie was introduced by Ford. The police package, however, was restricted to the Custom 300 and Fairlane models. The Custom 300 was the base trim level while the Fairlane was the intermediate trim level. For 1959, the wheelbase was extended to 118 inches for both the Custom 300 and Fairlane. This made a big difference at a time when longer wheelbases were assumed to be more stable at higher speeds than shorter wheelbases. Every inch counted.

By 1959, the horsepower race from the previous year's retail cars was over. Multiple carbureted V-8s were

gone. Compared to 1958, compression ratios were down slightly and so was horsepower. The drivetrain combinations were also fewer. The 4-bbl version of the 332-ci was gone. The 361-ci engine was no longer available. However, the 300-horsepower version of the 352-ci FE-block was carried over to 1959. Mercury police engines for use in the Monterey included the 322-horsepower, 383-ci, 4-bbl and the 345-horsepower, 430-ci, 4-bbl.

In 1959, a totally new rear end was introduced on Ford police cars: the Equa-Lock limited slip differential. The police literature explained, "Delivers the driving force equally to both rear wheels, providing better traction on slippery surfaces. Both wheels turn at the same speed instead of one spinning and the other standing still." While four axle ratios from 2.91 to 3.70 were available with the standard differential, the Equa-Lock was only available in 3.10 and 3.70 ratios.

Tyrex "super-rayon" cord 7.50x14-inch tires were standard on 1959 police cars.

In 1959, Ford maintained its dominance among state police and highway patrol agencies with over 70 percent of the market. For 1960, the Ford police sedans were totally redesigned. This was the first of the longer, lower, wider Ford sedans. The only features in common with the 1959 models were the engines and drivetrains. The wheelbase was increased 1 inch to 119 inches. For 1960, the police package was based on the Fairlane. This was now the base trim level.

In 1960, the Ford police package was available for the two-door and four-door Fairlane sedan and both the

The biggest engine for 1959 Ford police cars was the 352-ci, 4-bbl V-8. Many cruisers like this Nassau County, New York, Police unit used this 300-horsepower, dual-exhaust drivetrain. *Douglas Stiegelmaier*

Many city police cars like this 1959 Chicago Police Fairlane were powered by the 223-ci, 1-bbl Six. This economical engine made sense for many city police details. *Greg Reynolds*

For 1959, more than 70 percent of the state police and highway patrol agencies, such as the Indiana State Police, used Fords. *Jerry Parker*

Ranch Wagon and Country Sedan station wagons.

The 1960 chassis was 25 percent stronger than 1959, the rear suspension was redesigned with asymmetric leaf springs and the front and rear track was wider.

The 1960 police drivetrains including transmission options and axle ratios were basically a carryover from 1959. For 1960, a new 2-bbl version of the 352-ci rated at 235 horsepower replaced the 1959 2-bbl version of the 332-ci rated at 225 horsepower. Both this engine and the 292-ci, 2-bbl carried the name Thunderbird, but this was starting to lose its image of performance.

The 332-ci V-8 was discontinued. The 292-ci V-8 got smaller valves for better fuel economy and the result was slightly less power than 1959.

For 1960, the words "Police Special" were embossed in the valve covers of the 300-horsepower, 352-ci Police Interceptor V-8.

For 1960, the two available automatic transmissions were the two-speed Fordomatic and the three-speed Cruise-O-Matic. No official mention is made in the police literature about an alleged three-speed special-order version of the Fordomatic. Unlike the three-speed Cruise-O-Matic which can start off in either first or second, the three-speed Fordomatic, if it existed, was supposed to start off only in first gear.

New for 1960, the Cruise-O-Matic was a 12-inch torque converter that increased the stall speed and gave greater throttle response without affecting fuel economy.

Check out the Pinellas County, Florida, Sheriff's fleet. Sheriffs departments and county police all over the county drove Fords in 1959. *Robert Helmick*

In 1960, the Washington State Patrol used Fords. So did the state police or highway patrol in Colorado and Alaska. *Darryl Lindsay*

For 1960, 15x5-inch wheels were back in the police lineup. The 14-inch wheels were widened to 5.5 inches. The top tires were the 7.10x15 used on the 300-horsepower, 352-ci powered cars and the 8.00x14 used with the 235-horsepower, 352-ci mill.

For 1960, Ford increased the width of the drum brakes. The lining area was increased from 180 square inches to 226 square inches for most engines and to 248 square inches for the Interceptor version of the 352-ci.

The 1958 Fords were used by the Indiana State Police; Fairfax County, Virginia, Sheriff; North Carolina Highway Patrol; and Washington State Patrol. In 1959, Fords were used by the Pinellas County, Florida, Sheriff; Santa Clara County, California, Sheriff; Indiana State Police; Chicago Police; Los Angeles Police; Cook County, Illinois, Sheriff; Iowa State Patrol; Illinois State Police; Alaska State Troopers; Ohio State Highway Patrol; Alabama State Troopers; Idaho State Police; and Washington State Patrol. The 1960 Fords were used by the Kansas City, Missouri, Police; San Jose, California, Police; Washington State Patrol; Fairfax County, Virginia, Sheriff; Chicago Police; Alaska State Trooper; Colorado State Patrol; and Pinellas County, Florida, Sheriff.

For 1960, Ford police cars like this Nashville, Tennessee, Police cruiser got a redesigned rear suspension and a wider front and rear track. *Dave Dotson*

For 1960, Ford police cars powered by the 352-ci, 4-bbl V-8 like this Nashville, Tennessee, Police unit got 15-inch wheels for better brake cooling. *Dave Dotson*

1958 Ford and Mercury Police Drivetrains

Marque	layout	cid	carb	comp	horsepower	exhaust
Ford	I-6	223	1-bbl	8.6	145	single
Ford	V-8(Y)	292	2-bbl	9.1	205	single
Ford	V-8 (FE)	332	2-bbl	9.5	240	single
Ford	V-8 (FE)	332	4-bbl	9.5	265	dual
Ford	V-8 (FE)	352	4-bbl	10.2	300	dual
Ford	V-8 (FE)	361	4-bbl	10.5	303	dual
Mercury	V-8	383	4-bbl	10.5	312	single
Mercury	V-8	430	4-bbl	10.5	360	dual
Mercury	V-8	430	3x2-bbl	10.5	400	dual

Axles   2.69, 2.91, 3.10, 3.56, 3.70, 3.89

1959 Ford and Mercury Police Drivetrains

Marque	layout	cid	carb	comp	horsepower	exhaust
Ford	I-6	223	1-bbl	8.4	145	single
Ford	V-8	292	2-bbl	8.8	200	single
Ford	V-8	332	2-bbl	8.9	225	single
Ford	V-8	352	4-bbl	9.6	300	dual
Mercury	V-8	383	4-bbl	10.0	322	dual
Mercury	V-8	430	4-bbl	10.0	345	dual

transmission: 3-speed, Overdrive, 2-speed Fordomatic, 3-speed Cruise-O-Matic
axles: 2.91, 3.10, 3.56, 3.70

1960 Ford and Mercury Police Drivetrains

Marque	layout	cid	carb	comp	horsepower	exhaust
Ford	I-6	223	1-bbl	8.4	145	single
Ford	V-8	292	2-bbl	8.8	185	single
Ford	V-8	352	2-bbl	8.9	235	single
Ford	V-8	352	4-bbl	9.6	300	dual
Mercury	V-8	383	4-bbl	10.0	280	dual
Mercury	V-8	430	2-bbl	10.0	310	dual

The top police engine for 1960 Ford police cars like this Mayberry replica was the 300-horsepower, 352-ci V-8. Mercury police cars could get the 345-horsepower, 430-ci V-8. *Quay Johnson*

Check out this black-and-white 1960 Ford used by a California movie studio. The San Jose, California, Police used cars exactly like this one. *Darryl Lindsay*

Chapter Six

1961-1962
The 390-ci FE-Block

In 1961, Ford offered 25 versions of police vehicles, each tailored to specific kinds of police duty. This included two versions of the Police Interceptor Sedan, 15 variations of its Police Wagons, and 8 varieties of the Police Sedan.

Ford took the police package concept beyond just a set of heavy-duty components. The company actually developed a number of complete police vehicle packages including the right engine for the job. One example is the Police Cruiser V-8 Package using the 300-horsepower, 390-ci, V-8 intended for high-speed patrol but not necessarily needing the Interceptor engine. Another example is the Guardian V-8 Package based on the 220-horsepower, 352-ci intended for general patrol work. Yet another example is the Utility Six Package using the 135-horsepower, 223-ci Six intended for light urban patrol or use by nonemergency personnel such as detectives.

This package concept involving the entire vehicle was an attempt to simplify the police-car ordering process. In 1990s terms, it would be called value pricing: putting together the most common combinations. Each package came with its own list of standard equipment, highly recommended options, and other options.

However, any of the engine and trans combinations could be ordered even if the particular drivetrain did not fall under one of the neatly presented packages.

For 1961, the police package was available on the two-door and four-door 119-inch wheelbase Fairlane and all three versions of the station wagon.

In 1961, Ford introduced the famous 390-ci FE-series V-8 to both retail cars and police package cars. This was basically a 4.05-inch bore 361-ci V-8 stroked from 3.50 inches to 3.78 inches. The rest is police engine history. The 390-ci V-8-powered police cars through 1971.

The 390-ci V-8 was a very popular street performance engine; however, the 375-horsepower and 390-horsepower solid lifter versions and the 401-horsepower, three-two barrel versions of the 390-ci V-8 were never police package engines.

In 1961, the 390-ci V-8 was available in two versions for police use. One was the 300-horsepower "Thunderbird 390 Special." The other was the extremely popular 330-horsepower "Interceptor" V-8. Both had 4-bbl carbs, 9.6:1 compression, and dual exhaust. The 330-horsepower version had a special high-lift cam and header-type cast-iron exhaust manifolds borrowed from the 375-horsepower,

An exact replica of the 1961 Mayberry sheriff Ford Fairlane used on the TV series *The Andy Griffith Show. TAGS* enthusiasts form a strong core of Ford fans.

The 1961 Ford Fairlane, like this Mayberry replica, was the third major restyling in three years.

A 1961 Ford Fairlane used by the Montreal, Quebec, Police. The 1961 Fords had a 119-inch wheelbase. *John Carroll*

The Massachusetts State Police used the Ford in 1961. So did the Arkansas State Police; St. Louis County, Missouri, Sheriff; and Atlanta, Georgia, Police. *Darryl Lindsay*

390-horsepower and 401-horsepower engines. The 335-horsepower V-8 included solid lifters, high rpm valve springs, and low back-pressure mufflers.

The 390-ci V-8 was not available with the Fordomatic, while it was available with the three-speed stick, Overdrive, and three-speed Cruise-O-Matic. New for 1961, the Cruise-O-Matic got an aluminum housing. A heavy-duty version of the Cruise-O-Matic was developed for the 335 horsepower version of the 390 ci. It had a faster upshift at higher rpms. The rear axle ratio for all Cruise-O-Matic cars was 3.00:1 except for the 292-ci engine. The Equa-Lock limited slip axle was not available with the 335-horsepower Interceptor V-8.

Again, improvements were made in the chassis for 1961. The steering was up to 25 percent easier thanks to a 30 to 1 ratio on nonpower steering units. Bodies were 17 percent more rigid. Self-adjusting brakes were new for 1961. The 14-inch rims were widened to 6 inches and six-ply nylon tires were back on the option list. The use of 15-inch wheels was also recommended for better cooling of brakes.

Radiators were beefed up for 1961 with thicker tubes and reinforced brackets. Universal joints had self-aligning needle bearings.

In 1961, Ford introduced a 101-horsepower, 170-ci, I-6 for use with the retail Falcon. This was a stroked version of the 144-ci I-6 released in 1960 along with the Falcon. For 1962, this 170 ci became the standard equipment powerplant in the police Fairlane. Axle ratios varied from 3.00 for most automatics to 3.56 and 3.89 for most manual transmissions.

For 1962, the police package for full-size cars was based on the two-door and four-door Galaxie. The Galaxie retained its 119-inch wheelbase. Ford presented 26 police vehicle packages including full-size sedans, midsize sedans, and station wagons.

New for 1962 was Ford's first midsize police car, the 115.5-inch wheelbase Fairlane. With the new, little police car came two unique powerplants: the 170-ci I-6 and the 221-ci V-8. The 221-ci V-8 represented brand-new thin-wall casting technology. As a midyear release, Ford introduced its 260-ci V-8.

How the times have changed! In 1962, the 115.5-inch wheelbase Fairlane was a midsize car that most cops thought was too small for police work. In 1997, the 114.4-inch Crown Vic is the last of the full-size cop cars and is ideal for police work.

In 1962, Ford again designed vehicle packages around car and engine combinations. The Fairlane "Ranger" included the 145-horsepower, 221-ci V-8 while the Fairlane "Sentry" was based around the 101-horsepower, 170-ci I-6. The midyear Fairlane "Defender" used the 160-horsepower, 260-ci V-8. The Fairlane police car was available in both two-door and four-door versions.

The midsize Fairlane was roughly 12 inches shorter than the full-size Galaxie yet 8 inches longer than the compact Falcon. The 1962 Falcon was not available with a police package.

The new Fairlane used a unitized body structure with integral body torque boxes to help stiffen the chassis. The unibody was not new to law enforcement. Chrysler Corporation introduced it in 1960.

However, the unibody was a very hard sell for cops who strongly preferred the body-on-frame design.

The "single-unit body" was a welded, integral body and frame that used special torque boxes under each corner of the underbody structure to absorb shock and vibration.

The 1962 Fairlane engines were teamed with the three-speed stick, Overdrive, or the two-speed Fordomatic. The three-speed Cruise-O-Matic was not available.

The Fairlane used 6.50x13 tires with the six-cylinder engine and 7.00x13 tires with either of the V-8s. The 14-inch wheels were a recommended option and a requirement with heavy-duty brakes.

In the early 1960s, a horsepower race and a fuel economy race were going on at the same time. On one hand, compression ratios and engine sizes would increase. On the other, downsized, short wheelbase cars with even smaller six-cylinder engines were released.

The 1962 Fairlane was released at the same time as the 1962 Plymouth Savoy in an attempt to capture the light-duty, urban patrol market.

While the concept was right, cops were reluctant to accept these smaller vehicles. Less than 1,000 a year were sold. That is a relatively small number, considering around 60,000 police package cars are sold each year.

Perhaps the biggest news of 1962 was the first Windsor small-block engine, the 221-ci V-8. Future Windsor V-8s would be the 260-ci, 289-ci, 302-ci, and 351-ci. All of these engines have 4.38-inch cylinder bore centers. This series of engines remained in service until the late 1990s, powering thousands of full-size, midsize, four-wheel-drive, and Mustang police cars. This small-block V-8 eventually would be replaced in most patrol cars by the 4.6L "modular" SOHC V-8. The 302-ci Windsor does, however, power the 1997 police Explorer.

In 1962, Ford police cars were available with the four-speed stick for the first time. This Missouri State Highway Patrol commission, however, had a three-speed Cruise-O-Matic. *Jim Post*

The 1962 Ford police cars were based on the 119-inch wheelbase Galaxie, like this Dallas Police squad. The 115.5-inch midsize Fairlane was also available with the police package.

This 1962 Dallas Police Ford Galaxie is powered by the 330-horsepower, 390-ci V-8. The 406-ci FE-block was never used in police cars.

A 1962 Ford used by the Nassau County, New York, Police. The extra speedometer and fender lights indicate this is a big-block highway patrol unit. *Douglas Stiegelmaier*

Ford introduced the 221-ci "Fairlane V-8" to police and retail customers alike in 1962. The 221-ci small-block V-8 had a much different bore and stroke than the first flathead V-8; however, it had exactly the same displacement.

The small-block V-8 was needed as a powerplant for Ford's new midsize car, thus the name Fairlane V-8. The deep skirt, Y-block was far too large for such a car even debored and destroked. The 1962 221-ci V-8 was actually Ford's belated response to the 1955 Chevy small-block V-8. However, Ford took advantage of the latest thin wall casting techniques for both the block and overhead-valve head. The result was an engine that was both smaller and lighter than the Chevy small-block.

Like the Y-block V-8 and unlike the flathead V-8, Ford was very careful to fully develop its new small-block. More than 17,000 hours were spent on the dynamometer by over 500 prototype and preproduction engines. Over 250,000 miles were logged both at the Ford proving grounds and on public streets and highways.

In mid-1962, Ford released what would be a more famous version of its small-block, the 260-ci V-8. The 260-ci was simply a bored-out 221-ci. The 160-horsepower 260-ci was only available in the Fairlane in 1962. However, by 1963 it would find its way into the full-size Galaxie as an economy engine for urban patrol.

In 1962, Ford joined the horsepower race with its 405-horsepower, 406-ci big-block. A bored-out 390-ci engine, the 406 ci was never used in police cars.

New for 1962 was the option of a four-speed manual shift transmission. This was unusual in police work. While Chevrolet also offered a four-speed stick in 1959, no Dodge or Plymouth police car ever came with a four-speed. The four-speed was available with the 352-ci and 390-ci V-8s. When this was used, the rear axle ratio was 3.56 to 1. The three-speed and overdrive cars got either 3.56 or 3.89 gears while the Fordomatic and Cruise-O-Matic cars got 3.00 and 3.56 gears.

Once again for 1962, Ford was law enforcement's number one choice for police vehicles. Ford ads claimed that more Ford police cars were sold than all other makes combined.

The 1961 Ford was used by the St. Louis County, Missouri, Sheriff; Arkansas State Police; South Carolina Highway Patrol; Baltimore, Maryland, Police; Omaha, Nebraska, Police; Massachusetts State Police; and Atlanta Police. In 1962, Fords were used by the Dallas Police; Nebraska State Patrol; Kansas City, Missouri, Police; Wisconsin State Patrol; St. Louis County, Missouri, Sheriff; New Orleans Police; Tennessee Highway Patrol; and Missouri State Highway Patrol.

1961 Ford Police Drivetrains

Layout	cid	carb	comp	horsepower	exhaust
I-6	23	1-bbl	8.4	135	single
V-8	292	2-bbl	8.8	175	single
V-8	352	2-bbl	8.9	220	single
V-8	390	4-bbl	9.6	300	dual
V-8	390	4-bbl	9.6	330	dual

1962 Ford Police Drivetrains

Layout	cid	carb	comp	horsepower	exhaust	model
I-6	223	1-bbl	8.4	138	single	Galaxie
V-8	292	2-bbl	8.8	170	single	Galaxie
V-8	352	2-bbl	8.9	220	single	Galaxie
V-8	390	4-bbl	9.6	300	dual	Galaxie
V-8	390	4-bbl	9.6	330	dual	Galaxie
I-6	170	1-bbl	8.7	101	single	Fairlane
V-8	221	2-bbl	8.7	145	single	Fairlane
V-8	260	2-bbl	8.7	160	single	Fairlane

Chapter One

1963-1965
The 260-ci and 289-ci Small-Block

In 1963, the Ford police fleet was made up of the 119-inch wheelbase full-size Galaxie and the 115.5-inch midsize Fairlane. Both were available in two-door and four-door sedans.

From the Ford 300 Police Interceptor, to the Fairlane Sentry with the 170-ci I-6 to the six-passenger police package station wagons, in 1963 Ford offered a total of 31 different police models.

In 1963, the base trim level for the full-size Ford was the Ford 300. The Galaxie was the intermediate trim level. The police package was available for both models. In the past, Ford offered a variety of two-door and four-door police station wagons in various trim levels. For 1963, the police package was restricted to the four-door Galaxie Country Sedan. The wagon was available in powerplants from the 223-ci I-6 to the 390-ci Police Interceptor V-8.

For 1963, the 170-horsepower, 292-ci Y-block was replaced by the 164-horsepower, 260-ci small-block V-8. The 289-ci small-block, introduced on 1963 retail Fords, was not yet available as a police engine. The 292-ci engine had been in police cars since 1955.

The early 1960s was the so-called Super Stock era when carmakers developed multiple carb, high-compression engines for use in full-size cars. This was different from the Muscle Car era of the late 1960s when high-performance engines were put in midsize and pony cars. In response to the 400-plus horsepower engines from Chevrolet and Dodge, in 1963 Ford released the most powerful production engines it ever made: the 410-horsepower and 425-horsepower versions of the overhead-valve 427-ci V-8. However, these 11.5:1 compression engines were never used in police cars.

The top cop engine for 1963 remained the 330-horsepower Police Interceptor 390-ci V-8. The Ford police literature said, "The Interceptor 4-V/390 V-8 is a specially engineered 330 horsepower powerplant designed exclusively for and sold only to law enforcement agencies."

While the valve covers said Thunderbird, this was a unique engine. The two hot 390-ci Thunderbird Special V-8s at the time were a 9.6:1, 4-bbl engine rated at 330 horsepower and a 10.5:1, 6-bbl engine rated at 340

In 1963, the 260-ci V-8 was a popular choice for urban police cars like this Montreal, Quebec, Police unit. *John Carroll*

horsepower. It appears the Police Interceptor used the triple-deuce engine with a single 4-bbl carb. It did have a high lift cam, solid lifters, high-rpm valve springs, header-type cast exhaust, low restriction mufflers, and dual exhaust. For 1963 police cars, this was quite the setup!

In 1963, Ford introduced the Synchro-Smooth Drive. This was the first fully synchronized three-speed manual transmission. While the first to second and second to third shifts had been synchronized for some time, going into first gear had not been. The ease of getting into first without grinding gears made these cars much easier to drive.

For 1963, the four-speed stick was also available with the 352-ci and 390-ci engines. The three-speed stick was a column shift while the four-speed was a floor shift. The four-speed Cruise-O-Matic was available with all of the V-8s. The two-speed Fordomatic was restricted to the Sixes and the small-block V-8s. As a rule, the manual shift cars got 3.50 or 3.89 rear axles while the automatic trans cars got 3.00, 3.25, or 3.50 to one rear gears.

In 1963, Ford was once again the United States' number one police car.

In 1964, Ford began its famous theme: Total Performance. The company would emphasize Total Performance throughout the rest of the 1960s and into the 1970s. It perfected the concept of Total Performance with the Mustang. The Mustang was not

An exact replica of the 1963 Ford Galaxie used on the TV series, *The Andy Griffith Show.* The crest in the center of the grille was the hood release.

The 1963 Ford, like this Mayberry sheriff replica, was the fifth major restyle in as many years.

always the fastest compared to the Camaro, Firebird, 'Cuda, and Challenger. However, it did have the best balance of performance.

So it was with Ford's police fleet. In the ABCs of vehicle performance (acceleration, braking, cornering), Ford set out to have the best overall performance. They would never accelerate like a Dodge or brake like a Chevy or corner like a Pontiac. However, the goal was to do well enough in all categories to give the best Total Performance.

In 1964, the full-size Ford police car was based on the 119-inch wheelbase Custom and Custom 500 in both two-door and four-door sedans. The Galaxie nameplate was only used in 1962 and 1963. It would resume in 1969. The police package remained available for the 115.5-inch wheelbase two-door and four-door Fairlane. The police station wagon was available in six-passenger and nine-passenger versions.

For 1964, all the models using the optional, larger V-8s had that engine emblem on the lower front fender.

Two new engines joined the police fleet for 1964, the 289-ci V-8 used in both the Custom and Fairlane and the 200-ci I-6 for the Fairlane.

The 289-ci is one of Ford's most famous retail engines; however, the Mustang's 271-horsepower 289-ci "Hi-Po" was never a police engine. Neither was the 306-horsepower Shelby version of the 289-ci ever used in police cars.

The 289 ci was introduced on retail cars in 1963. It was basically a 260-ci V-8 bored out to 4.00 inches. While the 289 ci became a popular high-performance engine in the Mustang, its reputation did not carry over to police cars for two reasons. First, the full-size cars used by most cops were too heavy for the 289-ci small-block. It really took a 352-ci for reasonable performance from the four-door sedan. The 390-ci was even a better fit for most

police use. The second reason was the output from the 289 ci itself. While the 4-bbl version was available on the low volume Fairlane, the full-size Custom used 2-bbl versions of the 289 ci for best economy. As a result, the 289 ci became known as a durable and economical small-block for urban patrol, not as a high-performance engine for rural sheriffs and state police.

Simply put, the 195-horsepower, 289 ci, 2-bbl V-8 was intended for "routine police work," "thrifty performance on regular gas," and "routine patrol work." You do not generally gain fame for doing a good job of something routine.

The 200-ci I-6 was new for police cars in 1964. This inline Six was originally designed for the Mustang. It was called the "Mustang Six," as opposed to the 223-ci "Ford Six" used in the full-size cars, and the 170-ci "Fairlane Six" used in the Falcon and Fairlane. The 200-ci I-6 was a bored and stroked version of the 170-ci I-6 and not at all related to the 223-ci I-6. The two smaller Sixes had seven main bearings while the larger Six had just four. The new 116-horsepower, 200-ci I-6 was used as an optional engine in the Fairlane, which now had its choice of two Sixes and two V-8s.

The transmissions and axle ratios were a carryover from 1963 with one big exception: The two-speed Fordomatic was no longer available in the full-size Custom. It was only available in the midsize Fairlane and only with the 200-ci I-6 and 260-ci V-8. This was the last year for the Fordomatic in a police car.

The available transmissions were the three-speed stick, Overdrive, four-speed stick, and Cruise-O-Matic. For the first time the four-speed stick and three-speed Cruise-O-Matic were optional but only with the 289-ci-powered Fairlane.

As a rule, the rear axle ratios were 3.00, 3.25, and 3.50 with the automatics and 3.50, 3.89, and 4.11 with the manual shift transmissions.

The 1963 Ford was used by the Missouri State Highway Patrol. Fords were also driven by officers with the Nebraska State Patrol, South Dakota Highway Patrol, and Pennsylvania State Police. *Darryl Lindsay*

New for 1963, the 260-ci Windsor V-8 was available on the full-size Galaxie. Most police cars, however, like this Cook County, Illinois, Sheriff's Department unit used the 352-ci or 390-ci V-8. *Darryl Lindsay*

For 1964, Ford was once again the United States' most popular police car.

For 1965, Ford expanded its police fleet to a total of 41 different "kit-priced Police Packages." This included the two-door and four-door Custom and Custom 500 in five different engines, the two-door and four-door Fairlane with three different engines and three kinds of police station wagons with five different engines.

In 1965, Ford continued with the Total Performance theme. The full-size Custom police car remained at 119 inches while the midsize Fairlane grew slightly to a 116-inch wheelbase.

In 1965, the Custom had police engines in nice and neat power increments: 150 horsepower, 200 horsepower, 250 horsepower, 300 horsepower, and 330 horsepower. The Fairlane went from the mild 200-ci I-6 to the wild 289-ci, 4-bbl V-8.

In 1965, the full-size Custom got a larger in-line six-cylinder as the base engine. This 150-horsepower, 240-ci I-6 was a bored and stroked version of the Fairlane's 200-ci Six. This was not a bored out 223-ci Six used in the 1964 Ford. The 223-ci I-6 had only four main bearings and it had a "square" bore and stroke. This means the 3.62-inch bore equaled the 3.60-inch stroke. The new 240-ci I-6 had a larger 4.00-inch bore and a short 2.87-inch stroke. The new I-6 also had seven main bearings like the Fairlane-Mustang versions.

The V-8 lineup for the 1965 Custom was a carryover from 1964 with one exception. The 289-ci, 2-bbl was bumped in compression enough to gain 5 horsepower for a 200 horsepower rating. The top cop mill remained the 330-horsepower, Interceptor 390-ci, 4-bbl V-8.

Big changes took place among 1965 Fairlane engines. First, the 170-ci I-6 engine was dropped. The 200-ci I-6 was bumped in compression enough to get a 120-horsepower rating. The 260-ci, V-8 was no longer available. The 289-ci, 2-bbl filled the role for an economical

New for 1964, the 289-ci Windsor V-8 was available on the full-size Galaxie. Most police cars, however, like this Manteca, California, Police cruiser used the 352-ci or 390-ci V-8. *Darryl Lindsay*

V-8. Big news for the midsize Fairlane was the 225-horsepower version of the 289-ci V-8 thanks to a 4-bbl carb and dual exhaust. This drivetrain combo made for a quick car for the time.

By 1965, all of Ford's police cars had been converted over from a generator to an alternator-based electrical system. The Interceptor 390 ci used a dual belt drive alternator while all other engines used a single belt drive. Alternators up to 60 amps were limited production options while 100-amp alternators were special order options.

In 1965, Ford also switched from a rear leaf spring to rear coil spring suspension. The all-coil suspension was supposed to give better control at pursuit speeds with less tendency to bottom out than a rear leaf system. The all-coil suspension was also smoother riding and quieter on a variety of road surfaces. This

The North Carolina Highway Patrol used the 390-ci Ford Galaxie in 1964. The Chicago Police, Washington State Police Patrol, and Texas Highway Patrol also drove 1964 Fords. *M. K. Holcomb*

A Mayberry-marked 1964 Ford Galaxie. *The Andy Griffith Show* Rerun Watchers Club is a hard-core group of early-1960s Ford enthusiasts.

The Pennsylvania State Police, Dearborn Police, and Columbus Police all used Ford police cars in 1964. *Monty McCord*

This 1965 Indiana State Police Ford Custom is powered by the 390-ci Interceptor V-8. Notice that this cruiser is a two-door. *Jerry Parker*

In 1965, the full-size Fords like this two-door Michigan State Police unit were converted from a leaf spring to a coil spring rear suspension. *MSP*

The Ohio State Highway Patrol used Ford police cars in 1965. So did the Illinois State Police, Dallas, Texas, Police, and Maryland State Police. *Darryl Lindsay*

The top cop mill in the 1965 Fords was the 330-horsepower, 390-ci V-8. That is the powerplant for this San Francisco Police cruiser. *Darryl Lindsay*

In 1965, the 200-ci Six was bored and stroked to 240 ci. This powered many urban police cars. This Nassau County, New York, Police unit has a V-8. *Ned Schwartz*

A beautiful Mayberry-marked 1965 Ford Custom. The 1965 Fords all had alternators and a new power steering system. *Jack Fellenzer*

was the first time the big Fords ever used a coil spring rear suspension.

In 1965, Ford released a single overhead-cam (SOHC) 427-ci V-8 with hemi-heads and 12.1 to 1 compression. The single 4-bbl version was rated at 616 horsepower while the dual quad version cranked out 657 horsepower. These were over-the-counter race engines, not retail engines and certainly not police engines. However, in 1992, Ford would indeed release a SOHC V-8 for police use. As a point of fact, the Ford 427-ci FE-block was never used in police cars of any year.

In 1965, a new trim level was announced for the retail-only Galaxie 500, the LTD. The LTD nameplate would be the basis for police package cars starting in 1975.

For 1965, Ford was once again the United States' top selling police car. The 1963 Ford was the choice of the Cook County, Illinois, Sheriff; Chicago Police; Pinellas County, Florida, Sheriff; Iowa State Patrol; North Carolina Highway Patrol; Missouri State Highway Patrol; Nebraska State Patrol; Pennsylvania State Police; Dallas Police; South Dakota Highway Patrol; San Francisco Police; St. Louis County, Missouri, Sheriff; and the Los Angeles Police. The largest user of the midsize Fairlane was the Columbus, Ohio, Police.

In 1964, Fords were used by the Pennsylvania State Police; Washington State Patrol; North Carolina Highway Patrol; Dearborn, Michigan, Police; Columbus, Ohio, Police; Chicago Police; Iowa State Patrol; and the Texas Highway Patrol.

The 1965 Ford was the choice of the Washington State Patrol; St. Louis County, Missouri, Sheriff; Maryland State Police; New York State Police; Louisville, Kentucky, Police; Los Angeles County Sheriff; Ohio State Highway Patrol; Illinois State Police; Iowa State Patrol; Michigan State Police; Dallas Police; San Francisco Police; Nassau County, New York Police; Missouri State Highway Patrol; and the Indiana State Police.

1963 Ford Police Drivetrains

Layout	cid	carb	comp	horsepower	exhaust	model
I-6	223	1-bbl	8.4	138	single	Galaxie
V-8	260	2-bbl	8.7	164	single	Galaxie
V-8	352	2-bbl	8.9	220	single	Galaxie
V-8	390	4-bbl	10.5	300	dual	Galaxie
V-8	390	4-bbl	10.5	330	dual	Galaxie
I-6	170	1-bbl	8.7	101	single	Fairlane
V-8	221	2-bbl	8.7	145	single	Fairlane
V-8	260	2-bbl	8.7	164	single	Fairlane

Transmission: 3-speed stick, Overdrive, 4-speed stick, 2-speed Fordomatic, 3-speed Cruise-O-Matic

1964 Ford Police Engines

Layout	cid	carb	comp	horsepower	exhaust	model
I-6	223	1-bbl	8.4	138	single	Custom
V-8	289	2-bbl	9.0	195	single	Custom
V-8	352	4-bbl	9.3	250	dual	Custom
V-8	390	4-bbl	10.1	300	dual	Custom
V-8	390	4-bbl	10.1	330	dual	Custom
I-6	170	1-bbl	8.7	101	single	Fairlane
I-6	200	1-bbl	8.7	116	single	Fairlane
V-8	260	2-bbl	8.8	164	single	Fairlane
V-8	289	2-bbl	9.0	195	single	Fairlane

Transmission: 3-speed, Overdrive, 4-speed, Fordomatic, Cruise-O-Matic
Axles: 3.00, 3.25, 3.50, 3.89, 4.11

1965 Ford Police Engines

Layout	cid	carb	comp	horsepower	exhaust	model
I-6	240	1-bbl	9.2	150	single	Custom
V-8	289	2-bbl	9.3	200	single	Custom
V-8	352	4-bbl	9.3	250	dual	Custom
V-8	390	4-bbl	10.1	300	dual	Custom
V-8	390	4-bbl	10.1	330	dual	Custom
I-6	200	1-bbl	9.2	120	single	Fairlane
V-8	289	2-bbl	9.3	200	single	Fairlane
V-8	289	4-bbl	10.0	225	dual	Fairlane

Transmissions: 3-speed, Overdrive, 4-speed, Cruise-O-Matic
Axles: 3.00, 3.25, 3.50, 3.89

A 1965 Missouri State Highway Patrol Ford Galaxie 500. In 1965, Ford was the United States' best-selling power car. *Ken Kerrick*

This 1965 Custom 500 was used by the Iowa Highway Patrol. The New York State Police and Suffolk County, New York, Police also drove 1965 Fords. *Bob Parks*

Chapter Eight

The 428-ci FE-Block V-8

In 1966, the Ford police package was based on the 119-inch Custom and Custom 500 in two-door and four-door versions, and the 116-inch Fairlane, also in two-door and four-door models. The midsize Fairlane was dramatically restyled for 1966 and now sported vertical headlights.

The big police news for 1966 was a new big-block engine, the 428-ci FE-block, "a real scorcher that turns out 360 horsepower with top speeds well in excess of 100 miles per hour." Top speeds, in fact, were well over 125 miles per hour.

The 428-ci FE-block and the 427-ci FE-block are frequently confused. These are not the same engine. The 427 ci is a 390 ci bored out to 4.23 inches but with the same 3.78-inch stroke. The 428 ci is a 390 ci bored out to 4.13 inches and stroked to 3.98 inches. Both the 427 ci and 428 ci were seriously hot-rodded by the factory; however, only the 428-ci version was used in police cars.

Like the Interceptor 390 ci, upon which the Police Interceptor 428 ci was based, the 428 ci engine contained all the latest go-fast goodies: 4-bbl carb, solid lifter, high lift cam, high rpm valve springs, dual exhaust, and low back-pressure mufflers. This was the last year for solid lifters. The Interceptor 428 ci was only available with the four-speed manual transmission and 3.25 or 3.50 rear gears or the three-speed Cruise-O-Matic and 3.00 or 3.25 rear gears. By this time, most police agencies ordered the automatic transmission regardless of the engine.

Retail cars used the term, "7-litre" for the 428-ci FE-block. Retail cars were limited to the 345-horsepower version. The retail cars had hydraulic lifters, standard lift cam, and standard back pressure exhaust. This would be an optional police engine in 1967.

The 352-ci V-8 was a retail engine in 1966 but it was no longer used in police cars. In 1966, Ford started an unusual strategy for its police engines. Ford offered a 1-bbl Six and a 2-bbl small-block V-8 for economical, urban patrol. Ford offered two versions of its big-block engines for high-speed police work.

However, for the first time in 1966, they offered a 2-bbl version of the 390-ci big-block. This was supposed to give 2-bbl economy for routine patrol and big-block performance for pursuit work. This theory about police powertrains was disproved in 1974 by *Motor Trend*'s John Christy who did extensive technical work with the Los Angeles County Sheriff. At least Ford equipped this 1966 2-bbl, 390-ci big-block with dual exhausts. For 1967, this compromise big-block engine would come with single exhaust.

In 1966, Ford introduced its "C6" big-block-version of the three-speed Cruise-O-Matic. Until then, the "C4" Cruise-O-Matic was used for all engines, big and small. This was the last year for the four-speed manual transmission in a full-size Ford police sedan.

The other big news for the big Fords in 1966 was the availability of front disc brakes. Dodge released front discs in 1965. By mid-1965, the big Plymouth got them. However, Chevrolet did not get front discs until 1967. For the record, Ford would be the first to get rear discs in 1976, 1977, and 1978 and then again in 1992. Chevrolet got rear discs in 1994. No Dodge nor Plymouth police sedan ever had rear discs.

Disc brakes are less likely to fade during repeated stops because they cool off faster. Disc brakes are also less likely to pull to one side or the other during hard braking. They are also much less affected by dust and water compared to drums. However, discs require more pedal effort for the same stopping performance. As a result, vacuum-assisted power brakes were required with front disc brakes.

This Arkansas State Police Ford Custom is powered by the 315-horsepower, 390-ci FE-series big-block V-8. *Darryl Lindsay*

New for 1966 was the option of front disc brakes. It gave police cruisers like this Cook County, Illinois, Sheriffs unit fade-resistant brakes and straight-line stops. *Greg Reynolds*

The 428-ci v-8 in this 1966 Iowa Highway Patrol unit is a bored and stroked version of the 390-ci V-8. *Robert Parks*

The Fairlane was dramatically restyled for 1966 and now sported vertical headlights. The Fairlane kept the same 116-inch wheelbase but was longer, lower, and wider. The Fairlane retained a rear leaf spring suspension. The big news, literally, for the 1966 Fairlane was the availability of the 335-horsepower, Interceptor 390-ci V-8 complete with 4-bbl carb and dual exhaust. This was called the "Trooper Package." However, no state police or highway patrol used the Fairlane in 1966.

A 2-bbl version of the 390-ci V-8 was also available for the Fairlane. This 2-bbl engine came in two versions depending on the transmission. The V-8 teamed with the three-speed or four-speed stick was rated at 265 horsepower. The same engine teamed with the three-speed Cruise-O-Matic had 275 horsepower.

In 1965, photos of the Falcon Station Bus van appeared twice in the police car literature. However, no mention was made of a police package for the van. This changed for 1966. The Falcon Club Wagon was available in standard and extended body version. The "paddy wagon" vans were available with either the 170-ci or 240-ci I-6 and either the three-speed stick or three-speed Cruise-O-Matic.

In 1966, Ford was the United States' number one police car.

For 1967, the Ford police package was available for the 119-inch wheelbase Custom in two-door and four-door sedans and the 116-inch wheelbase Fairlane in two-door and four-door sedans. Three versions of the Ford station wagon and two versions of the Falcon Club Wagon van came with the police package.

New for 1967, the four-wheel drive Bronco pickup, wagon, and roadster were available in official police trim. This was the first four-wheel-drive vehicle offered by any auto maker with a police package. The 4x4 Police Bronco was almost 30 years ahead of its time given the mid-1990s enthusiasm for police sport/utes. The four-wheel-drive Bronco was available with either the 105-horsepower, 170-ci I-6 or 200-horsepower, 289-ci V-8. It was only available with the three-speed stick.

New for 1967, every Ford police car came with the "Energy-Absorbing" steering wheel with deeply padded center hub.

For 1967, two 428-ci V-8s were available for the Custom. One was the 360-horsepower Interceptor version

Check out the window mounted radar used by the Iowa Highway Patrol. The 428-ci V-8 in this cruiser was new for 1966. *Robert Parks*

Ford was the number one police car in 1966. In addition to the Suffolk County, New York, Police, the New York State Police and Virginia State Police also used 1966 Fords. *Ned Schwartz*

carried over from 1966. While the 1967 engine had the same power output, it now used hydraulic lifters. The Interceptor 428-ci was only available with the three-speed Cruise-O-Matic and 2.80 rear gears. Ford now claimed this combination produced a "top speed well in excess of 120 miles per hour."

The other 428-ci engine was the 345-horsepower version that was used in 1966 retail cars. This mill had the same 4-bbl carb and 10.5 to 1 compression as the Interceptor engine. However, the 345-horsepower version used a standard lift cam and standard back-pressure dual exhausts. This 345-horsepower version of the 428-ci was only used in police cars during 1967.

In 1967, two versions of the 390-ci big-block were available in the Custom. One used a 4-bbl, 10.5:1 compression and dual exhausts with a rating of 315 horsepower. The other used a 2-bbl, 9.5:1 compression and single exhaust. The output from the 2-bbl big-block was 270 horsepower.

The strategy of offering a 2-bbl, single exhaust version of a big-block V-8 was both unique to Ford, and a hallmark of Ford's police selections from 1967 through 1978. Other big-block V-8 engines that followed this compromise theme were the 400-ci, 2-bbl and the 429-ci, 2-bbl. All 460-ci V-8s came with 4-bbl carbs.

For 1967, the four-speed stick was no longer available in the Custom. The transmission selections were the three-speed stick, three-speed with Overdrive, and three-speed Cruise-O-Matic. The three-speed stick was still available with all of the engines except the 428-ci V-8. The Overdrive was restricted to the 289-ci V-8 and 240-ci I-6. This was the last year for the three-speed Overdrive in a Ford police car. In the Fairlane, the four-speed was still available with the V-8s. Axle ratios varied from the 2.79 and 2.80 up to the 3.50.

Oddly, in 1967, manual front discs were available on the Custom. Power brakes were not a required option with front discs. This so greatly increased pedal effort that by 1968, the option of manual discs was removed. From then on, disc brakes were always power-assisted.

On the topic of brakes, in 1967, all Ford police cars came with a dual chamber master cylinder. Prior to 1967, the master cylinder had a single chamber. A leak anywhere in the system caused the entire brake system to

With the 360-horsepower, 428-ci V-8, this 1967 Massachusetts State Police Ford Custom had a top speed well in excess of 120 miles per hour. *Darryl Lindsay*

fail. A dual master cylinder was like having two independent braking systems. The front brakes and the rear brakes were separate. A leak or failure in one system still allowed the other system to provide some braking.

The 1967 drivetrain combinations for the 116-inch midsize Fairlane were basically the same as for 1966. The top cop Fairlane engine was a 320-horsepower version of the 390-ci 4-bbl V-8. The 428-ci was not available in the Fairlane. The Fairlane got front disc brakes in 1967.

In 1967, radial tires were used for the first time as original equipment on a Ford police car. However, these tires were restricted to the 289-ci V-8 and 240-ci I-6 versions of the full-size Custom. Radials were used to reduce rolling resistance for better fuel economy and for extended tire mileage to lower operating costs. The big-block Custom, however, got four-ply "Tyrex" rayon cord bias tires. The 7.75x15 was standard on the Custom while 7.35x14 was standard on the Fairlane.

In 1967, *Motor Trend* tested the Ford Galaxie 500, Chevrolet Impala SS, and Plymouth Sport Fury. These three were all two-door hardtops, and none had the police package. However, they all used the same platform as their police cars, and all had big-block engines used in many police cars. All had 119-inch wheelbases. All three cars performed surprisingly close to one another.

Make	Ford	Chevrolet	Plymouth
Model	Galaxie 500	Impala SS	Sport Fury
Engine, ci & carb	390, 4-bbl	396, 4-bbl	383, 4-bbl
Horsepower	315	325	325
Torque, lb-ft	427	410	425
Trans	3-speed C6	3-speed THM	3-speed TF
Axle ratio	2.75	2.73	3.23
Weight, lb	4,243	4,340	4,319
0–60 mph, sec	9.2	9.1	9.6
1/4-mile ET, sec	17.4	17.0	17.4
1/4-mile speed, mph	82	83	81

A highway patrol officer with the Nassau County, New York, Police assisting a motorist. Notice the McDermott light rack. *Ned Schwartz*

In 1967, some Ford police cars came with radial tires. The 390-ci-powered cruisers, like this Hudson County, New Jersey, Sheriff's unit ran a 17-second quarter-mile. *Ned Schwartz*

In 1967, Ford was still the number one brand of police car in the United States.

In 1968, the Ford police package was available for the two-door and four-door Custom and Custom 500, on the two-door and four-door Fairlane, on the Econoline van, Bronco, and all three station wagons. The Custom and Fairlane retained their 119- and 116-inch wheelbases, respectively. Both the Custom and Fairlane were restyled again. This time both had horizontal quad headlights. The big drivetrain change for 1968 is the replacement of the 289-ci small-block by the 302-ci V-8, aka 5.0L. The 289-ci would continue to be a 1968 retail engine but was not used in either the police Custom or the police Fairlane. It was, however, still an optional engine on the police Bronco.

The 302-ci V-8 had very humble beginnings. In 2-bbl form, it was simply added to the police lineup as an economical V-8 for urban patrol: "A good combination of smooth V-8 power and a measure of economy." The 302-ci V-8 would become one of the backbones of the Ford police fleet. It would power all of the "special service" Mustang pursuit cars between 1982 and 1993.

The 302-ci V-8 was simply a stroked version of the 289-ci V-8. Both shared the same bore. The police vehicles used only the 210-horsepower, 2-bbl version; however, a 230-horsepower, 4-bbl version was used in some retail cars. For the record, the Boss 302 introduced in 1969, was never a police engine.

Here is how the Ford 4.38-inch bore center small-block V-8s compare:

For 1968, Ford's top cop engine was the 428-ci V-8. This only came in the full-power Interceptor version cranking out 360 horsepower. The 4-bbl, high-lift cam,

In 1968, the 428-ci Mercury Monterey was extremely popular among state cops. The Indiana State Police became famous for their big-block Mercury cruisers. *Jerry Parker*

10.5:1 compression, low restriction dual exhaust version of this FE-block "is built to provide very fast takeoffs and sustained high speed driving in day-to-day patrol work. Speeds in excess of 120 miles per hour are well within the range of this powerplant."

Other Custom big-block engines included the 390-ci, 4-bbl, dual exhaust; the goofy 390-ci, 2-bbl, single exhaust; and the urban-oriented 302-ci V-8 and 240-ci I-6.

By 1968, tire sizes had started to grow in response to the 360-horsepower big-block engines, power front disc brakes and 120-miles-per-hour plus top speeds. The 7.75x15 was standard for the small-block and Six. The 8.15x15 was standard for the big-block cars. However, the 8.45x15 was a "highly recommended" limited production option. All the wheels were 6-inch heavy-duty steel.

Year (police)	1962	1963	1964	1968	1970
cid	221	260	289	302	351
bore	3.50	3.80	4.00	4.00	4.00
stroke	2.87	2.87	2.87	3.00	3.50
horsepower (2-bbl)	145	164	195	210	250

The Iowa Highway Patrol used 1968 Fords powered by the 360-horse-power, 428-ci V-8. Even with a twin rotator Vis-A-Bar lightbar, top speeds were well over 120 miles per hour. *Bob Parks*

This beautifully-restored 1968 Custom 500 with a 302ci V-8 is the pride of the Bay-area's Menlo Park, California Police. The rare red gumball is not a rotating light. Instead, it oscillates back and forth. *Darryl Lindsay*

The drivetrain for the 1968 police Fairlane was a carryover from 1967. The top mill was the 325-horsepower, 4-bbl, dual-exhaust version of the 390-ci FE-block. The Fairlane was discontinued as a police car after 1968. Police departments large and small continued to favor the longer wheelbase squad cars. The most popular cruisers were 119 to 122 inches. Departments would return to 116-inch wheelbase police cars, but it would be in the mid-1970s.

In 1968, *Popular Science* tested four "family" sedans typical of the platforms used for full-size police cars. These upscale four-door sedans included the Galaxie 500, Impala, Fury III, and Ambassador SST. These all had small-block V-8s that were widely used by urban sheriff departments and city police departments as a balance between V-8 power and good gas mileage.

Again in 1968, more U.S. law enforcement agencies used the Ford police package than any other police car.

In 1966, Fords were used by the Iowa State Patrol; Arkansas State Police; Cook County, Illinois, Sheriff; Illinois State Police; Tennessee Highway Patrol; New York State Police; Washington State Patrol; Detroit Police; and the Virginia State Police. For 1967, the Washington State Patrol, Iowa State Patrol, and Massachusetts State Police selected Fords. By 1968, Mercury became a credible patrol car for state police and highway patrols. The big Mercury was the choice of the Indiana State Police and Missouri State Highway Patrol. Indiana would become famous for their use of Mercury cruisers. Fords were used in 1968 by the Washington State Patrol and Iowa State Patrol.

Make	Ford	Chevrolet	Plymouth	AMC
Model	Galaxie 500	Impala	Fury III	Ambassador
Engine, ci & carb	302, 2-bbl	307, 2-bbl	318, 2-bbl	290, 2-bbl
Horsepower	210	200	230	200
Trans	3-speed C4	2-speed PG	3-speed TF	3-speed SC
Axle	2.80	3.08	2.94	3.15
Weight, lb	3,685	3,900	3,650	3,128
0–60 mph, sec	13.2	14.0	11.2	12.1
Lane change, mph	60	60	55	60
Slalom, mph	22	25	22	20
60–0 mph, ft	181	150.8	172.3	149
EPA city mpg	15.3	15.1	14.7	16.2

1966 Ford Police Engines

Layout	cid	carb	comp	horsepower	exhaust	model
I-6	240	1-bbl	9.2	150	single	Custom
V-8	289	2-bbl	9.3	200	single	Custom
V-8	390	2-bbl	9.5	275	dual	Custom
V-8	390	4-bbl	10.5	315	dual	Custom
V-8	428	4-bbl	10.5	360	dual	Custom
I-6	200	1-bbl	9.2	120	single	Fairlane
V-8	289	2-bbl	9.3	200	single	Fairlane
V-8	390	2-bbl	9.5	265	single	Fairlane
V-8	390	4-bbl	10.5	335	dual	Fairlane

Transmissions: 3-speed stick, Overdrive, 4-speed stick, Cruise-O-Matic
Axles: 2.80, 3.00, 3.25, 3.50

1967 Ford Police Engines

Layout	cid	carb	comp	horsepower	exhaust	model
I-6	240	1-bbl	9.2	150	single	Custom
V-8	289	2-bbl	9.3	200	single	Custom
V-8	390	2-bbl	9.5	270	single	Custom
V-8	390	4-bbl	10.5	315	dual	Custom
V-8	428	4-bbl	10.5	345	dual	Custom
V-8	428	4-bbl	10.5	360	dual	Custom
I-6	200	1-bbl	9.2	120	single	Fairlane
V-8	289	2-bbl	9.3	200	single	Fairlane
V-8	390	2-bbl	9.5	270	single	Fairlane
V-8	390	4-bbl	10.5	320	dual	Fairlane

Transmissions: 3-speed stick, Overdrive, 4-speed stick, 3-speed Cruise-O-Matic
Axles: 2.79, 2.80, 3.00, 3.25, 3.50

1968 Ford Police Engines

Layout	cid	carb	comp	horsepower	exhaust	model
I-6	240	1-bbl	9.2	150	single	Custom
V-8	302	2-bbl	9.0	210	single	Custom
V-8	390	2-bbl	9.5	265	single	Custom
V-8	390	4-bbl	10.5	315	dual	Custom
V-8	428	4-bbl	10.5	360	dual	Custom
I-6	200	1-bbl	8.8	115	single	Fairlane
V-8	302	2-bbl	9.0	210	single	Fairlane
V-8	390	2-bbl	9.5	265	single	Fairlane
V-8	390	4-bbl	10.5	325	dual	Fairlane

Transmissions: 3-speed stick, 4-speed stick, 3-speed Cruise-O-Matic
Axles: 2.80, 3.00, 3.25, 3.50

Chapter Nine

1969-1972
The 429-ci 351 Windsor, and 351 Cleveland

In 1968, the first of the new, lightweight 385-series big-blocks was developed for the retail Thunderbird. It displaced the 429 ci. With a 4-bbl carb and 10.5:1 compression, this big-block exactly equaled the 360-horsepower output of the 428-ci Police Interceptor.

In 1969, the 429-ci V-8 became the newest Ford police engine. However, it was pushed back to second place behind the 428-ci Police Interceptor. Why? The brand-new, canted-valve big-block was only available with a 2-bbl carb and single exhaust! Oddly enough, it had the full 10.5:1 compression, which was as high as any Ford police engine had been to date. This odd high-compression, 2-bbl, single-exhaust V-8 produced 320 horsepower.

Ford introduced the 429-ci V-8 in 1968 retail cars. The only other engine ever to appear in this 385-series of big-blocks was the 460 ci introduced in 1973. The 460 ci had the same bore but a longer stroke. The 385-series big-block engines had a large, 4.90-inch bore spacing compared to 4.63 inches for the FE-block.

For the new 385-series, Ford eliminated the deep skirt block design that dated back to 1955. It used thin-wall casting techniques for the 429-ci big-block originally developed for the 221-ci small-block.

The biggest difference with the 385-series of blocks was the incredible canted valvetrain. This is in response to Chevrolet's 1966 396-ci "porcupine" valve big-block engine that would grow to 402 ci, 427 ci, and 454 ci. Ford and Chevrolet were the only ones to offer canted-valve police engines. Dodge, Plymouth, Pontiac, and Buick remained with the in-line valvetrain design.

The 429-ci "Thunder Jet" had wedge combustion chambers and stud-mounted rocker arms. "The canted valves open in the direction of the gas flow for free-breathing efficiency." That was indeed true. Next to a pure hemi-head engine, the canted valvetrain allows the best airflow at all engine speeds.

The 429-ci engine used larger main bearing and rod bearing diameters than comparable FE-block engines. The 429 ci was built for maximum airflow through the heads and the maximum loads on the crankshaft. The 429-ci engine was more "robust" than either the police 428-ci or the retail 427-ci V-8s. In spite of lightweight casting methods, the bulletproof 429 ci was 75 pounds heavier than the 428 ci. It had bigger bearings, heavier crank, larger rods, and heavier pistons. The 429 ci would not "wrap up" as rapidly as the lighter reciprocating 428 ci; however, it made a better overall police engine by being both powerful and durable.

In 1969, cops had their choice of not one but two big-block powertrains with very odd induction and exhaust systems. The 390-ci FE-block and the 429-ci 385-series were only available with a 2-bbl carb and single exhaust. Other engines included the urban-patrol 240-ci I-6 and 302-ci V-8.

In 1969, the top cop engine was the 360-horsepower, 428-ci V-8 powering this Indiana State Police Mercury Monterey. The Iowa State Patrol also drove 1969 Monterey police cars. *Jerry Parker*

In 1969, the 429-ci, 385-series big-block V-8 was introduced to police work. However, this Missouri State Highway Patrol Monterey was powered by the 428-ci V-8. *Darryl Lindsay*

This 1969 South Carolina Highway Patrol Galaxie 500 is powered by the 428-ci V-8. This engine wrapped up faster than the more robust 429-ci V-8. *Charles Johnson*

The big news for 1969 was an increase in wheelbase from 119 to 121 inches for full-size Fords like this South Carolina Highway Patrol unit. *Charles Johnson*

For 1970, the 428-ci Police Interceptor used in this Nassau County, New York, Highway Patrol unit was the same engine as the Super Cobra Jet. *Ned Schwartz*

For 1969, the top cop mill remained the 428-ci Police Interceptor with 360 horsepower. It was available only with the three-speed Cruise-O-Matic. A 3.00:1 rear gear ratio was standard while 2.80:1 gears were optional. These cars had impressive top speeds.

The 1969 Ford police package was based on the base trim level Custom and Custom 500 and on the intermediate trim level Galaxie 500. The last Galaxie police car was 1963. The police package was available in both two-door and four-door sedans for all three models.

The police package was also available for three versions of the station wagon, three versions of the Econoline van, and two versions of the Bronco four-wheel-drive. The Fairlane series, which had shrunk to a 113-inch wheelbase for 1969, was not available with the formal police package.

The big news, literally, for 1969 was the wheelbase on the full-size Ford. It was stretched from 119 inches to 121 inches. It grew to 119 inches in 1960. It would shrink back to 114.4 inches in 1979. The 1969 to 1978 Fords were the longest and heaviest cars ever built by Ford Division.

In 1969, the transmission selection was down to either the three-speed manual or the three-speed Cruise-O-Matic. However, the Cruise-O-Matic was a required option with both the 428-ci and 429-ci engines. The three-speed stick would continue to be standard equipment for some police engines on the full-size Ford through 1971.

In 1969, *Popular Science* tested four full-size family sedans from Ford, Chevrolet, Plymouth, and Pontiac. All four of these automakers made police cars based upon the platforms tested by Norbye & Dunne. These were not police package cars; however, each of these four-door sedans used powertrains found in many police cars.

In fact, what made this test so significant is the choice of drivetrain. All of the sedans were powered by a big-block V-8 fitted with a 2-bbl carb and lowest numeric axle ratio available. This was the thinking of the late 1960s and early 1970s for how to get both performance and economy. Police departments bought this concept lock, stock, and barrel. It was not until 1974 that *Motor Trend* editor and the LA Sheriff's reserve deputy, John Christy, proved that a 4-bbl V-8 with a higher numeric axle ratio gave both better performance and fuel economy for police work.

These four-door sedans with 2-bbl big-blocks were extremely typical of city and county police cars from the

Make	Ford	Chevrolet	Plymouth	Pontiac
Model	Galaxie	Impala	Fury III	Catalina
Engine, ci & carb	390, 2-bbl	396, 2-bbl	383, 2-bbl	400, 2-bbl
Horsepower	265	265	290	290
Trans	3-speed C6	3-speed THM	3-speed TF	3-speed THM
Axle ratio	2.75	2.56	2.76	2.29
Weight, lb	4,206	4,218	4,172	4,267
0–60 mph, sec	11.6	11.3	11.0	10.6
Lane change, mph	60	58	58	58
Slalom, mph	28	30	25	28
60-0 mph, ft	198.8	195.2	175	161.5
EPA city mpg	10.2	11.4	12.1	11.7

late 1960s. These results also show why the Pontiac was so popular with some agencies. It had the best straight-line performance even from the 2.29 rear gears, the best brakes, very good handling, and nearly the best fuel economy.

For something like 37 years in a row, Ford had been the United States' number one police car. This changed in 1969 when Plymouth became the top-selling squad car. Plymouth would keep that honor until the mid-1980s when Chevrolet captured the top spot. Chevrolet remained the number one police car until after 1996, when Ford regained the title.

In 1970, Ford's "Police Special" package was available on the 121-inch wheelbase Custom and Custom 500 four-door sedans and the Galaxie 500 two-door hardtop and four-door sedan. The police package was also offered on all the station wagons, all the vans and two versions of the Bronco.

New for 1970, Ford had a midsize police car after sitting out 1969. The new car was the 117-inch wheelbase Torino. Actually, the police version was based on the Fairlane 500. This was the intermediate trim level in the Fairlane/Torino series. The base trim level was actually called the Falcon. Compared to the 1968 Fairlane, the 1970 Fairlane 500 had a longer wheelbase, longer overall length, and wider track. The Fairlane 500 had a selection of police engines that was very different than the police engines used in the Custom and Galaxie.

In 1970, the top cop engine for the full-size Custom and Galaxie was the 360-horsepower, 428-ci Police Interceptor. This was the last year for the 428-ci FE-block in police cars. In retail terms, the 428-ci Police Interceptor was the exact engine as the 428-ci Super Cobra Jet. The 428-ci Super Cobra Jet produced 360 horsepower, compared to the 428-ci Cobra Jet at 335 horsepower. The other high-compression big-block for the full-size Ford cruisers was the 320-horsepower, 429-ci V-8. This was the 2-bbl, single exhaust mill that was called the Cruiser engine in police cars and the Thunder Jet in retail cars.

The top police engine for the midsize Fairlane was a 370-horsepower, 4-bbl version of the 429-ci V-8. That's right. The midsize police car had an engine that was more powerful than the full-size car. The Custom and Galaxie got the faster-wrapping 428-ci FE-block at 360

In 1970, the top Ford police engine was the 370-horsepower, 429-ci V-8 available only in the midsize cars like the Torino/Fairlane and this Los Angeles Police Department Montego. *John Bellah*

horsepower, while the Fairlane 500 got the heavy-duty 429-ci 385-series block at 370 horsepower. This was the first time an engine larger than 390-ci was available in one of Ford's midsize police cars.

The 370-horsepower 429-ci Police Interceptor V-8 is different than two other popular 429-ci, 4-bbl engines in 1970. One is the 360-horsepower, 10.5 to 1 compression, 4-bbl retail engine. The other is the 375-horsepower, 11.3 to 1 compression Boss 429 engine. Neither were used in 1970 police cars. The 370-horsepower, 429-ci Police Interceptor would become the top cop engine for both midsize and full-size cars in 1971.

New in the police cars for 1970 was the 351-ci "Windsor" V-8. This small-block was made at the engine plant in Windsor, Ontario, Canada. At 351-ci, this was the largest displacement achieved from the small-block bore centers. Chevrolet pushed its small-block to 400 ci, which most agree was too far. Chrysler's largest small-block was 360 ci.

Also in 1970 for police cars, Ford released a totally different 351-ci V-8 engine, the 351 "Cleveland." Built in

The CHP used a FoMoCo product as an E-class vehicle just one time between the early 1950s and early 1980s. It was this 1970 Mercury Monterey. *Chris Watson*

The 1970 Mercury Monterey is shown at the CHP Motor Transport Division in Sacramento being fitted with radio gear, emergency lights, and shotgun racks. *Chris Watson*

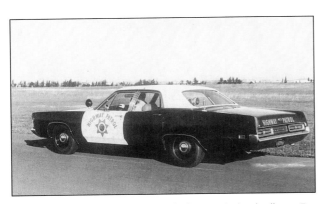

The 1970 CHP Mercury Monterey had a 124-inch wheelbase. For years, the CHP required its E-class cars have at least a 122-inch wheelbase and weigh 3,800 pounds. *Chris Watson*

Cleveland, Ohio, this is sometimes referred to as a big-block engine. The bore and stroke on the 351W and 351C were identical. Both V-8s eventually came in both 2-bbl and 4-bbl versions.

These engines were extremely difficult to tell apart from spec sheets and police car literature. Ford often treated them as interchangeable when it came to filling orders for 351-ci engines. Horsepower ratings were often the same. However, these engines were drastically different: The 351 Cleveland had a high rpm-oriented "canted" valvetrain.

The 351-ci Windsor was introduced to retail cars in 1969. It would be available in both 2-bbl and 4-bbl versions. As a rule, the 351-ci Windsor would go in full-size police cars. The 351-ci Cleveland would go in midsize police cars. There were exceptions and Ford often treated these engines interchangeably, but this was the trend. The 351-ci Windsor became a police engine in 1970.

The 351-ci Windsor had a very conventional valvetrain. The valves were parallel to one another in a standard wedge head. The 351-ci Cleveland was very different. Both engines shared the same 4.00-inch bore and 3.5-inch stroke. However, nearly everything else about the engines was different including the deck height (the distance from the centerline of the crank to the top of the engine block) and the center to center distance on the con rods.

The 351-ci Cleveland was introduced in both retail and police cars in 1970. What made it special was the canted valvetrain. Each intake valve was tilted 9.5 degrees in and canted 4.2 degrees up. Each exhaust valve was tilted 3 degrees back. This improved airflow into and out of the combustion chambers. The 351-ci Cleveland came in both 2-bbl and 4-bbl engines. As a rule, the 2-bbl engines used an "open" combustion chamber with smaller intake and exhaust valves. The 4-bbl Cleveland engines came with "quench-type" combustion chambers and larger intake and exhaust valves.

In 1970 and most of 1971, the 4-bbl Cleveland V-8 had two-bolt main bearing caps just like the 2-bbl version of the Cleveland V-8. However, in mid-1971, the 4-bbl Cleveland engines came with four-bolt mains. This 4-bbl, four-bolt main engine was called the 351-ci Cobra Jet. And that was used in police cars. The 2-bbl Cleveland engines retained the two-bolt main design through 1974. In 1974, Ford stopped making the 351-ci Cleveland V-8 all together. It was replaced by the 351-ci "Modified."

The 300-horsepower 351-ci Cleveland 4-bbl used in the Fairlane police car was exactly the same engine used in the famous 1970 Mustang Mach 1.

In mid-1971, the 351-ci "Cobra Jet" 4-bbl V-8 was released. This was a more durable engine than the 4-bbl but two-bolt main version of the 351-ci Cleveland. The 351-ci Cobra Jet used in police cars and the Boss 351 V-8 shared the same engine block. The 1971 Cobra Jet engine used the larger intake and exhaust valves from the 4-bbl version, but used the "open" combustion chamber from the 2-bbl version to improve emissions. For 1972, the name "Cobra Jet" itself was dropped. However, the 351-ci "Cleveland" 4-bbl engine kept the same four-bolt block.

The 351-ci Cleveland with its canted valvetrain and four-bolt main bearing block was viewed for what it was: a performance engine. In the mid-1970s, high performance was out. Emission controls, fuel economy, and lower insurance premiums were in.

The 351-ci Windsor is the largest displacement engine in the Windsor family of small-block V-8s that also includes the 221 ci, 260 ci, 289 ci, and 302 ci. This whole family of engines can be correctly referred to as the Windsor family; however, most people save that label for just the 351 ci engine to distinguish it from the 351-ci Cleveland big-block.

The 351-ci Windsor was introduced for retail cars in 1969 and made its first appearance in police cars for the 1970 model year. The 351-ci Windsor would power full-size police cars from 1970 through 1992 when it was replaced midyear by the 4.6L modular SOHC V-8. In fact, the 351-ci Windsor would be the largest Ford police engine available from 1979 through 1992.

The 351-ci Windsor is directly related to the 289-ci and 302-ci small-blocks. They all use an in-line valvetrain and rectangular head ports. All have the same 4.380-inch cylinder bore spacing. However, the 351-ci version of the Windsor small-block has a 1.3-inch taller deck height than the other small-blocks. The deck height is from the centerline of the crankshaft to the top of the block deck or bottom of the cylinder head. While the 351-ci Windsor appears to be a stroked 302-ci Windsor, the longer stroke required a taller deck and a unique block.

The 351-ci Windsor also has larger main and rod bearing diameters than the other Windsor small-blocks. The 351-ci crank was beefed up to handle the increase power and torque. The 351-ci Windsor also has a different firing order than other Windsor small-blocks. With the small-block firing order, the front two cylinders fired one right after the other. Ford engineers felt the extra power from the 351-ci engine would put too much stress on the number one main bearing. This was not a problem on the smaller displacement engines, but Ford wanted to avoid a problem with the 351 ci so the company changed the firing order to level out the load on the main bearings. The 351 ci is the only engine in the Windsor family with a unique firing order.

A great deal of confusion exists between the 351-ci Windsor and the 351-ci Cleveland. Part of the confusion is because the displacement, including bore and stroke, is identical. Adding to the confusion is that both engines were available in 2-bbl and 4-bbl versions. Both engines were available at the same time. Sometimes, Ford used the engines interchangeably.

Part of the confusion between the 351-ci Windsor and 351-ci Cleveland is also related to the wide variety of Ford's block sizes. The police engines from Chevrolet, and to a lesser degree from Plymouth, fell neatly into one of two categories, small-block V-8 and big-block V-8. Yes,

The Iowa Highway Patrol used this long and powerful 1970 Mercury Monterey as its primary cruiser. The police 428-ci V-8 was indeed the Cobra Jet engine. *Robert Parks*

This 1971 Lyman, South Carolina, Police Custom 500 is powered by a 370-horsepower, 429-ci canted-valve Police Interceptor V-8. This was the same engine as the retail 429-ci Cobra Jet. *Shane Bryant*

The 1971 full-size Fords, like this Cook County, Illinois, Sheriff's Police Custom, were available with the 351-ci Windsor V-8. The midsize Torino got the 351-ci Cleveland. *Greg Reynolds*

In 1971, the Indiana State Police prowled the highways in the 429-ci V-8 powered Mercury Monterey. This had an 11.3 to 1 compression and 370 horsepower. *Jerry Parker*

Mopar had its B-blocks and "raised" B-blocks. Yes, the Chevy 400-ci small-block had a unique casting with Siamesed cylinders. For the most part, however, it was either small-block or big-block and many of the engine components were interchangeable.

Not so with Ford. Since 1955, Ford has had five different series of overhead-valve V-8 engines. These include Y-block, Windsor 90-degree small-block, FE-series big-block, 385-series big-block and 335-series Cleveland big-block. The 351-ci Windsor was in the Windsor small-block series even if it had a deck height more than an inch taller than the other 90-degree V-8 small-blocks. The 351-ci Cleveland was in its own big-block series, which included only the 351-ci Cleveland, 351-ci Modified, 400-ci Cleveland, and Boss 351. As a rule, no engine parts are interchangeable between the 351-ci Windsor and 351-ci Cleveland.

The 351-ci Cleveland was the first engine in the 335-series of big-blocks. The Cleveland was a hybrid engine, a cross between the production small-block and the NASCAR version of the 429-ci big-block. The 351-ci

A 1972 Suffern, New York, Police Custom. For 1972, the compression ratio on Ford police engines dropped from an average of 9.7 to 1 to 8.5 to 1. *Ned Schwartz*

Cleveland was introduced in 1970 and used in police cars through 1974.

Sources vary as to what engine was used in what car line. Some references indicate the 351-ci Windsor was used interchangeably with the 351-ci Cleveland and later the 351-ci Modified. Most sources, however, draw a sharp distinction between the end use of the Windsor small-block series and the 335-series of Cleveland big-blocks.

Pay attention. There will be a quiz at the end of the book. As a general rule, the 351-ci Cleveland was only used in midsize cars and not in full-size cars nor in trucks. The 351-ci Windsor was only used in full-size cars. The 351-ci Modified was used mostly in trucks, not cars. The 400-ci Cleveland was used in midsize cars, full-size cars and trucks.

Since the 351-ci Windsor and 351-ci Cleveland were so similar but frequently confused and different in performance, it is critically important to be able to tell one from the other. The Cleveland has wider valve covers than the Windsor. The Windsor has six valve cover bolts while the Cleveland has eight valve cover bolts. The 351-ci Cleveland had 14 millimeter spark plugs compared to 18 millimeter for the 1970–1974 351-ci Windsor.

An even bigger visual difference exists in the timing chain housing. The Windsor uses a traditional bolt-on timing chain cover. The Cleveland has the housing cast into the block that includes water passages and the thermostat. A flat steel stamping serves as the front cover.

Internally, the 351-ci Windsor and 351-ci Cleveland have similar rod journals but very different main bearing diameters. Other major internal differences exist between the Windsor and Cleveland series of engines. First, the Windsor head ports are rectangular while the Cleveland uses rounded ports. By far, the most significant difference between these two engines is the valvetrain. The Windsor series uses conventional, in-line valves. The Cleveland uses the staggered or canted valvetrain.

The 351-ci Cleveland, however, shares bore spacing, head bolt pattern and thin-wall casting techniques with the Windsor small-blocks.

The 351-ci Cleveland was produced in both 2-bbl and 4-bbl versions. In spite of obviously better breathing ability, the 351-ci Cleveland and 351-ci Windsor were often given the same horsepower rating, all else equal. Like the difference between the 428 ci and the 429 ci, the 351-ci Cleveland would always out-accelerate, or wrap up, faster than a 351-ci Windsor even when both had the same horsepower rating.

Even the 351-ci Cleveland 4-bbl came in a number of variations. In 1971, Ford produced a "Boss" and a "Cobra Jet" version of the 351-ci Cleveland. The Boss 351 was not used in police cars but the 351-ci Cobra Jet sure was. In 1972, Ford released a variation called the 351-ci High Output.

The hottest Ford police engine in 1972 was the 248-horsepower, 351-ci Cleveland V-8 available only in the Torino, like this New York City Health and Hospitals Police unit. *Kirby McElhearn*

All Cleveland blocks are cast to accept four-bolt main caps. All that is needed to convert a two-bolt main Cleveland to a four-bolt main engine is a precise drilling and tapping operation for the extra bolts, and the four-bolt main bearing caps themselves.

In 1970, the 302-ci, 2-bbl, V-8 was only available in the police Fairlane 500 and not in the full-size police cars. In a like manner, the 390-ci, 2-bbl V-8 was only available in the Custom and Galaxie and not in the mid-size cars. As a rule, the 351-ci "Windsor" was used in the full-size Custom and Galaxie. The 351-ci "Cleveland" was used in the midsize Fairlane. This was true even though both 351-ci, 2-bbl V-8s were rated at 250 horsepower. The 1970 model year marked the last for a six-cylinder engine in a full-size Ford police car.

In 1970, Ford tried to use the same marketing hype with cops as they did with the retail enthusiasts. Using the success from the 1969 Boss 302 Mustang and the anticipated popularity of the 1970 Boss 302 Mustang, Ford used the term "Boss of the Road" repeatedly in its 1970 police literature. It never caught on.

In 1970, the full-size Ford with the 428-ci Interceptor engine also came equipped with a rear stabilizer bar to help resist body roll in high-speed curves. The use of a rear sway bar was pioneered by the Los Angeles Police Department in 1969. The police package from all makes and models, depending on the engine, has included a rear sway bar ever since then. The midsize Torino with the 429-ci Interceptor got its rear sway bar in 1971.

In 1970, Ford severely restricted the axle ratios used on its police drivetrains. No optional ratios appear to be available. The 360-horsepower, 428-ci and the 360-horsepower, 429-ci were teamed with 3.00 rear gears. All other police engines got 3.25 to one ratios.

In 1970, the Mercury Division captured the ultimate police car contract. They won the bid for the California Highway Patrol (CHP). This was the first time since the 1940s that a Mercury was selected as the Enforcement Class vehicle. It would turn out to be the last time.

The last FoMoCo product to earn the E-Class honor was the 1952 Ford. The next E-Class Ford would be the 1984 Crown Victoria. By all accounts, the 1970 CHP Mercury holds a special place in both Ford and California police car history.

The CHP's Monterey was powered by FoMoCo's 428-ci, 4-bbl rated at 360 horsepower. The Monterey had a 124-inch wheelbase compared to 121 inches for the Custom and Galaxie. The 360-horsepower, 428-ci engine in the police Monterey was totally unique among 1970 Mercurys. The Cyclone and Marauder could have a 429-ci, 4-bbl, while the Marquis got the 429-ci, 2-bbl. The retail Monterey was available only with the 390-ci, 2-bbl. Only the cop cars got the 360-horsepower, 428-ci Cobra Jet. The CHP bought 1820 of these 1970 Montereys for $2,478 each.

Unfortunately, the CHP had more than their fair share of fleet maintenance problems with the Monterey. The mechanical woes started in August 1970. The CHP had been experiencing a high rate of left side engine mount failures. No, this was not the big-block torque at work. Instead, the rubber-bonded mount itself was defective from the supplier. The CHP wanted the engine mounts replaced on the failed units and a chain or cable installed on all units to prevent future failures. Instead, Mercury changed all the CHP mounts with Goodyear-made mounts and the problem was solved.

In November 1970, the problems became more serious. Three of the Montereys suffered broken lower right ball joints. Yes, that is because state troopers and highway patrolmen jump medians and turn left for a living. However, the ball joints are supposed to take that kind of normal abuse. The ball joints had become loose even though the cotter pin was still in place. This looseness caused fatigue failures. Mercury replaced all loose ball joints under warranty. They also sent the CHP new control arm and ball joint assemblies and spindles for all the rest of the Montereys in the CHP fleet.

Also in November 1970, the CHP discovered three cracked or broken wheels. The cracks occurred in the wheel spider halfway between the rim and lug bolt holes. Mercury eventually agreed to replace all the wheels on the CHP Monterey fleet to ones of a heavier duty design.

In January 1971, the CHP experienced cracking of the C-6 transmission case. In some instances, this caused simply a fluid loss. In a couple of instances, the cracked case caused a total failure of the transmission. These cracks occurred with as little as 49,000 miles. The CHP simply inspected the transmissions. The Monterey was well out of its one-year warranty and most of the patrol units had already chalked up enough miles for them to be auctioned off.

In 1971, Ford police car performance peaked. Some would argue it peaked with the 428-ci Police Interceptor

A 1972 Massachusetts State Police Custom. Eight other state agencies like the Montana Highway Patrol, Georgia State Patrol, and Florida Highway Patrol drove Fords. *Darryl Lindsay*

in 1970. However, in terms of rated horsepower, the top year for the full-size cruisers was 1971 with the 429-ci Police Interceptor engine. With an 11.3:1 compression, 4-bbl carb, dual exhaust, this top cop engine for 1971 put out 370 horsepower. This was the most horsepower a Ford-marque police engine would ever produce. The reign of the 370-horsepower, 429-ci Police Interceptor V-8 was a short one. Compression would fall from 11.3 in 1971 to just 8.5 in 1972. Stroking the engine to 460 ci for 1973 did not help.

The history of Ford police car performance has two bleak eras, the loss of high-compression engines starting in 1972 and the loss of big-block engines starting in 1979. Ford held onto its high-compression engines a year longer than Chevrolet. The Bowtie canted valve, 454-ci V-8 was a high-compression powerhouse only in 1970. For 1971, the Chevy 454-ci mill was cut back to 365 horsepower. Plymouth kept its compression ratios high until 1972. The 1971 Mopar 440-ci V-8 produced 370 horsepower.

The 370-horsepower Ford 429-ci Police Interceptor was the same exact engine as the retail 429-ci Cobra Jet. Again, the 360-horsepower, 429-ci 4-bbl V-8 was not a police engine, neither was the 375-horsepower, 429-ci Super Cobra Jet.

In 1971, the 390-ci FE-block was still available in full-size police cars. However, this was its last year in both the police and retail market. The 390-ci was replaced by the 400-ci "Cleveland" V-8. Both were available in 1971 full-size police cars.

In 1971, a new engine was introduced in the 335-series, the 400-ci Cleveland. The 400-ci Cleveland V-8 was a 351-ci Cleveland stroked by a full half inch. The 400-ci engine was true "square" design. Both the bore and the stroke were 4.00 inches. This new 400-ci engine had a deck height 1.09 inches taller than the 351-ci

engine. In 1974, the 400-ci Cleveland was destroked back to 351 ci, resulting in the 351-ci Modified, the third engine in the 335-series. This same year, the 351-ci Modified replaced the 351-ci Cleveland. However, the 351-ci Windsor was still in use. In 1971, the 351-ci Windsor 2-bbl was generally used in the full-size police cars while the 351-ci Cleveland 2-bbl was generally used in the midsize cruisers. Both were rated at 240 horsepower in spite of the better breathing heads on the Cleveland version. The Torino was also available with a 285-horsepower version of the 351-ci Cleveland 4-bbl V-8. This engine would become the four-bolt main 351-ci Cobra Jet late in the model year. The most famous 351-ci engine in 1971 was the Boss 351 version of the Cleveland V-8 rated at 330 horsepower. This was not available in police cars.

In 1971, no six-cylinder engine was available for a full-size Ford police car. A brand-new, 250-ci Six was, however, standard on the midsize Torino.

In 1971, the "Police Special" package was available for the full-size Custom and Custom 500 four-door sedan and Galaxie 500 two-door hardtop and four-door sedan. New for 1971, the Police Special package was also available for the midsize Torino in both two-door hardtop and four-door sedan. The Torino replaced the Fairlane nameplate as Ford's midsize police car. The wheelbase for the Custom was once again 121 inches while the Torino retained the 117-inch wheelbase from the 1970 Fairlane.

Ford pointed to the NASCAR success of the Torino in its police literature: "Win after win has proven Torino's ability to stand up under the tortuous high speeds, continuous operation and rapid accelerations of stock car racing . . . the same characteristics often needed in police work." When discussing the Cobra Jet–based 429-ci Police Interceptor, they wrote, "The 429 police package is the maximum duty vehicle capable of sustained high speed chase and exceptionally fast acceleration. The Police CJ engine is a derivative of the 429-ci Ford engine that has been so successful on the stock car racing circuit."

The 1971 model year marked the last of the 2-bbl versions of the 429-ci big-block. From now on, the 429-ci would have a 4-bbl; however, only the Police Interceptor version had dual exhausts. The 400-ci Cleveland only came with a 2-bbl and single exhaust.

For 1971, the Torino with the 351-ci and larger engines and the Custom with the 429-ci Interceptor engine came standard with a rear antisway bar. This reduced body roll in the turns and produced less understeer and more neutral steering at all vehicle speeds.

In 1971, the Police Special package was also available for two versions of the Bronco 4WD, three models of the station wagon and six styles of Club Wagon and Econoline van. The Bronco used either a 170-ci I-6 or the

205-horsepower, 302-ci V-8. The vans were powered by a 240-ci I-6 or a 302-ci V-8.

In 1971, the Fordomatic transmission made a surprise appearance as a limited production option. This automatic had a first gear lockout. This eliminated the possibility of holding the transmission in first gear and over-revving the engine. The Fordomatic went through the 3-gear sequence automatically when in "Drive." The three-speed SelectShift Cruise-O-Matic started in first gear when in either "Drive" or "First" and started off in second gear when the selector was placed in "Second." The Fordomatic would be available just through 1972.

In 1971, seven of the ten powertrains for the full-size and midsize police cars required an automatic transmission. The three-speed stick was only available with the 351-ci engine in the Custom and the 250-ci and 302-ci mills in the Torino.

In 1971, Lee Iacocca, father of the Mustang, became president of Ford Motor Company.

In 1972, the Ford police package was available on the full-size Custom and Custom 500 four-door sedan and Galaxie 500 two-door hardtop and four-door sedan. The police package was also available on the midsize Torino two-door hardtop and four-door pillared hardtop. The station wagons, vans, and Bronco were also available with the heavy-duty cop gear.

In 1972, police car performance began its sharp fall. It would bottom out in 1981 and only slowly improve throughout the 1980s. Neither an increase in engine size from 429 ci to 460 ci in 1973 nor a reduction in wheelbase from 121 to 114.4 inches in 1979 did much to reverse the performance slide.

In the early 1970s, compression ratios were cut, vehicle weight was increased, emission standards were toughened and the demand for more fuel-efficient engines increased. Engine output and vehicle performance took a back seat among retail cars. Since police cars depend almost entirely upon retail cars for their powertrains, police car performance also fell sharply.

In 1972, retail engines were required to run on regular gas instead of premium. To do this the compression ratio had to be lowered on all engines. Just about this time, the cops found out the reality about "police" engines. With rare exception, the police-only engine no longer existed. The cops simply used retail engines. When the compression ratios on retail engines fell, then compression ratios on police engines fell. Gone were the days when the car companies would make an engine with a special cam or special carb or special compression to fill a police contract. Dodge did that for the California Highway Patrol in the 1960s. With the onset of emission controls and other regulations, by 1972, that kind of special treatment was not possible.

For 1972, the compression ratio on Ford police engines was dropped to an average of 8.5:1. No police

The 351-ci Windsor was standard equipment on 1972 full-size Fords, like this NYC-Housing Police Custom. *Ned Schwartz*

engine had a compression higher than 8.6:1. In comparison, the average compression in 1971 was 9.7:1 with some engines as high as 11.3:1.

In 1972, it was politically incorrect to mention race track victories in sales brochures, even to police officers. In fact, the whole vocabulary in describing Ford engines changed. Gone was any reference to a "Cobra Jet" or a "Boss." In its place, Ford reverted back to what has meant performance ever since 1955, Thunderbird. The top 429-ci, 4-bbl engine used in police car was the 212-horsepower Thunderbird V-8.

For 1972, the Torino was restyled to have even more of a "Coke-bottle" or "fuselage" body shape. The wheelbase was lengthened from 117 inches to 118 inches on the four-door "pillared hardtop." However, the wheelbase was shortened from 117 inches to 114 inches on the two-door hardtop.

Along with the wheelbase changes, the rear suspension was changed from leaf spring to a new four-

This unmarked 1972 Ford Custom is retired from the Kentucky State Police. It is powered by the 429-ci Police Interceptor, now rated at 212 horsepower net.

A 1972 Long Island Rail Road Police Custom. In 1972, compression ratios were cut to allow all police engines to run on regular gas. *Ned Schwartz*

link coil spring system. The four-link system was supposed to provide better longitudinal and lateral stability. It better absorbed acceleration and braking forces and controlled the side to side movement of the axle while cornering.

The 351-ci engines were widely used in 1972 Ford police cars. The 153-horsepower 351-ci Windsor 2-bbl was standard equipment on the full-size Custom. The 163-horsepower, 351-ci Cleveland 2-bbl was an option on the midsize Torino.

The top cop engine in the entire Ford lineup, in fact, was a 351-ci V-8, even though two 4-bbl versions of the 429-ci were available in both police cars. The hottest engine of the year was the 351-ci Cleveland 4-bbl V-8 available only in the Torino. This 351-ci engine produced 248 horsepower compared to the 429-ci Police Interceptor at 212 horsepower. The big-block had a torque advantage over the Cleveland V-8, but only a small one, 322 pounds per foot versus 306 pounds per foot All-in-all, the fastest police car in Ford's 1972 fleet was the midsize Torino with this Cobra Jet-inspired 248-horsepower dual exhaust engine.

The 429-ci V-8 was available in two power levels for both the full-size and midsize police cars. The 429-ci 4-bbl was rated at 208 horsepower in the Custom while the same basic engine had a 205-horsepower rating in the Torino. The 429-ci 4-bbl Police Interceptor cranked out 212 horsepower in both cars.

The top 351-ci retail engine in 1972 was an 8.6:1, 4-bbl version of the 351-ci Cleveland called the High Output. The 351-ci HO was rated at 266 horsepower. This was more than any 429-ci or 460-ci engine in 1972. However, the 351-ci HO was not offered in police cars.

The 1972 model year is best known as the time horsepower rating methods changed. Before 1972, the "brake" or SAE gross horsepower of an engine operating without any drive accessories became its rating. In 1972, the system changed to "SAE net" horsepower. SAE test method J245 involved all or most of the driven accessories installed and included the transmission and some kind of exhaust. The sheer power level dropped for 1972 due to lower compressions to meet emission standards but not as much as the published horsepower ratings indicated.

The Cruise-O-Matic transmission became standard equipment with all police engines on the full-size Fords in 1972. A three-speed stick was available, but only with the 302 V-8 and only in the Torino. This was the last year for any manual transmission until the 1982 arrival of the Special Service package Mustang.

In 1969, Ford police cars were used by the North Carolina Highway Patrol and Maryland State Police. Mercurys were used by the Missouri State Highway Patrol, Iowa State Patrol, and Indiana State Police. The 1970 Fords were used by the Kansas Highway Patrol and the Maryland State Police who used the Torino. The 1970 Mercury Montego was used by the Los Angeles Police while the Mercury Monterey was the choice of the California Highway Patrol and Iowa State Patrol. In 1971, the Indiana State Police patrolled in Mercurys while the Cook County, Illinois, Sheriff and Nassau County, New York, Police used Fords.

In 1972, the state police and highway patrol in nine states used the Ford Custom and Galaxie including Kentucky, Maryland, Kansas, Montana, Connecticut, Massachusetts, South Carolina, Florida, and Georgia. The Indiana State Police and Nebraska State Patrol used the Mercury Monterey. Seventeen states used Plymouth, eight states used Dodge, three used Chevrolet, and the rest used AMC, Oldsmobile, and Chrysler police cars.

1969 Ford Custom and Galaxie Police Engines

Layout	cid	carb	comp	horsepower	exhaust	axle
I-6	240	1-bbl	9.2	150	single	3.25
V-8	302	2-bbl	9.5	220	single	3.25
V-8	390	2-bbl	9.5	265	single	3.00, 3.25
V-8	429	2-bbl	10.5	320	single	2.75, 3.25
V-8	428	4-bbl	10.5	360	dual	2.80, 3.00

transmissions: 3-speed stick, 3-speed Cruise-O-Matic

The Yonkers, New York, Police used this four-door Ford Custom in 1972. By this year, the three-speed Cruise-O-Matic was standard equipment on all full-size Fords. *Kirby McElhearn*

1970 Ford Police Engines

Layout	cid	carb	comp	horsepower	exhaust	axle	model
I-6	240	1-bbl	9.2	150	single	3.25	Custom
V-8	351W	2-bbl	9.5	250	single	3.25	Custom
V-8	390	2-bbl	9.5	265	single	3.25	Custom
V-8	429	2-bbl	10.5	320	single	3.25	Custom
V-8	428	4-bbl	10.5	360	dual	3.00	Custom
I-6	240	1-bbl	9.2	150	single	3.25	Fairlane
V-8	302	2-bbl	9.5	220	single	3.25	Fairlane
V-8	351C	2-bbl	9.5	250	single	3.25	Fairlane
V-8	351C	4-bbl	11.0	300	dual	3.25	Fairlane
V-8	429	4-bbl	11.3	370	dual	3.00	Fairlane

1971 Ford Police Engines

Layout	cid	carb	comp	horsepower	exhaust	axle	model
V-8	351W	2-bbl	9.0	240	single	3.25	Custom
V-8	390	2-bbl	8.6	255	single	3.25	Custom
V-8	400	2-bbl	9.0	260	single	3.25	Custom
V-8	429	2-bbl	10.5	320	single	3.25	Custom
V-8	429	4-bbl	11.3	370	dual	3.00	Custom
I-6	250	1-bbl	9.0	145	single	3.25	Torino
V-8	302	2-bbl	9.0	210	single	3.25	Torino
V-8	351C	2-bbl	9.0	240	single	3.25	Torino
V-8	351C	4-bbl	10.7	285	dual	3.25	Torino
V-8	429	4-bbl	11.3	370	dual	3.25	Torino

1972 Ford Police Drivetrains

Layout	cid	carb	comp	horsepower	exhaust	axle	model
V-8	351W	2-bbl	8.6	153	single	3.25	Custom
V-8	400	2-bbl	8.4	172	single	3.25	Custom
V-8	429	4-bbl	8.5	208	single	3.25	Custom
V-8	429	4-bbl	8.5	212	dual	3.00	Custom
I-6	250	1-bbl	8.0	95	single	3.00	Torino
V-8	302	2-bbl	8.5	140	single	3.25	Torino
V-8	351C	2-bbl	8.6	161	single	3.25	Torino
V-8	351C	4-bbl	8.6	248	dual	3.25	Torino
V-8	400	2-bbl	8.4	168	single	3.25	Torino
V-8	429	4-bbl	8.5	205	single	3.25	Torino
V-8	429	4-bbl	8.5	212	dual	3.00	Torino

Chapter Ten

1973-1978
The 460-ci-series Big-Block

For 1973, the Ford Police Special package was available for the Custom 500 four-door pillared hardtops and Galaxie 500 four-door pillared hardtops and two-door hardtops. Again for 1973, the police package was available for the Torino two-door hardtop and four-door pillared hardtop. As in the past, the station wagons, vans, and Broncos were also available with these specialized, heavy-duty components.

Again for 1973, the Custom and Galaxie used a 121-inch wheelbase while the four-door Torino was built on a 118-inch chassis and the two-door Torino on a 114-inch chassis.

In 1972, Ford introduced a new big-block in the 385-series, the 460-ci V-8. This was strictly a retail engine in 1972 and not a police engine. Ford needed the extra cubic inches to make up for the loss in compression ratio. The 460-ci V-8 was made by stroking the 429-ci V-8 from 3.59 inches to 3.85 inches while keeping the same 4.36-inch bore. For 1973, this engine became the 460-ci Police Interceptor. Unlike the 429-ci big-block, the 460-ci always came with a 4-bbl carb.

The 460-ci was the largest police engine ever built by Ford Motor Company. The 460-ci V-8 calculates to 7.5

liters of interceptor power, compared to the 4.6 liter V-8 used in the 1992–1997 Crown Victoria police car. The 1973 460-ci, overhead-valve, 4-bbl police V-8 produced 219 net horsepower. As a comparison, the 1997 281-ci, overhead-cam, fuel-injected police V-8 produced 210 net horsepower. With today's engine technology, the old big-block could have easily produced 350 net horsepower.

Both the 429-ci, 4-bbl Police V-8 and the 460-ci, 4-bbl Interceptor V-8 were available in the full-size Custom and Galaxie and the midsize Torino. These big engines were required because the compression ratios and horsepower ratings continued to fall to meet emission standards. The 460-ci Interceptor was rated at 219 horsepower compared to 201 horsepower or 202 horsepower for the 429-ci V-8. The 460-ci also produced a hefty 15 pounds per foot more torque than the 429-ci. This was the last year for the use of a 429-ci V-8 in a Ford police car.

The 460-ci Police Interceptor included a large flow Motorcraft 4-bbl, free-breathing intake manifold, high-lift cam, canted valvetrain, forged aluminum pistons, specially balanced crankshaft, heavy-duty oil pump, electric fuel pump, engine oil cooler, 90-amp alternator, and dual exhaust. Ford said, "This engine is designed for the maximum requirements of highway and expressway patrol duty." Unlike the Plymouth 440-ci V-8 and the Chevrolet 454-ci V-8, the Ford 460-ci V-8 was never available with high-compression. Between 1973 and 1978, the compression ratio remained at 8.0:1.

The 460-ci Police Interceptor was the heavy-hitter in the engine lineup. However, the 351-ci Cleveland 4-bbl V-8, available only in the Torino, was an extremely popular police engine. The 351-ci 4-bbl was the only engine other than the 460-ci 4-bbl to have dual exhausts. The Cobra Jet-inspired Cleveland V-8 had a special carb, special intake manifold, special valve springs, modified cam, and 2 1/2-inch diameter exhaust pipes. This was the only police engine to use four-bolt main bearings for the maximum crankshaft rigidity at high engine speeds. The 266-horsepower 351-ci Cleveland 4-bbl engine used in the Torino police cars was indeed the 351-ci Cobra Jet, or what was left of it.

In 1972, Ford gave its engines slightly different ratings depending upon which model of engine was

New for 1973 police cars like this South Carolina Highway Patrol Galaxie 500 was the 460-ci, 385-series big-block Police Interceptor V-8. *Quay Johnson*

A 1973 Danbury, Connecticut, Police Ford Custom. In 1973, all Ford police engines had an 8 to 1 compression ratio. *Ned Schwartz*

This 1973 Burlingame, California, Police Ranch Wagon was used to transport a police canine. Many police station wagons used the 400-ci Cleveland V-8. *Darryl Lindsay*

installed. This trend was more pronounced in 1973. As body size and weight increased between models, the horsepower ratings also increased. Engine ratings for the same engine varied from 1 horsepower to 17 horsepower depending on the model. For example, the 400-ci 2-bbl installed in the police Custom and Galaxie was rated at 171 horsepower while the same basic 400-ci 2-bbl in the police Torino was rated at 168 horsepower.

Again for 1973, all police engines were designed to run on regular gasoline. Regular gas was defined as having an octane rating of at least 91 using the Research Method.

In 1973, every single Ford police engine had a compression ratio of 8.0:1. This was the lowest since 1955. Low compression was viewed as the solution to ever-toughening emission standards. The 1973 engines were further detuned using leaner carbs and less aggressive cam timing. With the addition of emission control accessories and equipment, 1973 marked the period of the worst vehicle performance and the worst fuel economy.

The 1973 police Torino came standard with the 98-horsepower, 250-ci Six. This was almost never used. In fact, this was the last year for an in-line six-cylinder engine in a Ford police car until the 1979 Fairmont.

In 1973, the Fordomatic was replaced for the second time by the Cruise-O-Matic. The Fordomatic had been used with a first gear lockout. For 1973, that feature was transferred to the Cruise-O-Matic and the Fordomatic was dropped. The first gear lockout prevented the Cruise-O-Matic from being manually held in first gear and over-revving the engine. With the lockout, the Cruise-O-Matic started off in first with the selector in "Drive" and started off in second with the selector in "Second." Even still, a first gear lockout "delete" was available as a limited production option.

For 1973, the heavy-duty Cruise-O-Matic was standard on all police cars and was the only available transmission. The three-speed stick was available with the six-cylinder engine on the retail Torino. However, the Ford police package for the Custom, Galaxie, and Torino specified the Cruise-O-Matic.

For 1973, the Custom and Torino had massive front and rear bumper systems. These were required to meet new federal standards for impact resistance and damage protection. These heavy bumpers prevented sheet metal damage in the event of a 5-miles-per-hour frontal impact and a 2.5-miles-per-hour rear impact.

For 1973, the Fords came with big tires. The police package included 15x6.5 heavy-duty steel wheels. The G78x15 tires were standard on the midsize Torino while H78x15 was standard on the full-size Custom and Galaxie. The police Torino with 351-ci and larger engines got H78x15 rubber, while the police Custom with the 460-ci engine got the J78x15 tires normally used on station wagons.

In 1973, radial tires were used for the first time as original equipment on retail cars. The full-size LTD used HR78x15 steel-belted radials. Police cars would get radials in 1974.

New for 1973 were batteries up to 80 amps and alternators up to 90 amps, a coolant recovery system, inside hood release, and an engine oil cooler with the 460-ci engine. The auxiliary power steering oil cooler was first used on the 400-ci, 429-ci, and 460-ci engines in 1973.

In 1974, the Ford police package was available on the full-size, 121-inch wheelbase Custom 500 four-door pillared hardtop, the Galaxie 500 four-door pillared hardtop and two-door hardtop. Once again, the police package was also available for the 118-inch Torino four-door pillared hardtop, and the 114-inch Torino two-

The 1973 Torino, like this San Francisco Police unit, was available in powerplants ranging from the 250-ci Six to the 460-ci V-8. *Darryl Lindsay*

The New Jersey State Police used the Mercury Monterey in 1973. This had a 219 horsepower, 460-ci V-8. *Michael Fay*

A New York State Police Mercury Monterey. The emblem with the outline of the state means this was a Thruway unit. *Ned Schwartz*

door hardtop. In 1974, all Ford police cars were powered by a V-8 engine. The police package was also available for the station wagons, vans, and Bronco. For 1974, the 460-ci Police Interceptor had a horsepower rating worthy of the term "big-block" and the title "Police Interceptor." The top-of-the-line 460PI cranked out 260 horsepower,

which was quite impressive for the times. In comparison the Mopar 440-ci wedge V-8 produced 275 horsepower and the Chevy 454-ci "porcupine head" V-8 produced 235 horsepower. As a more modern-day reference, the dominating 1994 to 1996 Chevy "LT1" 350-ci police V-8 was also rated at 260 horsepower.

The 460-ci Police Interceptor wrested the top cop engine title away from the 351C 4-bbl V-8. The 260-horsepower, 460-ci had 5 more horsepower than the Cleveland V-8. At 380 pounds per foot, the 460-ci also had 90 pounds per foot more torque than the Cleveland V-8. Torque wins drag races. The 1974 model year was the last for the 351-ci Cleveland engine in police cars. In 1975, it would be replaced by a destroked 400-ci Cleveland that also happened to displace 351 ci. To avoid confusion with the 351 Windsor and 351 Cleveland, the new engine would be known as the 351-ci Modified, 351M.

In 1952, Ford heralded its "short stroke" 215-ci six-cylinder engine with its improved efficiencies. In 1954, Ford bragged that its Y-block V-8 also had high revving abilities thanks to its "short-stroke" design. By 1974, engine marketing had come full circle. The 400-ci was noted for being a "long stroke" engine. The Ford Police literature said, "There is ample power and the low end torque is exceptionally good, a characteristic of the long stroke engine." Recall that the 400-ci Cleveland had a "square" design. The bore and stroke were identical; the piston diameter (bore) equaled the piston travel (stroke).

Due to emission control standards unique to the state of California and the high cost of certifying an engine to those standards, some 1974 police engines were not available in the Golden State. These included the 302-ci, 351-ci 4-bbl, and the 460-ci Interceptor used in the Torino and the 460-ci Interceptor used in the Custom and Galaxie. The largest police engine available for California cops was the 460-ci 4-bbl Police (non-Interceptor).

In 1974, Ford introduced a solid-state, breakerless ignition system on police cars powered by the 351-ci, 400-ci, and 460-ci engines. The days of "breaker points and condenser" tune-ups were over. Solid-state ignition provided a stronger spark for starting, longer plug life, and reduced hydrocarbon emissions. This was a big step forward in achieving a "maintenance-free" drivetrain.

For 1974, Ford took its impact resistant bumper systems to the next higher level. They still met the 5-miles-per-hour frontal impact standards. However, rear impact resistance was increased from 2.5 miles per hour to 5 miles per hour. The new bumpers also complied with 3-miles-per-hour corner impact requirements.

In 1974, HR78 and JR78x15 steel-belted radials were limited production options for all Ford police cars except those with the 460-ci PI V-8 engine. The Custom and Torino with the 460-ci Police Interceptor had

The Indiana State Police became famous for their use of Mercury police cars, like this 1973 Monterey. The 460-ci engine in this unit was the largest FoMoCo police car engine ever built. *Jerry Parker*

The performance-fuel economy trade-off pointed out that it's what's inside the engine that counts rather than sheer size and axle ratio.

Torino's giant 460 cubic incher blew the doors off the field—well let's say the car rattled them a bit—with an 8.91 second 0–60-miles-per-hour time, and managed to clock a 14.3 mpg mileage figure.

Torino suffers from a psychological handicap. With 355 ft/lbs of torque available at only 2600 rpm, there is a very large temptation to use more gas pedal than you really need. It will spin the tires on any standing start. Lots of self restraint needed.

Motor Trend gave equal time to the full-size big-block sedans in 1974. Again, the exact models they tested had the upscale trim packages as opposed to the Spartan, entry-level trim found in most police cars. Their quick review pitted the LTD against the Caprice and Gran Fury.

With 121- to 122-inch wheelbases and 4,300 to 4,800 pound curb weights, these four-door sedans were about as large as police cars ever got. The exceptions were the 124-inch Mercury Monterey, 124-inch Chrysler Newport, and 125-inch Mercury Marquis. No Ford, Dodge, Plymouth, or Chevrolet police car ever had a wheelbase longer than 122 inches. Even still, the 121- to 122-inch sedans needed big-block, 4-bbl engines! The quarter-mile times in the 17-second bracket are typical for the very fastest full-size cruiser of that day. The 460-ci LTD turned in the best performance of the three. As a side note, the Gran Fury had the 205-horsepower, 400-ci engine. A 275-horsepower 440-ci was available.

In 1975, the Ford police package was based on the Custom 500 four-door pillared hardtop and the LTD two-door and four-door pillared hardtop. The police package was also available on the Torino and Gran Torino two-door hardtop and four-door pillared hardtops. As in past years, the police package was also available for a wide variety of station wagons, and vans, and for the Broncos.

LR78x15 steel-belted radials as an option. The Chevrolet police cars were also available with radials except those with the 454-ci engine, which oddly never came from the factory with radials.

In 1974, *Motor Trend* tested a mixed bag of 116- to 118-inch wheelbase "midsize" sedans. The full-size police cars in this era had 121- to 122-inch wheelbases. These midsize cars were indeed used by law enforcement. The Los Angeles County Sheriff used the 401-ci-powered AMC Matador in 1973 and 1974. The Los Angeles Police used the 401-ci Matador from 1972 through 1974. The San Francisco Police used the 1974 Torino. A few agencies used the Chevelle, while many used the Coronet.

The 360-ci small-block to 460-ci big-block midsize cars tested by *Motor Trend* were not police package cars but the straight-line performance and gas mileage were representative of police cars. With quarter-mile times in the 15 second bracket, these test results explain why the 401-ci Matador was popular. It was not reliable but it was fast!

Well into the era of low compression, low-performance engines, *Motor Trend* made refreshing observations about the 460-ci Torino.

Make	Ford	Chevrolet	AMC	Dodge
Model	Torino	Chevelle	Matador	Coronet
Engine, ci & carb	460, 4-bbl	400, 4-bbl	401, 4-bbl	360, 4-bbl
Horsepower	220	180	255	200
Trans	3-speed C6	3-speed THM	3-speed TC	3-speed TH
Axle ratio	3.00	2.73	3.54	2.71
Wheelbase, in	118	116	118	118
Weight, lb	4,530	4,100	4,055	3,850
0–60 mph, sec	91	11.20	8.50	9.45
1/4-mile ET, sec	16.47	18.27	15.96	16.60
1/4-mile speed, mph	84.9	76.5	87.4	84.7
60–0 mph, ft	130	141	160	125
EPA city mpg	14.3	15.6	12.2	13.2

Make	Ford	Chevrolet	Plymouth
Model	LTD Brougham	Caprice Classic	Gran Fury
Engine, ci & carb	460, 4-bbl	454, 4-bbl	400, 4-bbl
Horsepower	200	235	205
Transmission	3-speed C6	3-speed THM	3-speed TF
Axle ratio	3.00	2.73	3.23
Wheelbase, in	121.0	121.5	122.0
Weight, lb	4,860	4,373	4,676
0–60 mph, sec	10.8	9.6	10.4
1/4-mile ET, sec	17.6	17.9	18.2
1/4-mile speed, mph	80	82	78
60–0 mph, ft	139	133	139

The 460-ci powered Fords, like this 1974 Custom from Texas, ran the quarter-mile in the 16-to-17-second bracket. *Terry Fiene*

This 1974 San Francisco Police Torino had a 118-inch wheelbase. Engines ranged from the 302-ci V-8 to the 460-ci Police Interceptor. *Darryl Lindsay*

In 1975, the 351-ci Modified replaced the 351-ci Cleveland for use in midsize police cars. The 351-ci Windsor was still used in full-size police cars.

The 351-ci Modified was a destroked 400-ci. The 351-ci Modified was the third engine in the 335-series of Cleveland big-blocks. The 351-ci Modified and the 400-ci engine are very closely related. Here is the chronology: In

1970, the original 351-ci Cleveland was released. In 1971, Ford stroked the 351-ci Cleveland to 400 ci. However, to handle the extra piston travel, Ford raised the deck height of the basic 351-ci Cleveland block by 1.09 inches. The main journals for the 400-ci were increased to the 3-inch diameter used by the 351-ci Windsor.

For 1975, the stroked and raised block 400-ci was destroked back to 351 ci. This became the 351-ci Modified. In very loose terms, the 351-ci Modified is a raised block, but severely detuned, 351-ci Cleveland. All engines, of all vintages and carb options in the 335-series Cleveland family have the canted valvetrain.

For 1975, the top cop engine for both the full-size and midsize Ford police cars was the 460-ci Police Interceptor. This low compression big-block was rated at 226 horsepower. Only this one version of the 460-ci big-block was available.

In this model year, a 4-bbl was not available for either of the 351-ci engines. Both the 351-ci Modified used in the Torino and the 351-ci Windsor used in the Custom and LTD were rated at 148 horsepower. These were the base engines for the police fleet. For the first time since its introduction in 1968, the 302-ci V-8 was not available in a police car. At merely 129 horsepower in retail trim, the 302-ci would not have had the power to move these heavy police cruisers.

In 1975, for the first time, both 460-ci 4-bbl engines came standard with dual exhaust. This was done both to get the most power out of these low-compression engines and to achieve a slight improvement in fuel economy.

For 1975, performance was down and so was fuel economy. To make up for this, larger 24.3-gallon gas tanks were introduced. An 8-gallon "extended range" tank was option on the full-size cars. In 1975, every Ford police car had a catalytic converter and required the use of unleaded gasoline.

Anyone remember vacuum gauges used as fuel economy reminders? In 1975, a "Fuel Sentry" vacuum gauge was optional on the Custom "to help departments get the most out of their fuel dollar by indicating when drivers are getting the best gas mileage." A low vacuum

A 1975 Custom on-duty with the Louisiana State Police. The front fender emblems show this trooper is serious about his job. *Darryl Lindsay*

The top cop engine in 1975 Fords, like this Rhode Island State Police Custom, was the 226-horsepower, 460-ci V-8. *Darryl Lindsay*

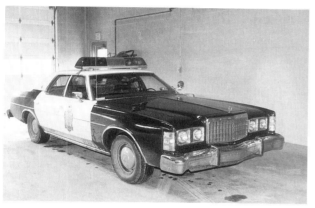

In 1976, the full-size Custom was available for the first time with rear wheel disc brakes. This put Ford 18 years ahead of Chevrolet. *Darryl Lindsay*

For 1977, the axle ratio for 351-ci powered LTDs, like this Brooklyn, Ohio, Police detective unit, was lowered to just 2.50 to 1 to improve gas mileage. *Darryl Lindsay*

warning light called a Fuel Monitor was available on the Torino. These devices showed Ford was at least a little out of touch with most troopers and road deputies!

In 1975, Ford police cars were again available with radial tires, except this time they were fabric-belted, not steel-belted. A steel-belt separated on a radial tire and resulted in the death of a state trooper. As a result, police departments insisted on fabric belted tires for nearly the next decade.

In 1976, the Ford police package was based on the Custom 500 four-door pillared hardtop, and LTD two-door and four-door pillared hardtop. The Torino and Gran Torino two-door and four-door pillared hardtops were also available with this special performance package. Station wagons, vans and Broncos could also get the police package.

The 1976 Ford police cars were straight carryovers in terms of drivetrains and chassis from the 1975 model year. The engines remained the 351-ci Windsor, 351-ci Modified, 400-ci Cleveland, 460-ci 4-bbl, and 460-ci Police Interceptor. The wheelbases for the Custom and

Torino were unchanged at 121 inches and 118 inches/114 inches, respectively.

In spite of no major changes, even to the exterior styling, Ford engineers made one huge advancement. For 1976, Ford developed a braking package for its full-size police cars that was nearly 20 years ahead of Chevrolet: rear wheel disc brakes. From 1976 through 1978, these were a regular production option. The four-wheel discs were available with either standard organic pads or with police-spec, heavy-duty semi-metallic brake pads. This four-wheel disc setup on a production police car was quite an engineering accomplishment.

In 1976, *Popular Science* tested four midsize, four-door sedans. All had 116- to 118-inch wheelbases. These were not police package cars. However, these midsize sedans were powered by the same medium displacement V-8s as many police cars. In 1976, even the California Highway Patrol ran a midsize cruiser. For decades, they had insisted upon a 122-inch wheelbase, 3,800-pound minimum four-door sedan for their Enforcement-Class vehicle. The 440-ci Coronet met the weight requirement

Make	Ford	Dodge	Chevrolet	AMC
Model	Torino	Coronet	Chevelle	Matador
Engine, ci & carb	400, 2-bbl	318, 2-bbl	305, 2-bbl	360,4-bbl
Horsepower	144	150	140	180
Transmission	3-speed	3-speed	3-speed	3-speed
Axle ratio	2.75	2.45	2.73	3.15
Wheelbase, in	118	117	116	118
Weight, lb	4,362	4,010	4,413	3,670
0–60 mph, sec	12.2	14.0	13.5	11.6
60–0 mph, ft	153	120	170	163
Lane change, mph	49.9	56.3	53	53
Slalom, mph	25	26	26.4	23.9

but had only a 117-inch wheelbase. Full-size four-door sedans were on their way out. By 1979, they would be history. Midsize four-door sedans with 112.7- to 116-inch wheelbases and 318-ci to 351-ci engines were the future.

For 1977, the only drivetrain or chassis change to the full-size LTD or the midsize Torino was to the axle ratios. In 1976, the rear gears were 3.25:1 for the 351-ci and 400-ci engines, and 3.00:1 for both 460-ci engines. In 1977, the 351-ci Windsor and 351-ci Modified used an incredibly low 2.50:1 ratio.

The 400-ci 2-bbl came with lower, 3.00 gears while the non-Police Interceptor version of the 460-ci 4-bbl got 2.75 rear cogs. The 302-ci V-8 was back in the police line-up for 1977 in both the LTD and Torino. It, too, got a low, 2.75:1 ratio.

The single reason for the lowered rear axle ratios was to increase fuel economy by allowing the engine to operate at lower rpms while cruising. At least that was the theory. In 1974, John Christy, editor of *Motor Trend* and Los Angeles County Sheriff's technical reserve deputy, proved that these low ratios actually produced worse gas mileage when used in police cars. Cops spend more time accelerating and less time cruising at a steady speed than civilians. These low axle ratios hurt acceleration, making cops give the cars even more gas. The gas mileage they lose trying to get up to speed is not made up by lower engine speeds while cruising. Even still, the pressure to gain better gas mileage was so intense, many fleet managers ignored the LASD/*Motor Trend* findings. They in turn, pressured Ford for axle ratios that give the best mileage in nonpolice scenarios. After 1977, Ford switched to aluminum intake manifolds on 351-ci 2-bbl engines strictly to save weight.

Ford Fleets' best kept police car secret is the existence of an official police package for the 1977 Maverick. These compact cars were powered by either the 250-ci, 1-bbl Six or the 302-ci, 2-bbl V-8. Both engines were teamed up with the Cruise-O-Matic transmission and 2.79:1 rear gear. The police package included a heavy-duty suspension (springs, shocks, rear away bar), certified speedometer, 61-amp alternator, 875 CCA battery, special body-to-frame reinforcements, extra heavy-duty seat fabric, extra capacity fuel tank, and extra capacity

A 1977 Milpitas, California, Police LTD. Once again, four-wheel disc brakes were an option on the full-size police Ford. *Darryl Lindsay*

The Kentucky State Police used the 460-ci powered, full-size Ford in 1977. So did the Georgia State Patrol, Alabama State Troopers, Connecticut State Police, and Mississippi Highway Patrol. *Darryl Lindsay*

cooling system with three-core radiator and six-blade fan, and front-disc brakes.

The Ford police literature made it clear that the Maverick was intended for suburban, nonpursuit assignments. The Maverick was used as a detective unit by the New York City Police, as a patrol car by the Fort Dix, New Jersey, Military Police, and as a highway patrol cruiser by the Ontario Provincial Police. With the small-block V-8, the police Maverick had good straight-line performance, and with the 2.79 rear gears, it had good gas mileage. However, the balance of the car was all wrong. The front end was heavy, the rear end was light, and a limited slip differential was not available. Even with a heavy-duty suspension and rear sway bar, the handling was deplorable. These cars were a real handful to drive during wet or snowy road conditions. In fact, the Mavericks were so dysfunctional as police cars, the New York Police Department (NYPD) is reported to have returned their units to Pearl Motors in the city demanding their money back.

In mid-1977, the midsize LTD II, like this Brown County, Indiana, Sheriff's unit, replaced the midsize Torino. The LTD II shared the same 118-inch wheelbase. *Bill Hattersley*

The 1978 model year was the last for any big-block Ford V-8 and the last for rear wheel discs. This Brooklyn, Ohio, Police LTD has the 460-ci Police Interceptor. *Darryl Lindsay*

This 1978 Rhode Island State Police LTD is the last of the long wheelbase Ford police cars. For 1979, the wheelbase would shrink from 121 inches to 114.4 inches. *Darryl Lindsay*

This 1978 Newbergh Heights, Ohio, Police LTD II was powered by the 400-ci Cleveland. This was the last year for police car engines greater than 351-ci. *Darryl Lindsay*

Ford produced about 350 police package 1977 Mavericks. The complaints about the car were so numerous and the car was so unpopular that Ford halted production of the police version by mid-year. These Mavericks may be the rarest of all Ford police cars. Fewer police package Mavericks were sold than the 1982 special service package Mustang. What was criticized in 1977 may now be one of Ford's most collectible police cars.

The big news for 1977 was the midyear release of the midsize LTD II, which replaced the Torino. The LTD II S-series replaced the Gran Torino. Like the Torino, the four-door pillared hardtop LTD II had a 118-inch wheelbase. The two-door hardtop LTD II checked in with a 114-inch wheelbase. This was a sheet metal change and not a change to either the drivetrain or chassis. The full-size LTD retained its 121-inch wheelbase.

In 1977, rear wheel disc brakes with either organic or semimetallic brake pads were again available on the full-size LTD.

The 1978 model year was extremely significant to cops and to big-block and police car enthusiasts alike. This was the last year of the long wheelbase Ford police car. For 1979, the LTD wheelbase would shrink from 121 inches to 114.4 inches. It would stay at 114.4 inches through the end of the century. For 1979, the midsize

LTD II was dropped from the police car line, and along with it the 118-inch wheelbase. Regardless of the drivetrain changes in the future, the 1978 Ford marked the end of the era of BIG Fords.

The 1978 model year was also the last for big-block engines of any kind. It was the last for the 351-ci Modified and 400-ci Cleveland. Both were in the 335-series of Cleveland big-blocks. The 1978 model year was also the last for the 460-ci V-8 of any kind. These 385-series big-blocks would be gone forever.

The largest police interceptor engine available after 1978 would be the 351-ci Windsor small-block V-8. Even this would eventually be dropped in favor of a 281-ci modular block V-8.

In 1977, the LTD II replaced the Torino. The top powerplant for these midsize cars became the 400-ci V-8. The LTD II was not available with either of the 460-ci engines.

The 1978 model year also marked the last for four-wheel disc brakes on the full-size Ford. For 1979, the full-size and midsize Fords were only available with rear drum brakes. Fords would remain disc/drum until after the 1992 changeover. When Fords got rear discs again, they also gave Antilock Braking Systems and Traction Assist as options.

As a clear sign of the times, in mid-1978, Ford released a brand-new kind of police car, the 105.5-inch wheelbase, four-door Fairmont. Mercury also released a police package for its 105.5-inch Zephyr. These compact cars were powered by either the 200-ci I-6 or 302-ci V-8. Downsized, four-door police sedans were the trend in large urban police departments whether police officers liked it or not. And most did not like it. It was one thing to patrol in the 108-inch 350-ci, 4-bbl Chevy Nova that popularized the use of compact police cars in urban areas. It was quite another to patrol in an 85-horsepower Fairmont or Zephyr.

The Fairmont and Zephyr were intended for general patrol, ordinance enforcement, investigations, and other non-high speed and nonpursuit assignments. "An efficient, tough compact performer," the Fairmont and Zephyr were claimed to have enough room to seat five adults in comfort that they had 90 percent of the head, leg, and shoulder room of most large cars.

The compact cars did indeed come with a full police package, complete with auxiliary trans and power steering coolers, 90-amp alternators, police heavy-duty suspension including heavier springs and shocks and both front and rear sway bars, and 70-series police-spec radials. Ford tried. However, these compacts became some of the least popular police cars of any make, model, or vintage. The cops just were not ready yet.

The Fairmont was not a popular police car, but it sold in the retail market even better than the Mustang in its first year. It was Ford's top-selling car line in 1978.

In mid-1978, a police package was released for the 105.5 inch Fairmont and Zephyr. This Milpitas, California, Fairmont is powered by a 200-ci Six. Note the door shield is on the rear fender. *Darryl Lindsay*

In 1978, the Michigan State Police began their famous series of annual patrol vehicle tests. Under their test procedure, a certain percentage of the car's bid price was weighted by a performance factor. Using the MSP method, a more expensive police car would win the "low bid" contract if its vehicle performance was high enough. The 1978 MSP test phases included acceleration to 100 miles per hour, absolute top speed, braking distances, road racing course lap times, an ergonomic evaluation, and the EPA city fuel mileage.

In 1978, the Michigan State Police set a minimum acceleration standard for its patrol cars. They had to reach 60 miles per hour in 12.5 seconds or less and 100 miles per hour in 38 seconds or less. Cars that failed to meet these standards were disqualified from bidding. However, the MSP completed all the tests even on disqualified cars as a service to police agencies whose requirements for acceleration or top speed differed from the MSP.

The 1978 400-ci Ford LTD II was tested by the MSP along with a 350-ci Buick LeSabre, 350-ci Chevrolet Impala, 400-ci Dodge Monaco, 400-ci Pontiac Catalina, and 440-ci Plymouth Fury. The 400-ci LTD II met the

MSP requirement for 0 to 60-miles-per-hour acceleration but did not get to 100 miles per hour fast enough. Both the LTD II and Buick were disqualified for acceleration that was too slow. The MSP did not test any of the 460-ci Police Interceptor-powered Fords or Mercurys. They should have.

In 1973, the Kentucky State Police used the big Ford while the San Francisco Police and Pinellas County, Florida, Sheriff used the Torino. Mercurys were the choice of the Stockton, California, Police; Iowa State Patrol; New Jersey State Police; and Indiana State Police. The Pinellas County, Florida, Sheriff used the Torino again in 1974 and 1975. Also in 1975, the Washington State Patrol cruised in Fords. For 1976, the Louisiana State Police, Wyoming Highway Patrol, and South Carolina Highway Patrol selected Fords. In 1977, Fords were the choice of the Alabama State Troopers, Connecticut State Police, Kentucky State Police, Massachusetts State Police, Mississippi Highway Safety Patrol, South Carolina Highway Patrol, and Georgia State Patrol. In the last year of the big-block V-8, the New Jersey State Police selected the LTD II while the Missouri State Highway Patrol went for the Mercury.

1973 Ford Police Drivetrains

Layout	cid	carb	comp	horsepower	exhaust	axle	model
V-8	351 W	2-bbl	8.0	156	single	3.25	Custom
V-8	400	2-bbl	8.0	171	single	3.25	Custom
V-8	429	4-bbl	8.0	202	single	3.25	Custom
V-8	460	4-bbl	8.0	219	dual	3.00	Custom
I-6	250	1-bbl	8.0	98	single	3.00	Torino
V-8	302	2-bbl	8.0	138	single	3.00	Torino
V-8	351 C	2-bbl	8.0	159	single	3.25	Torino
V-8	351 C	4-bbl	8.0	266	dual	3.25	Torino
V-8	400	2-bbl	8.0	168	single	3.25	Torino
V-8	429	4-bbl	8.0	201	single	3.25	Torino
V-8	460	4-bbl	8.0	219	dual	3.00	Torino

1974 Ford Police Drivetrains

Layout	cid	carb	comp	horsepower	exhaust	axle	model
V-8	351 W	2-bbl	8.0	162	single	3.25	Custom
V-8	400	2-bbl	8.0	170	single	3.25	Custom
V-8	460	4-bbl	8.0	195	single	3.25	Custom
V-8	460 PI	4-bbl	8.0	260	dual	3.00	Custom
V-8	302	2-bbl	8.0	140	single	3.00	Torino
V-8	351 C	2-bbl	8.0	163	single	3.25	Torino
V-8	351 C	4-bbl	8.0	255	dual	3.25	Torino
V-8	400	2-bbl	8.0	170	single	3.25	Torino
V-8	460	4-bbl	8.0	195	single	3.25	Torino
V-8	460 PI	4-bbl	8.0	260	dual	3.00	Torino

Note: The only axle available in California was the 3.00:1. All police cars used the 3-speed Cruise-O-Matic.

1975 and 1976 Ford Police Drivetrains

Layout	cid	carb	comp	hp	exhaust	axle	model
V-8	351 W	2-bbl	8.2	148	single	3.25	Custom
V-8	400	2-bbl	8.0	158	single	3.25	Custom
V-8	460	4-bbl	8.0	218	dual	3.00	Custom
V-8	460 PI	4-bbl	8.0	226	dual	3.00	Custom
V-8	351 M	2-bbl	8.0	148	single	3.25	Torino
V-8	400	2-bbl	8.0	158	single	3.25	Torino
V-8	460	4-bbl	8.0	218	dual	3.00	Torino
V-8	460 PI	4-bbl	8.0	226	dual	3.00	Torino

1977 and 1978 Ford Police Car Engines

Layout	cid/liter	carb	hp	axle	model
V-8	302/5.0	2-bbl	137	2.75	LTD
V-8	351W/5.8	2-bbl	149	2.50	LTD
V-8	400/6.6	2-bbl	173	3.00	LTD, Marquis
V-8	460/7.5	4-bbl	197	2.75	LTD, Marquis
V-8	460PI/7.5	4-bbl	202	3.00	LTD, Marquis
V-8	302/5.0	2-bbl	134	2.75	Torino, LTD II, Cougar
V-8	351M/5.8	2-bbl	152	2.50	Torino, LTD II, Cougar
V-8	400/6.6	2-bbl	166	3.00	Torino, LTD II Cougar
I-6	200/3.3	2-bbl	85	2.73	1978 Fairmont
V-8	302/5.0	2-bbl	139	2.47	1978 Fairmont
I-6	250/4.1	1-bbl	98	2.79	1977 Maverick
V-8	302/5.0	2-bbl	130	2.79	1977 Maverick

1978 Michigan State Police Patrol Vehicle Test Results

Make	Buick	Chevrolet	Dodge	Ford	Plymouth	Pontiac
Model	LeSabre	Impala	Monaco	LTD II	Fury	Catalina
Engine, ci & carb	350, 4-bbl	350, 4-bbl	400, 4-bbl	400, 2-bbl	440, 4-bbl	400, 4-bbl
Hp, SAE	155	170	190	166	255	180
Axle ratio	2.73	3.08	3.21	3.00	2.71	3.08
Weight, lb	4,77	3,996	4,369	4,611	4,413	4,057
Wheelbase, in	115.9	116	117.4	118	117.4	115.9
Road course lap time, sec	96.6	92.7	93.6	93.5	91.1	93.7
0–100 mph, sec	46.4	33.7	34.4	41.0	24.8	34.6
Top speed, mph	110	115	117	115	133	110
EPA city mpg	15	15	13	13	10	14
Adjusted bid price, $	disqual.	5,679	5,582	disqual.	5,397	5,663

Here's a beautifully restored 1973 Mercury Montego MX used by the Arizona Highway Patrol. The mid-size Merc is powered by a 351ci, 4-bbl Cleveland V-8.—*DG Development*

Chapter Eleven

1979-1981
The Downsized Fords

Ford fielded three main police cars for 1979. These were the LTD two-door and four-door sedan, LTD II two-door hardtop and four-door pillared hardtop, and the Fairmont two-door and four-door sedan. The LTD II, which was a midsize car in 1978, retained its 118-inch wheelbase. As such, the LTD II was the "big Ford" in 1979.

For 1979, the LTD, which was the full-size car in 1978, was downsized from a 121-inch wheelbase to a 114.4-inch platform. The "full-size" LTD was now actually shorter than the "midsize" LTD II. The Fairmont compact police car remained at a 105.5-inch wheelbase.

Chevrolet was the first out with a downsized and lighter weight full-size sedan. The Impala was dropped from 122 inches to 116 inches for the 1977 model year. Chrysler was next. The 121.5-inch 1977 Plymouth Gran Fury became the 117.4-inch Fury for 1978. Oddly, for 1979, the Plymouth Fury was replaced by the 118.5-inch Chrysler Newport and Dodge St. Regis.

Retail sales were down by 15 percent because Ford lagged behind Chevy and Plymouth in reducing the size of its full-size car. Of course, the police were just the opposite from the public. They continued to demand the largest V-8 and the longest wheelbase cars. Regardless of the police enthusiasm for long wheelbases, in January 1979, the production of the 118-inch wheelbase LTD II ceased due to lack of retail demand. From 1979 through 1997, with this half year exception of the LTD II, the largest Ford police sedan has had a 114.4-inch wheelbase. When the LTD II was dropped, so was the 351-ci Modified. From then on, the 351-ci V-8 would be the Windsor.

The new, downsized LTD was the result of 270 hours of wind-tunnel testing. It was Ford's ninth totally new full-size car in the company's history. In spite of a 7-inch shorter wheelbase, the 1979 LTD actually had more interior room than the larger 1978 LTD.

From 1979 through 1982, Ford had two different grille and headlight assemblies for the full-size LTD. The base model LTD or the fleet-oriented LTD "S," had single rectangular headlights. The mid-trim level LTD and the upscale LTD Crown Victoria had dual rectangular headlights. Since most police departments purchased the lower-priced model, during this era the Ford police

cars generally had single headlamps. This looks a little unusual today since the upscale LTD from 1979 through 1982 and all LTD police cars after 1982 had dual headlights. Since Plymouth was at its peak of popularity in this era, these Ford police cars are fairly rare.

The 1979 and 1980 LTD had single headlights with grille slots in the front bumper. The 1981 LTD had single headlights and a solid front bumper. The 1982 LTD had single headlights, a solid bumper, and the blue Ford oval in the grille on the driver's side.

The large displacement big-block engines were history for all makes of police cars by 1979. The top Ford engine was the 351-ci Modified 2-bbl at 151 horsepower. This Ford V-8 was the same size but had much less power than the Mopar 360-ci, 4-bbl at 195 horsepower and the Chevrolet 350-ci, 4-bbl with 170 horsepower. Only some of the horsepower difference can be traced to Ford's use of a 2-bbl instead of the 4-bbl used by the competition. The rest of the difference is outright detuning: cam grind, ignition timing, and head design. The 151-horsepower 351-ci Modified was available only in the long wheelbase LTD II. This was the last year for any Cleveland big-block engine in any Ford police car. Recall

The downsized 1979 LTD-S like this Brooklyn, Ohio, Police unit, had a 114.4-inch wheelbase but more interior room than the long wheelbase 1978 LTD. Note the single headlight per side. *Darryl Lindsay*

In 1979, the midsize LTD II with a 118-inch wheelbase, like this Baldwin, Illinois, Police unit, was actually larger than the full-size 114.4-inch LTD. *Dave Dotson*

that the 351-ci Modified was a destroked 400-ci Cleveland raised-deck, big-block.

The downsized LTD was available with the 351-ci Windsor 2-bbl at 142 horsepower. The 302-ci V-8 was available in all three police cars. Oddly enough, the more powerful 140-horsepower version was available in the Fairmont while the less powerful 129-horsepower version came in the LTD.

In 1979, a variable venturi 2-bbl carburetor became standard on 351-ci Windsor engines. The 302-ci would be fuel injected on 1983 police cars. However, the 351-ci Windsor would keep its variable venturi carb until the engine was replaced by the 4.6L SOHC with fuel injection in mid-1992.

All of the 1979 Ford police cars were slow. Tests on all makes and most models of police car have been conducted each year since 1956 by the Los Angeles County Sheriff and each year since 1978 by the Michigan State Police. The LASD test vehicles have the California emissions packages, while the MSP test cars have Federal engines, the so-called "Other 49" emissions controls.

The 151-horsepower LTD II tested by the MSP had a 0 to 60-miles-per-hour time of 14.8 seconds. Its 0 to 100-miles-per-hour time was 66.7 seconds. In comparison the competition from Chevrolet and Chrysler hit

The midsize LTD II, like this Amelia, Ohio, Police cruiser, was produced for just half a model year. This was the last year for any canted valve, Cleveland-based V-8. *Bill Hattersley*

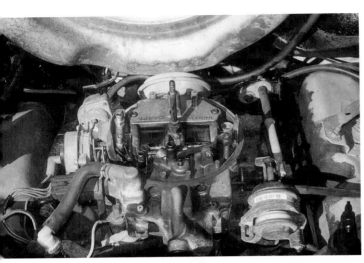

New for 1979 police engines in 1979 was this unique Motorcraft "Variable Venturi" 2-bbl carb. This was used on 351-ci Windsor police engines through 1991.

100 miles per hour in 30 to 35 seconds. The long wheelbase LTD II had a top speed of 111 miles per hour compared to 122 miles per hour from the competition.

The 142-horsepower LTD was no different. It was only slightly faster than the LTD II to 100 miles per hour but had a top speed of merely 105 miles per hour. These cars were disqualified from bidding for failing to reach 100 miles per hour in 43 seconds. Out of five full-size cars tested by the MSP around the Michigan International Speedway road racing course, the LTD and LTD II came in fourth and fifth. The MSP contract was awarded to the Dodge St. Regis.

The Los Angeles County Sheriff found a similar lack of performance from the LTD, LTD II, and Fairmont. With the 149-horsepower California emissions version of the 351-ci Modified, the LTD II reached a top speed of just 99 miles per hour. The 138-horsepower, 351-ci

Here is one of the 1979 Fairmonts in service during the CHP Special Purpose Vehicle Study. To the surprise of most cops, the CHP found the 105.5 inch police car could be used for police work. *Darryl Lindsay*

Windsor-powered LTD hit just 102 miles per hour. Oddly enough, the 302-ci Fairmont outran both the bigger Fords with a top speed of 108 miles per hour. The big Fords came in fourth and last behind the St. Regis, Chrysler Newport, and Chevy Impala. Among the midsize cars at the LASD tests, the Fairmont came in last behind the Dodge Aspen, Plymouth Volare, and Chevy Malibu. This was an all-time low for Ford police cars. Things would get better.

Ford used more aluminum castings in its V-8 police engines for 1979 to reduce weight and improve mileage. The 302-ci got an aluminum intake while the 351-ci Windsor lost 40 pounds by switching to an aluminum intake, water pump, and rear cover.

Soon after the 1979 model year began, Henry Ford II fired Lee Iacocca as president of Ford Motor Company. A few months later, Iacocca was named president of Chrysler Corporation.

The period immediately after the demise of the big-block was an especially rough one for state troopers and highway patrol officers. For 50 years, these officers had nearly the most powerful cars on the road. Now, they had midsize and full-size four-door sedans with a small-block V-8 choked off with emission gear. In the late 1970s and mid-1980s, the fastest police four-door sedans produced top speeds well under 120 miles per hour.

The California Highway Patrol was the first to be affected by this loss of power. The patrol lost their 440-ci V-8 after 1978. The 1979 CHP Dodge St. Regis used a 360-ci V-8. The 1979 St. Regis was bigger than the 1978 Fury, so the 1979 Dodge was even slower than the engine sizes show. Top speeds dropped from 133 miles per hour to 123 miles per hour. The news for the CHP in 1980 was worse yet. Top speeds with the 318-ci-powered, 118.5-inch wheelbase St. Regis were just 115 miles per hour.

The big news for 1979 was the Special Purpose Vehicle Study conducted by the California Highway Patrol. This study was a direct result of the loss of the big-block V-8 and the downsizing from 122-inch wheelbase cars to 116- and 117-inch wheelbase cars. One of the alternatives on how to deal with the changing police cars was a mixture of vehicles with different designs within one fleet. Some of the vehicles would be smaller four-door sedans with multipurpose abilities. Others would be special purpose vehicles like sports coupes and station wagons that would be intended for specific police tasks. In late 1978, using 1979 model vehicles, the Special Purpose Vehicle Study began.

CHP executive management wanted to include vehicle designs that would probably be available after 1985, which appeared to be a stability point in the pattern of vehicle change. By using 1978 manufacturer forecasts, the following models were selected for testing.

In an effort to simulate mixed fleet management conditions, three of each of the 1979 models were

Sport Coupe	1979	Chevrolet	Z28 Camaro,	350 ci	V-8
Compact Sedan	1979	Chevrolet	Malibu	305 ci	V-8
Compact Sedan	1979	Ford	Fairmont	302 ci	V-8
Station Wagon	1979	Plymouth	Volare	318 ci	V-8

The 1979 Fairmont tested by the CHP was powered by a 133-horsepower, 302-ci V-8. It had a faster quarter-mile speed than the 1979 360-ci E-class St. Regis. Note the experimental twin strobe lights. *Darryl Lindsay*

assigned to four test areas throughout the state. This resulted in a total of 12 test vehicles in each area. The balance of each local fleet consisted of the basic police sedan.

The test areas were selected because they represented a sampling of statewide operating conditions. Roadway design, topography, climate, and traffic patterns were incorporated into the selection process. It was hoped that potential problems arising from a specific model's inability to perform in a particular region could be documented. The four test areas included Redding, Bakersfield, West Los Angeles, and El Centro.

Redding area: This area is located in rural northern California. Its topography includes both long mountain grades and the northern Sacramento valley. The climate changes seasonally from severe cold and snow in winter to extreme 100 degree plus heat in summer.

Bakersfield area: This Area is located in the central portion of the state and is the high-speed link between northern and southern California. Aside from freeways, the Bakersfield area also has a variety of suburban and rural roadways. Climate ranges from rainfall in winter to severe heat in summer.

West Los Angeles area: Located in the more densely populated Los Angeles metropolitan area, much of the area is older freeway with little or no shoulder. Extremely heavy traffic volumes are frequently present, especially during commute hours.

El Centro area: Located just north of the California–Mexico border, most of the El Centro area is open desert with extreme heat

Testing of the 1979 Camaro turned out to be extremely important for Ford. The CHP concluded that a sport coupe was needed for select traffic enforcement duties. The qualified success of the Camaro during the CHP Study resulted in an open bid to all V-8 powered pony cars. Ford won the first bid with what would become its most famous police car, the 5.0L HO Mustang—the Ford that chases Porsches for a living.

From 1979 through 1982, Ford used one headlight per side for the fleet-oriented LTD-S, like this 1980 Ross Township, Ohio, Police patroller, and two headlights per side on the upscale LTD. *Bill Hattersley*

A 1981 LTD-S in-service with the Alabama State Troopers. These were all powered by the 351-ci High Output V-8. *Greg Reynolds*

More about the Special Service package Mustang in chapter 15.

The 302-ci Fairmont was not as glorious as the Mustang. However, it led to one of the most significant conclusions of the test: Downsized vehicles are capable of performing most enforcement duties. Downsized vehicles do not necessarily impair officer safety except when inadequate performance is present. Downsized four-door sedans do not significantly affect prisoner transportation.

At the time, the CHP used the 1979 Dodge St. Regis with a 118.5-inch wheelbase. The 1979 Fairmont had a 105.5-inch wheelbase. In comparison, the first generation Taurus, which was a credible urban police car, had a 106-inch wheelbase. The St. Regis was used throughout the study as a benchmark of performance.

The 1979 Fairmont was the lightest vehicle of the Study with a curb weight of 2961 pounds. The St. Regis

tipped the scales at 3,746 pounds. Remember, long ago the CHP had set its vehicle standards at 3,800 pounds and a 122-inch wheelbase. It was a real culture shock for the CHP to even consider the 105.5-inch 2,961 pound Fairmont!

The Fairmont was powered by a 302-ci, 2-bbl V-8 producing 133 horsepower. The CHP Study lists this as a 4-bbl engine. That was probably a typo. A 4-bbl was not an option on the 302-ci in 1979, and the CHP was careful to obtain test vehicles that were standard. A few modifications were done on the Camaro for safety and performance reasons. However, the CHP stated the Fairmont was a stock vehicle. For the record, this was a 2-bbl engine. Emission controls were the difference between the California rating of 133 horsepower and the Other 49 rating of 140 horsepower. The Fairmont had a three-speed Cruise-O-Matic and 2.73:1 rear gears.

This was indeed a police package vehicle. The Fairmont 55A police package included a three-speed auto with first gear block-out and auxiliary oil cooler, power front disc brakes with semimetallic pads, calibrated speedometer, heavy-duty suspension with rear stabilizer bar and upgraded frame supports, heavy-duty 5.5-inch wheels, 70-series police radials, heavy-duty cooling including power steering cooler, 77-amp battery and 100-amp alternator.

History has not been kind to the Fairmont, however, in terms of real performance, it was acceptable for the era. The 302-ci Fairmont had a good bottom end response even with 2.73 gears. It was almost as fast to 60 miles per hour as the 360-ci St. Regis. It was faster to 60 miles per hour and to 100 miles per hour than the 305-ci, 4-bbl Malibu. The 302-ci Fairmont even had a quarter-mile speed faster than the E-class 360-ci St. Regis. Its brakes got "excellent" and "above average" ratings.

The Fairmont, however, received marginal ratings for interior comfort. Some considered it "acceptable" while others rated it as "cramped."

The CHP kept detailed maintenance, downtime, and fuel mileage records for all test vehicles. CHP traffic officers logged between 15,000 and 76,000 on all 12 vehicles for a total of 537,000 test miles.

In addition to competitive performance, the Fairmont had two great advantages. One, it produced better gas mileage than any of the other test or control vehicles. In actual police service, it got 13.3 miles per gallon. That was big news in 1979 when the CHP was experiencing 10 miles per gallon or less in its current fleet.

The other strength was its fleet maintenance record. The Fairmont had the least downtime of any test or control vehicle and the lowest repair cost of any four-door sedan.

Overall, the results from the Fairmont in the study were very favorable. Nearly all officers considered the trunk large enough. Many recommended a split seat instead of the bench seat. Most believed the Fairmont

In 1981, all the full-size Fords, like this St. Charles Parish, Louisiana, Sheriff LTD-S, had four-speed overdrive automatic transmissions. *Bill Hattersley*

New for 1981 was a 255-ci V-8 in full-size cruisers like this Union Township, Clermont County, Ohio, Police LTD-S. This debored 302-ci engine got almost 20 miles per gallon. *Bill Hattersley*

was a durable and dependable car. The clear majority noted that downsizing did not have an effect on high-speed stability. (Longer wheelbases were once felt to be more stable at higher speeds, all else equal.) The CHP was disappointed in the 107-miles-per-hour top speed however, here is the concluding paragraph:

Despite these concerns (seats, top speed), field officers believed the Fairmont could be useful in enforcement work. Good handling and quick low end acceleration can be an asset for those beats not requiring frequent high speed operation. The Fairmont possessed these qualities and might be very effective on such beats.

In 1980, the police package was available on the fleet-oriented LTD "S" and the base-line LTD in both two-door and four-door sedans. The "S" edition had single square headlights per side while the LTD-series had dual rectangular headlights. Both models shared the same 114.4-inch wheelbase. The police package was also available for the four-door Fairmont.

The 118-inch wheelbase LTD II was discontinued in mid-1979. It did not return for the 1980 model year.

The LTD "S" and LTD had three police powerplants for 1980: the base 302-ci V-8, the single exhaust 351-ci V-8, and the 351-ci High Output V-8. The 351-ci HO had dual exhausts and a high lift, long duration cam. This was the first year for this HO version of the Windsor engine. The 351-ci HO produced over 30 horsepower more than the standard 351-ci V-8. That kind of horsepower was hard to come by in the gas economy and emissions-focused 1980s. The standard output 351-ci engine was teamed with a 3.08 axle, while the 351-ci HO got 2.73 rear gears.

The police Fairmont was available with the 200-ci In-Line Six or the brand-new 255-ci V-8. The new V-8 was a debored version of the 302-ci small-block.

Engine	Bore	Stroke
255-ci/4.2-L	3.68 inch	3.00 inch
302-ci/5.0-L	4.00 inch	3.00 inch

The goal of the new engine was to provide V-8 performance but from as small a displacement engine as possible to get the best gas mileage. This engine also powered the Mustangs in the early 1980s. This was not a noteworthy police engine.

The big news for 1980 was the option of Ford's new four-speed lockup torque converter, Automatic Overdrive Transmission, aka, AOT, aka, A4. This was a transition year for Ford transmissions, and the source of some parts confusion. Many of the retail LTD sedans got the four-speed AOT. It was optional with the 5.0L and 5.8L retail drivetrains. However, most of the police sedans got the Select-Shift, nonlockup, three-speed auto. Only the California 5.8L police package cars got the four-speed AOT. All the other police cars got the three-speed. While it may have changed by midyear, in the beginning of the model year, the four-speed AOT was not even available as an option with the non-California police packages.

Both the 351-ci Ford LTD "S" tested by the Michigan State Police and the 351-ci Ford LTD tested by the Los Angeles County Sheriff used the C-6 Select-Shift three-speed trans.

Popular Science discovered a problem with the 1980 four-speed AOT, which was corrected for 1981. In a high-speed panic stop in fourth gear, if the rear brakes locked quickly (before the torque converter unlocked), the engine would stall. This happened about 60 percent of the time. If rear wheel lockup was delayed or if only one wheel locked, the engine did not stall. Of course, the stalled engine cut power to the power steering and cut vacuum to the power brakes at a time when both were urgently needed.

The problem was not in the overdrive's fourth (0.67:1) gear. Instead, the lockup torque converter disconnect governor was at fault. This was the first year for the lockup torque converter. Here is what Dunne & Jacobs wrote:

The drivetrain coupling arrangement of AOT seems to be the culprit. As we reported in Aug. '79, in third gear, power flows from the engine to the transmission 40 percent through the torque converter (the usual coupling device in automatic transmissions) and 60 percent through direct, mechanical connection. That arrangement allows the torque converter to slip when the car or drive shaft and rear wheels stop, so the engine doesn't stall.

In fourth gear, however, the engine-transmission coupling is 100 percent mechanical, and allows no slippage. The transmission's centrifugally operated governor is designed to disconnect the linkup when road speed falls below 35 miles per hour, to allow the slippage that will bar stalling. If the rear wheels are solidly locked up too quickly, there isn't time for the governor to disconnect before the engine stalls. And there is no backup system.

Lockup torque converters on Chrysler products use the same disconnect system as Ford, but we noted no stalling in Chrysler cars under similar circumstances. Lockup converters on GM cars have two disconnect systems—one from manifold vacuum, and the other electrical, in conjunction with the brake-light switch.

By the time the four-speed AOT was standard across the board for all 1981 Ford police cars, the disconnect governor was fixed.

The combination of a lockup torque converter and a 0.67:1 overdrive fourth gear improved gas mileage by 19 percent over a comparable 1979 model. That was a big deal.

In 1980, the Michigan State Police expanded their testing to include a wide variety of police package midsize cars. They had two sets of vehicle performance standards. One for full-size cars with wheelbases from 114.4 inches to 118.5 inches and another for midsize cars with wheelbases from 105.5 inches to 112.7 inches.

The 255-ci Fairmont was quicker around the MIS road course than the 318-ci Aspen and Volare but not as fast as the 305-ci and 350-ci Malibu and 360-ci Aspen. It had almost the shortest stopping distances and the best EPA city economy ratings. However, the MSP disqualified the Fairmont for failing to meet their 0 to 60-miles-per-hour and 0 to 90-miles-per-hour acceleration standards. With 2.26:1 rear gears, acceleration was not what the Fairmont did best.

The 351-ci HO-powered LTD "S" did well during the MSP tests of full-size cars. It ran door-to-door with the 360-ci powered St. Regis and Gran Fury. In the final analysis, it was simply outbid by the Gran Fury.

The Los Angeles County Sheriff did not test any of the 360-ci-powered Mopars. As a result, the 351-ci HO LTD was by far the best performing police sedan. Again, both the LTD and Fairmont were outbid by the Malibu.

In 1980, only three police engines/chassis combinations met the California Air Resources Board (CARB) emission standards for California Highway Patrol "Enforcement" class squad cars. These were the 318-ci, 4-bbl in the Dodge Diplomat, the 350-ci, 4-bbl in the Chevy Malibu and the 351-ci HO, 2-bbl in the Ford LTD. A high stakes drag race was organized to see which cars, if any, could meet the CHP's new acceleration and top speed requirements.

The Ford LTD proved to be the quickest to 60 miles per hour in 12.76 seconds, the quickest to 100 miles per hour in 42.16 seconds, and had the fastest top speed at 116.4 miles per hour. The Malibu was disqualified by the CHP for failing to achieve the 110-miles-per-hour top end. In the final analysis, however, the Diplomat under-

In 1981, the top gun among all makes of police sedan was the LTD-S with the 351-ci HO, like this Orleans Parish, Louisiana, Sheriffs unit. Top speed, however, was only 116 miles per hour. *James Donohoe*

The 1981 police package Fairmont, like this Ford City, Illinois, Police patroller, was available with a Four, Six or V-8. The 255-ci V-8 Fairmont ran a 19-second quarter-mile. *Greg Reynolds*

A 1981 Missouri State Highway Patrol LTD. The die-cast emblem on the lower front quarter panel says "Overdrive." The overdrive was .67 to one. *Darryl Lindsay*

door and four-door sedan, and the Fairmont four-door sedan. As in the past, Econoline vans and Club Wagons with engines from the 300-ci I-6 to 460-ci V-8 were available to police specs. The police Bronco 4x4 with 302-ci and 351-ci engines was also available.

For 1981, both the police LTD and police Fairmont came standard with smaller engines. The LTD got the 255-ci V-8. The Fairmont got the 140-ci I-4.

In 1980, Chevrolet introduced a 229-ci V-6 for Impala police cars. At the time, the smallest engine available for the LTD was the 302-ci V-8. In mid-1980, Chevrolet upped the ante with a "special economy equipment package" for the Impala. This made the 229-ci Impala the first full-size, gasoline-powered car to have an EPA "city" rating of 20 miles per gallon. For urban police fleets that wanted both a full-size car and good mileage, this hurt Ford fleet sales. In 1981, Ford countered with the LTD now available with the 255-ci V-8. This was the first appearance of this debored 302-ci in a full-size police sedan. The engine was still a "V-8," but was rated at only 120 horsepower. This set the tone for the early 1980s police cars.

The other LTD engines were the 302-ci V-8 and one of the 351-ci V-8s. The standard output 145-horsepower, single exhaust 351-ci was only available in California and not the other 49 states. The 165-horsepower, 351-ci High

bid the LTD. Except for the 1982 Impala, 1984 Crown Victoria, and 1987 Caprice the Diplomat held onto the CHP contract through 1988.

As a sign of the times, a 40-channel CB radio was an option on the 1980 Ford police packages.

In 1981, the Ford police package was available for the fleet-priced LTD "S" four-door sedan, the LTD two-

The Missouri State Highway Patrol ran Mercury Marquis in 1980. Downsized in 1979, this has a 114.3-inch wheelbase.

A 1981 Missouri State Highway Patrol Mercury Marquis. These were powered by the 142-horsepower 351-ci V-8 using a Variable Venturi carb.

Output, was only available with Federal emissions and not with the California emissions package. Again the HO engine included dual exhausts, revised cam profile, engine oil cooler, premium bearings, special valves, and valve springs.

For 1981, all LTD "S" and LTD sedans came with the four-speed automatic overdrive trans. The three-speed auto was not available. Again, the LTD "S" had single headlamps while the LTD had dual headlamps. As a reference, this was the last year for a 351-ci engine in a retail sedan.

Ford was way ahead of the competition with its four-speed overdrive trans and lockup torque converter. The full-size Chevrolet did not get lockup torque converters and an overdrive automatic until 1983. Dodge and Plymouth went to a lockup converter in 1981 but never did produce a four-speed overdrive for the Diplomat and Gran Fury. They were discontinued after 1989.

The new engine for the Fairmont was the 140-ci, 2-bbl overhead-cam In-Line Four rated at 88 horsepower. This had the same horsepower as the 200-ci, 1-bbl I-6; however, it had much less torque, 118 pounds per foot versus 154 pounds per foot The transmission used in all Fairmont drivetrains was the three-speed nonoverdrive, nonlockup automatic. The four-speed AOT was not available even though the Fairmont and LTD shared a similar 255-ci V-8.

The LTD police package included a certified and calibrated 140-miles-per-hour speedometer. This was a cruel hoax. In 1981, no U.S. police package vehicle of any marque had a top speed over 120 miles per hour. This will put the sluggishness of these early 1980s police sedans in perspective: Vehicles that passed the MSP acceleration standards ran the quarter-mile as slow as 19.6 seconds!

In 1981, the top gun among police sedans was the 351-ci HO LTD. Michigan State Police troopers got the slick top LTD up to 116.4 miles per hour. The big Ford had excellent road course times and 0 to 100-miles-per-hour acceleration times. Plymouth fleet officials had the sharpest pencil, but not the highest performing police sedan.

The MSP tested the Fairmont powered by both the 200-ci I-6 and the 255-ci V-8 during its evaluation of midsize cars. This was a tough class. It included the 350-ci, 4-bbl Malibu and the 318-ci, 4-bbl Diplomat. Both of the Fairmonts were disqualified for failing to meet acceleration and top speed standards.

The early 1980s was the bleakest era of police car performance on record. Ford, Chevrolet, and Plymouth police cars first topped 120 miles per hour in the mid-1950s. Buick police cars exceeded 120 miles per hour in the early 1950s. While the police Mustang broke the 120-miles-per-hour barrier with its 1982 introduction, it would not be until 1984 that a four-door police sedan would top 120 miles per hour. That sedan was the fuel-injected, 302-ci LTD!

Among major departments, the Indiana State Police; South Carolina Highway Patrol; and Pinellas County, Florida, Sheriff used Fords in 1979. In 1980 and 1981, the Missouri State Highway Patrol selected Mercurys. Also in 1981, the Alabama State Troopers used Fords.

1979 Michigan State Police Vehicle Tests

Make	Chevy	Chrysler	Dodge	Ford	Ford
Model	Impala	Newport	St. Regis	LTD	LTD II
Engine , ci & carb	350,4-bbl	360,4-bbl	360,4-bbl	351,2-bbl	351, 2-bbl
SAE HP	170	195	195	142	151
Axle ratio	3.08	3.21	3.21	3.08	2.47
Weight, 2 on board, lb	4,398	4,520	4,530	4,332	4,882
Wheelbase, inches	116	118.5	118.5	114.4	117.9
Road course time, sec	93.46	91.36	91.65	95.14	97.88
0–100 mph, sec	35.3	31.5	30.2	63.3	66.7
Top Speed, mph	112.5	121.3	122.9	105.4	111.1
Braking, ft/sec^2	23.8	21.8	21.4	18.6	20.1
EPA city mpg	16	12	12	14	13
Results, overall	third	second	first	disqual.	disqual.

1979 Los Angeles County Sheriff's Midsize Vehicle Tests

Make	Ford	Chevy	Dodge	Plymouth
Model	Fairmont	Malibu	Aspen	Volare
Engine, ci & carb	302, 2-bbl	350, 4-bbl	360, 4-bbl	360, 4-bbl
Horsepower (CA)	133	165	190	190
Axle ratio	2.73	2.73	3.21	3.21
Weight, lb	3,250	3,560	3,920	3,930
Wheelbase, in	105.5	108.1	112.7	112.7
Top speed, mph	108.1	108.2	110.6	107.2
0–60 mph, sec	10.1	9.7	9.9	10.3
1/4-mile trap speed, sec	77.4	79.0	78.4	79.3
Brake power, g	.76	.88	.85	.78
Skid pad, 200 ft dia., g	.80	.80	.78	.81
Fuel economy, actual, mpg	14.4	13.4	12.3	11.7
Total score	59.5	60.6	64.1	62.4
Rank	fourth	third	first	second

1979 CHP Special Purpose Vehicle Study

Make	Chevrolet	Chevrolet	Ford	Plymouth	Dodge
Model	Camaro	Malibu	Fairmont	Volare SW	St. Regis*
Engine, ci & carb	350 ci, 4-bbl	305 ci, 4-bbl	302 ci, 2-bbl	318 ci, 4-bbl	360 ci, 4-bbl
Horsepower (CA)	160	125	133	155	195
Transmission	3-speed THM	3-speed THM	3-speed auto	3-speed auto	3-speed auto
Axle ratio	3.08	2.7	32.7	32.41	3.23
Wheelbase, in	108.0	108.1	105.5	112.7	118.5
Curb weight, lb	3,522	3,222	2,961	3,533	3,746
0–60 mph, sec	9.8	12.2	12.0	14.6	11.3
0–100 mph, sec	27.6	44.2	44.0	50.2	34.4
1/4-mile speed, mph	81.6	73.5	77.2	72.7	77.1
Top speed, mph	123.6	107.8	106.8	109.5	117.5
EPA city mpg	11.8	12.3	13.3	12.8	10.2
Repairs, $/K**	48.36	31.65	24.54	20.58	25.80
Downtime, hr/mo	51.6	34.0	20.2	32.3	30.2

*The Dodge St. Regis was the CHP E-class vehicle for 1979
**Maintenance dollars per 1,000 miles

1980 Michigan State Police Patrol Vehicle Tests
(114.4 to 118.5 inch wheelbase)

Make	Buick	Chevrolet	Dodge	Ford	Plymouth
Model	LeSabre	Impala	St. Regis	LTD-S	Gran Fury
Engine, ci & carb	350, 4-bbl	350, 4-bbl	360, 4-bbl	351, v/v	360, 4-bbl
SAE HP	155 n	165 n	185 n	172 n	185 n
Axle ratio	2.73	3.08	2.94	2.73	2.94
Weight, lb	4,146	3,934	4,100	4,030	4,053
Wheelbase, in	115.9	116	118.5	114.3	118.5
Road course					
lap time, sec	96.2	92.8	91.8	92.2	90.8
0–100 mph, sec	49.4	46.2	36.7	37.3	35.5
Top speed, mph	113.1	110.4	122.7	120.5	124.6
1/4-mile time, sec	19.5	19.1	18.4	18.5	18.2
1/4-mile speed, sec	74.3	73.3	77.5	77.8	76.8
Braking from 60 mph	1681	691	71.11	71.41	82.5
EPA city mpg	15	14	11	14	11
Adjusted bids, $	disqual.	disqual.	6,518	7,105	6,392

1980 Michigan State Police Patrol Vehicle Tests
(105.5- to 112.7-inch wheelbase)

Make	Chevrolet	Dodge	Ford	Plymouth	Chevrolet	Dodge
Model	Malibu	Aspen	Fairmont	Volare	Malibu	Aspen
Engine, ci & carb	305, 4-bbl	318, 4-bbl	255, 2-bbl	318, 4-bbl	350, 4-bbl	360, 4-bbl
SAE HP	155 n	155 n	119 n	155 n	165 n	185 n
Axle ratio	2.73	2.94	2.26	2.94	2.73	2.94
Weight, lb	3,484	3,673	3,109	3,673	3,01	3,734
Wheelbase, in	108.1	112.7	105.5	112.7	108.1	112.7
Road course						
lap time, sec	93.3	96.2	95.7	96.2	92.2	92.7
0–90 mph sec	33.4	32.3	49.1	29.4	31.9	25.7
Top speed, mph	113.4	117.3	111.6	120	110.8	122.2
1/4-mile speed, mph	73.5	73.3	68.5	74.8	74.3	77.5
1/4-mile ET, sec	19.2	19.6	20.7	19.3	19	18
Braking from						
60 mph, sec	64.11	77.31	58.11	67.81	56.11	61.7
EPA city mpg	17	16	18	16	14	13
Adjusted bids, $	6,109	6,110	disqual.	5,788	info only	info only

1981 Michigan State Police Patrol Vehicle Test Results
(midsize cars)

Make	Chevrolet	Chrysler	Chrysler	Dodge	Ford	Ford
Model	Malibu	LeBaron	LeBaron	Diplomat	Fairmont	Fairmont
Engine, ci & carb	350, 4-bbl	318, 4-bbl	225, 1-bbl	318, 4-bbl	255, 2-bbl	200, 1-bbl
SAE HP	165	165	85	165	115	88
Axle ratio	2.73	2.94	2.94	2.94	2.73	2.73
Weight, test, lb	3,579	3,856	3,694	3,851	3,156	2,944
Wheelbase, in	108.1	112.7	112.7	112.7	105.5	105.5
Road course						
lap time, sec	1:30.37	1:32.54	n/a	1:31.98	1:33.50	n/a
0–100 mph, sec	40.27	45.24	n/a	42.71	65.79	n/a
Top speed, mph	111.9	114.7	92.5	116.3	106.4	92.3
1/4-mile ET, sec	18.15	18.90	22.80	19.38	19.68	21.78
1/4-mile speed, mph	74.75	73.50	61.75	75.50	71.00	63.50
Braking, ft/sec^2	25.71	26.02	n/a	24.63	25.02	n/a
EPA city mileage, mpg	14.7	15.5	17.9	15.5	18.1	19.8
Adjusted bid price, $	7,531.48	7,691.79	disqual.	7,623.55	disqual.	disqual.

1981 Michigan State Police Patrol Vehicle Test Results (fullsize cars)

Make	Chevrolet	Buick	Dodge	Ford	Plymouth
Model	Impala	LeSabre	St. Regis	LTD	Gran Fury
Engine, ci & carb	350, 4-bbl	252,4-bbl	318,4-bbl	351,2-VV	318,4-bbl
SAE HP	165	125	165	165	165
Axle ratio	3.08	3.23	2.94	2.73	2.94
Weight, test, lb	3,927	3,834	4,086	4,060	4,090
Wheelbase, in	116.0	116.6	118.5	114.3	118.5
Road course lap time, sec	1:30.72	1:38.48	1:33.93	1:32.40	1:33.60
0–100 mph, sec	39.98	n/a	45.72	42.16	42.22
Top speed, mph	113.8	97.1	114.7	116.4	115.1
1/4-mile ET, sec	18.95	21.88	19.63	19.35	19.40
1/4-mile speed, mph	75.00	66.25	74.50	74.75	75.25
Braking, ft/sec^2	26.93	23.87	23.67	23.35	25.15
EPA city mpg	14.7	18.5	15.5	15.3	15.5
Adjusted bid price, $	7,560.90	disqual.	7,733.54	8,318.05	7,516.74

1979 Ford Police Drivetrains

Layout	cid/liter	carb	comp	hp	axle	model
V-8	302/5.0L	2-bbl	8.4	129	3.08	LTD
V-8	351W/5.8L	2-VV	8.3	142	3.08	LTD
V-8	302/5.0L	2-bbl	8.4	133	2.47	LTD II
V-8	351M/5.8L	2-bbl	8.0	151	2.47	LTD II
I-6	200/3.3L	1-bbl	8.5	85	2.73	Fairmont
V-8	302/5.0L	2-bbl	8.4	140	2.73	Fairmont

1980 Ford Police Drivetrains

Layout	cid/liter	carb	comp	hp	axle	model
V-8	302/5.0L	2-bbl	8.4	130	2.26	LTD-S, LTD
V-8	351W/5.8L	2-VV	8.3	140	3.08	LTD-S, LTD
V-8	351W/5.8L-HO	2-VV	8.3	172	2.73	LTD-S, LTD
I-6	200/3.3L	1-bbl	8.6	91	2.26	Fairmont
V-8	255/4.2L	2-bbl	8.8	119	2.26	Fairmont

1981 Ford Police Drivetrains

Layout	cid/liter	carb	comp	hp	axle	model
V-8	255/4.2L	2-bbl	8.2	120	3.08	LTD
V-8	302/5.0L	2-bbl	8.4	130	3.08	LTD
V-8	351W/5.8L	2-VV	8.3	145	3.08	LTD (Calif.)
V-8	351W/5.8L-HO	2-VV	8.3	165	2.73	LTD (Federal)
I-4	140/2.3L	2-bbl	9.0	88	3.08	Fairmont
I-6	200/3.3L	1-bbl	8.6	88	2.73	Fairmont
V-8	255/4.2L	2-bbl	8.2	115	2.73	Fairmont*

*NOTE: LTD used the 4-speed automatic overdrive, Fairmont used the 3-speed automatic.

Chapter Twelve

1982-1989
302-ci Mustang and LTD, 351-ci Crown Victoria

The 1980s are best described as a period of low vehicle performance and almost no change to the police vehicles from the Big Three. For the entire decade, Chrysler fielded its 112.7-inch wheelbase Dodge Diplomat and Plymouth Gran Fury powered by the 318-ci V-8. Chevrolet offered its 116-inch wheelbase Impala and then Caprice. Except for the addition of fuel-injection in 1989, the 350-ci V-8 was nearly unchanged for a decade. Ford had its LTD and later Crown Victoria powered by the 302-ci V-8 and 351-ci V-8. Just one major sheet metal change took place.

For 1982, the police package was available on the LTD "S" four-door sedan, the LTD two-door and four-door sedans and the Fairmont four-door sedan. This was the last model year for a two-door police package full-size sedan. This was also the last year the low-priced LTD "S" was a separate car line and the last year for single rectangular headlights. After 1982, the full-size Fords all had dual headlights.

The 1982 LTD "S" is unique among the single headlamp "S" series cars. It is the only model with the single headlight per side and the blue oval in the grille. The 1982 marked the return of the "Ford" script markings in the form of a blue oval found on the grille of all the LTDs. In 1982, the upscale LTD-series had dual headlights per side. Also in 1982, Ford opened an assembly plant in St. Thomas, Ontario, Canada. This production facility would later be used to build the 1992 and later police package Crown Victorias.

The 351-ci Windsor V-8 had been available in two versions, standard and High Output. The standard 351-ci was discontinued in retail and police cars alike after the 1981 model year. The only 351-ci remaining was the High Output and this was only available in police package cars.

The full-size police LTD was available in three powerplants, 255-ci, 302-ci, and 351-ci HO. The only transmission available was the four-speed automatic overdrive.

In 1982, the Fairmont was available with the 140-ci Four, 200-ci Six, and 255-ci V-8. For the first time, the Michigan State Police tested all three versions. New for 1982, the Six and V-8 got lockup torque converters for their three-speed Select-Shift automatics. The lockup would work in all three forward speeds. The 1982 Fairmonts were restyled with quad headlights.

The 1982 model year, however, is best known as the year of the CHP Mustang: the Ford that chased Porsches for a living. For the pursuit cars, the CHP set a new and tougher standard of performance. The pursuit pony had to accelerate to 60 miles per hour in 10 seconds maximum, get to 100 miles per hour in less than 30 seconds, and have a top speed of 120-miles-per-hour minimum. The CHP also required that the pursuit car be driven with Wide Open Throttle flat-out for 25 miles without any damage to drivetrain components.

Both the 350-ci Camaro Z28 and the 302-ci Mustang GL were fast enough to be eligible to bid for the CHP business. The 302-ci V-8 had replaced the 255-ci V-8 in mid-1982. In retail trim, the 302-ci, 2-bbl Mustang reached 60 miles per hour in 6.9 seconds, 100 miles per hour in 21.1 seconds, and had a top speed of 128 miles per hour. It ran the quarter-mile in 16.1 seconds at 87.2 miles per hour. Chevrolet bid $11,445 versus the $6,868 Ford bid. The CHP ordered 406 Mustangs. The rest is automotive, California, and police car history. See chapter 15.

The Mustang was powered by a 157-horsepower, 302-ci HO, 2-bbl V-8. The 1982 "severe" service package Mustang came with the GT suspension, GT steering,

This 1982 Chicago Police cruiser is the upscale LTD. Note the two headlights per side. These 351-ci HO sedans ran 116 miles per hour. *Greg Reynolds*

In 1982, Ford and the CHP revolutionized the high speed pursuit car with this Severe Service 5.0L Mustang. The Ford that chases Porsches for a living was born. *Ford Division*

A 1983 Ford on duty with the Alabama State Troopers. This was the first year for the Crown Victoria nameplate in police service. *Darryl Lindsay*

and Fairmont brakes and wheels. The package was renamed "Special Service" for 1983. The HO retail and police engine had a special marine cam with more lift and double duration roller timing chain, heavier valve springs, an oversize 351-ci HO air cleaner, and larger 356-cfm 2-bbl carb instead of 310 cfm.

A difference exists between the "Police package" and the "Special Service package." Ford, General Motors, and Chrysler all draw a similar distinction between these two classes of law enforcement vehicle. For the record, here is what Ford Fleet literature says:

"The special service vehicle does not meet Ford Motor Company durability requirements for police packages, and recommended use is for high-speed highway traffic law enforcement service."

During Michigan State Police testing, the 5.0 HO Mustang reached 60 miles per hour in 8.35 seconds, 100 miles per hour in 24.68 seconds, and had a top speed of 126.4 miles per hour. It ran the quarter-mile in 15.96 seconds at 84.0 miles per hour. After a year of the slowest

In 1983, the 302-ci V-8 used in the full-size Ford, like this Minnesota State Patrol Crown Vic, was converted to central fuel injection. *Greg Reynolds*

A 1984 CHP Crown Victoria. This was the first time since 1970 the CHP selected a FoMoCo product as their Enforcement-class vehicle. *Darryl Lindsay*

This is a tan, slick-top 1984 CHP Crown Vic used to enforce commercial truck regulations. Catching semi-trucks requires a stealth-mobile. *Darryl Lindsay*

police cars in 25 years, the performance from the 5.0 HO Mustang caused excitement in police circles from coast to coast.

During their annual police car tests, the MSP found all the V-8-powered police four-door sedans ran the quarter-mile in the 19-second bracket. The 351-ci HO LTD captured the heavily weighted road course test phase, but the 318-ci Gran Fury won the contract. Mustangs with four grille styles were used by police departments from 1982 to 1993. These styles are different than the ones familiar to most enthusiasts. This is because the Special Service package was based on the entry level LX, not the GT and not the SVO.

The 1982 police Mustang had a styling that was a carryover from the major restyling of 1979. The 1982 Mustang LX had deeply recessed, quad rectangular headlamps. The outer lights in the pair were set back farther than the inner headlights. The angled grille had a 10-by-5 hole crosshatch pattern. The word *FORD*, not the blue oval, was on the driver's side of the grille.

The 1983 and 1984 Mustang LX shared the same grille. Like the 1982 version, the 1983 and 1984 models had a crosshatch grille and quad headlamps. The only real change was the blue oval in the center of the grille instead of the word *Ford*.

The 1985 and 1986 Mustang LX also retained rectangular quad headlights. However, the grille was now a single wide slot. The blue oval was in the rounded panel just above the grille opening.

For 1987, the Mustang got the first major restyling since its debut in 1979. Dual flush mounted headlamps replaced the quad recessed lamps. This was available on the 1984 to 1986 Mustang SVO. The 1987 Mustang LX had the blue oval suspended on a single, body color crossbar in the center of the grille opening. The Mustang LX would retain this same front end styling through 1993.

In 1983, Ford made some very significant nameplate changes, wheelbase shuffles, and engine option changes.

The name of the full-size Ford was changed from LTD to LTD Crown Victoria, a name from the 1950s. This same year, a brand-new midsize car was introduced to the retail market, the LTD. One was a 114.4-inch LTD Crown Victoria. The other was a 105.5-inch LTD.

Cops across the country called this new short wheelbase sedan the "Baby LTD." It was strictly a retail car in 1983, but it became Ford's midsize police car in 1984. With the fuel-injected 302-ci, the Baby LTD was one of the fastest sedans to 100 miles per hour. The Florida Highway Patrol are best known for their use of these whip-quick Ford sedans.

For 1983, the police package was available on the LTD Crown Victoria "S" four-door sedan. The police package was not available on the upscale LTD Crown Victoria. Nor was the police package available on a two-door sedan for the first time in at least three decades.

The Crown Vic "S" came standard with the 302-ci V-8, four-speed overdrive automatic, power steering, and power front disc brakes. The 351-ci HO V-8 was the only optional engine. The 225-ci V-8 was no longer available for either the full-size Crown Vic or the midsize Fairmont.

Ford's midsize police car for 1983 was the four-door Fairmont. This was available with only the 140-ci overhead-cam I-4 or the 200-ci I-6. For 1983, the Four was switched from a Holley or Motorcraft 2-bbl carb to a Carter 1-bbl carb. This was the last model year for the rear-drive Fairmont. In 1984, it was replaced in the retail market by the front-drive Tempo and in the police market by the rear-drive Baby LTD.

The Fairmont never did live up to the expectations of the CHP Special Purpose Vehicle Study. Part of the reason was the interior layout of the dash and seats. The other part was the selection of low power engines. The Fairmont was only available with the 302-ci during the 1979 model year, the year of the CHP test. By 1983, it was not even available with a V-8. However, in 1984, the 302-ci-powered Baby LTD would prove the CHP correct. A powerful midsize vehicle could be a very effective police car.

The big news for 1983 was central fuel injection for the 302-ci V-8. The horsepower was almost unchanged, 132 horsepower for the 2-bbl and 130 horsepower for fuel-injection; however, the peak power occurred 200 rpm lower at 3,200 rpm. The torque was also similar, 236 pounds per foot for the 2-bbl and 240 pounds per foot for the CFI; however, the peak torque occurred 200 rpm higher at 2,000 rpm. The basic effect of the fuel injection was to "flatten" the torque curve and make the engine more responsive throughout the rpm range.

Chevrolet put fuel injection on the 262-ci V-6 used in the Impala. Dodge and Plymouth never did have fuel injection for their Diplomat and Gran Fury police cars even though police fleet managers begged for it and fuel injection was already used on a 318-ci V-8 retail engine. Chevrolet's 350-ci V-8 got fuel injection in 1989. The 351-ci Windsor was never fuel injected. For the next ten years, from 1983 to 1992, the powertrain on the full-size Crown Victoria would remain basically unchanged. The big V-8 would be the 351-ci HO with its Variable Venturi carburetor and 165 to 180 horsepower. The small V-8 would be the 302-ci with central, and later multiport, fuel injection and 130 to 160 horsepower.

In terms of sheer performance, the 351-ci HO Crown Victoria did very well during the Michigan State Police tests. Of the four-door sedans, once again, it clearly had the quickest course times. It had the second fastest acceleration to 100 miles per hour, the best ergonomics and competitive brakes, and top speed. The problem was the Gran Fury was just as strong and $600 less expensive.

By 1983, word on the Mustang 5.0L pursuit car reached across the country. Eleven states had adopted the Mustang as a special traffic enforcement pursuit car.

This 1984 South Dakota Highway Patrol cruiser is packing a 351-ci HO V-8. The top speed without lightbar was 118 miles per hour. *Greg Reynolds*

The Indiana State Police used this LTD Crown Victoria in 1984. It is easy to see why Hoosier cops call this car a Stripe. *Rick Hammer*

The 1984 302-ci EFI HO powered LTD, like this Florida Highway Patrol unit, was the highest performance four-door police sedan of the year. It hit 100 miles per hour 10 seconds faster than the 351-ci HO Crown Vic. *Greg Reynolds*

The 1984 Special Service package 5.0L Mustang, like this Oklahoma Highway Patrol pursuit, was available with central fuel injection or a 4-bbl carb. *Greg Reynolds*

The Indiana State Police used the LTD Crown Vic in 1985. Rated at 180 horsepower, the 351-ci HO V-8 made this cruiser the nation's most powerful full-size police sedan. *Rick Hammer*

By 1991, at least 35 state police and highway patrol departments and well over 100 major sheriffs departments used the 5.0L Mustang LX as a pursuit car. The Mustang grew to have the same reputation among cops as the old 440-ci big-block Dodges.

For 1983, the Special Service package Mustang received a 4-bbl carb that boosted the output from the 5.0L HO to 175 horsepower. The full-size police sedans of all marques ran the quarter-mile in the mid-18-second to low-19-second range. The 5.0L police Mustang ran the quarter in 16.7 seconds with two troopers on board. It had a top speed of 132 miles per hour. The last time any police vehicle topped 130 miles per hour was the 1978 440-ci Fury.

In 1984 the police package was available for the LTD Crown Victoria "S" four-door sedan and the mid-size LTD four-door sedan. The Bronco 4x4, Econoline van, and Club Wagon were also available with police gear. In its third year, the Special Service package was available for the Mustang LX.

The 105.5-inch LTD was built on the L-body platform, which it shared with the Granada and the Fairmont. This was a stretched wheelbase version of the same Fox-body platform used by the Mustang. The LTD was officially a five-passenger, four-door sedan.

The Baby LTD was much more aerodynamic than either the Granada or Fairmont. It had a 60-degree rear-window angle, wedge-style front grille, and aerodynamic decklid. The drag coefficient of 0.38 was very sleek for a four-door sedan. This new LTD used a rack-and-pinion steering instead of a worm-and-roller design.

The Baby LTD was available with two powerplants: the 140-ci Four and the 302-ci HO V-8. The LTD and Mustang shared exactly the same 165-horsepower fuel-injected V-8. The 140-ci Four was teamed with a three-speed automatic and 3.45 rear gears. The 302-ci HO CFI V-8 was mated to a four-speed overdrive automatic and 3.08 gears.

After decades of being an option in Ford police cars, the In-Line Six was no longer available in either police or retail cars. The retail cars had gone to the V-6. The last use in police cars of the Mopar Slant Six was 1983. The Chevrolet police In-line Six was dropped after 1979.

The 1984 Crown Victoria was mostly a carryover from 1983; however, the 351-ci HO was now rated 15 horsepower stronger at 180 horsepower. In comparison, the Impala's 350-ci had 155 horsepower and the 318-ci used in the Diplomat and Gran Fury had 165 horsepower. For the record, the 302-ci V-8 used in the Crown Vic was not the High Output version used in the Mustang and Baby LTD.

By far, the hottest Ford police sedan was the 302-ci HO-powered LTD. Of the 11 four-door police sedans tested by the Michigan State Police, the 302-ci HO LTD had the fastest 0-to-60-miles-per-hour time, fastest 0-to-100-miles-per-hour time, fastest quarter-mile elapsed time, highest top speed, and fastest road course lap times. The fuel-injected LTD exactly split the differences in overall performance between the 5.0L Mustang and the full-size police sedans. No wonder the 302-ci HO Baby LTD was so popular among cops. It has four doors and most of the space of a full-size sedan, yet it ran almost like a pursuit pony car.

As quick as the Fox-body Baby LTD was, it did have one serious drawback that it shared with its Fox-body twin, the Mustang LX. The drawback was brakes that were nowhere near up to the potential of the 302-ci HO engine. This was a widely known problem with the Mustang but less-known and even more severe problem for the LTD. Nothing short of a complete re-engineering of the entire rear axle and brakes would solve the problem. The Santa Monica, California, Police purchased the 302-ci LTD one year and sold them after just one year of service due to poor brakes. Officers were reluctant to get into a pursuit of more than a few city blocks due to

This 1985 Crown Victoria patrolled the hills and hollers of Tennessee. The 351-ci HO V-8 produced top speeds around 118 miles per hour. *Dave Dotson*

This 1985 LTD used by the Florida Highway Patrol was powered by the Mustang's 302-ci HO V-8. With a 17-second quarter-mile, the 302-ci LTD was a great cross between the two-door Mustang and the four-door Crown Vic. *Greg Reynolds*

severe brake fade. Veteran police officers point to the 1983–1984 Baby LTD as having the worst brakes of any car they have driven. In this regard, the 302-ci HO LTD, like the Mustang, was a better car for state police and rural sheriffs departments than urban sheriffs departments and city police where brake-critical pursuits are more common.

Oddly, this braking deficiency was not uncovered by the Michigan State Police vehicle tests, even though their test methods called for four 90-miles-per-hour stops before each of the two 60-miles-per-hour stops for score. For 1984, the 302-ci HO LTD stopped at a rate of 24.36 feet per second squared for a distance of 159 feet. For 1985, the rate increased to 26.47 feet per second squared and 146 feet. For both years, the Fox-body LTD turned in a braking performance that was the exact average for the police and special service vehicles.

For 1984, the Special Service Mustang was available with one of two 302-ci HO engines. The central fuel-injected engine produced 165 horsepower. The Holley 4-bbl engine was bumped from last year's 175 horsepower to this year's 205 horsepower. The fuel-injected engine came with a four-speed overdrive automatic. The carbureted engine came with a five-speed manual trans.

The 1984 model year was a breakthrough year for Ford police cars. The 351-ci HO Crown Victoria captured the influential California Highway Patrol contract for full-size, Enforcement-Class vehicles. The 302-ci EFI

LTD was awarded the equally influential Los Angeles County Sheriff Department contract for urban-sized police cars. These two police departments set the pace for vehicle selection for all of the western states.

In 1985, the police package was available on the full-size 114.4-inch LTD Crown Victoria "S" four-door sedan and the midsize 105.6-inch LTD four-door sedan. The Mustang LX was once again available with a Special Service package. The four-door sedans were mostly a carryover from 1984. The 1985 Crown Vic got nitrogen-charged, gas-filled shock absorbers for a better ride.

In 1985, Ford produced five different 302-ci V-8 engines.

Check out the elevated McDermott light rack mounted behind the lightbar on this 1985 Suffolk County, New York, Police Highway Patrol Crown Vic. The heavy-duty rear sway bar is also visible. *Ned Schwartz*

Engine	Induction	Horsepower	Vehicle	End Use
302 ci	efi	140	Crown Vic	police
302 ci	HO efi	155	Crown Vic	retail
302 ci	HO efi	165	LTD	both
302 ci	HO efi	180	Mustang	both
302 ci	HO 4-bbl	210	Mustang	both

This 1985 Cook County, Illinois, Sheriff's LTD was powered by the fuel-injected 302-ci HO V-8. These vastly underrated police sedans had a 123-miles-per-hour top end. *Greg Reynolds*

Odd as it seems, even though a High Output 302-ci was available for the Crown Vic, it was not available with the police package. The whole purpose of the 302-ci in a full-size squad car was V-8 performance at maximum fuel economy for urban patrol.

The Special Service package Mustang became a higher performance police car each year. For 1985, the 5.0L HO V-8 got a higher lift, longer duration cam, roller tappets, and a two-speed accessory drive system. The 4-bbl version was bumped from 205 horsepower to 210 horsepower. The fuel-injected version jumped from 165 horsepower to 180 horsepower.

Again, the injected 5.0L came only with the four-speed overdrive automatic. The carbureted 5.0L came only with the five-speed stick. For 1985, the five-speed stick got an entirely new set of gear ratios, including a stronger pulling first year and a tighter overdrive.

Gear	1984	1985
1st	2.95	3.35
2nd	1.94	1.93
3rd	1.34	1.29
4th	1.00	1.00
5th	.63	.68

In 1985, the fuel-injected Mustangs retained their P205/70R14 radials. However, the 4-bbl cars got P225/60VR-15 Goodyear Eagle "Gatorback" unidirectional radials on 15x7 wheels. By 1985, the state police and highway patrol in 15 states had adopted the Special Service Mustang.

At 180 horsepower, the 351-ci HO Crown Vic was the country's most powerful full-size sedan, while the 165-horsepower, 302-ci HO LTD was the nation's most powerful midsize sedan. At the annual Michigan State Police tests, the 302-ci HO LTD had the quickest road course time of any four-door sedan. The 351-ci HO

By 1985, 15 states used the Mustang as a pursuit car. This was the year the 4-bbl version got unidirectional Gatorback radials. Top speeds were over 135 miles per hour. *Motor Trend*

Crown Vic was just a half second behind and was ahead of every other full-size police sedan.

In 1985, the 4-bbl Mustang had the fastest quarter-mile acceleration of any police vehicle. The 302-ci HO LTD was the fastest accelerating midsize. The 351-ci HO Crown Vic grabbed the honors among full-size police sedans. The brakes on all three police vehicles were truly excellent this year.

New for 1986 was sequential fuel injection for the 5.0L Mustang, like this Idaho State Police unit. SEFI replaced both the 4-bbl carb and central fuel injection. *Bill Hattersley*

Sequential fuel injection flattened the horsepower and torque curves on the 5.0L V-8 used in Mustangs like this 1986 CHP commercial enforcement vehicle. The result was better overall performance. *Darryl Lindsay*

This 1986 South Carolina Highway Patrol Crown Vic had a 180-horsepower, 351-ci HO V-8 but a top speed of only 115 miles per hour. *Darryl Lindsay*

The 1987 Crown Vic, like this Medical Lake, Washington, Police unit, was the last of the square designs. With the 351-ci HO and 2.73 rear gears, it reached 115 miles per hour. *Bill Hattersley*

This was the last year for the red-hot 302-ci HO LTD. Midsize police cars have not been the same ever since. The 302-ci HO LTD was to the mid-1980s what the 350-ci-powered Nova was to the mid-1970s. These were truly powerful, well-balanced, fairly economical midsize police cars. Even though the Taurus sedan replaced the Baby LTD for 1986, the Taurus would never be the police car the midsize LTD was. Not even close.

For 1986, the police package was available only on the LTD Crown Victoria LX and "S" four-door sedans. A Special Service package was available for the Mustang. The Bronco, Aerostar, and Econoline van were all available in police trim. The Bronco was available with 300-ci I-6, 302-ci V-8 or 351-ci V-8 engines.

The midsize LTD was no longer available as a police car. It was replaced in the retail market in mid-1986 by the front-drive Taurus. The Taurus would not be available in a police package until 1990.

The big news for 1986 was sequential electronic multiport fuel injection, SEFI. SEFI replaced central fuel injection on the 302-ci used in the Crown Vic. Other changes included fast-burn combustion chambers, roller tappets, a viscous clutch cooling fan, and a half point more compression. This added up to 10 more horsepower and a 150-horsepower engine.

In 1986, sequential fuel injection replaced both the central fuel injection and the 4-bbl carburetion on the Mustang's 302-ci HO engine. Here is how they compared:

	Horsepower	Torque
1985 302-ci CFI	180@4,200	260@2,600
1985 302-ci 4-bbl	210@4,400	270@3,200
1986 302-ci SEFI	200@4,000	285@3,000

Sequential fuel injection flattened the horsepower curve and produced peak output at a lower rpm. SEFI also greatly increased the torque at roughly the same peak rpm.

The Special Service package Mustang was available with either a four-speed automatic overdrive or a five-speed stick. The four-speed cars came with a 3.27 rear axle ratio while the five-speed cars could have either 2.73 or 3.08.

The 200-horsepower SEFI 5.0L engine gave the Special Service Mustang the kind of performance known to most enthusiasts: 0 to 60 miles per hour in 7 seconds, 0 to 100 miles per hour in 19 seconds, a 15-second quarter-mile, and a top speed of 135 to 137 miles per hour. This performance would be generally unchanged from 1986 through 1993.

The 180-horsepower, 351-ci HO used in the Crown Vic was unchanged from 1985. As a postscript on history, the Treasury Department required law enforcement agencies to register with the Internal Revenue Service for a certification to be exempted from payment of the so-called "gas guzzler" tax when the 5.8L HO engine was selected. The EPA estimated this engine to produce 13 miles per gallon city and 18 miles per gallon highway.

Even though all four police car marques—Chevrolet, Dodge, Ford, and Plymouth—had carryover engines, all the sedans closed in on the performance of the 351-ci HO Crown Vic. All four cars were within 0.4 second of one another around the MIS road racing course. The 318-ci, 4-bbl Diplomat was the quickest to 100 miles per hour among the four-door sedans and had the highest top speed.

A Mopar would capture the Michigan State Police tests for the last time in 1986. After 1986, Chevrolet decided to get serious with its 350-ci small-block. Unfortunately, Ford rested on its laurels with its 351-ci HO. Chevrolet would outperform all the other marques of four-door sedan for the next 10 years straight.

For 1987, the police package was available only on the full-size, 114.3-inch wheelbase, LTD Crown Victoria "S" four-door sedan. A Special Service package continued for the Mustang LX.

The Crown Vic was a carryover from 1986 with the exception of its fuel-injected 302-ci base engine. Ford engineers tweaked an additional 10 horsepower out of the pushrod small-block. For 1987, the 302-ci EFI V-8 was rated at 160 horsepower. That horsepower would remain unchanged until the engine was dropped from the car line in mid-1992. The 351-ci HO was unchanged at 180 horsepower.

Two big changes took place with the 1987 Mustang. First, it was restyled from deeply recessed quad headlights to flush-bezel dual headlights. This was the first major restyling since the Mustang replaced the awful Mustang II in 1979. The second change was a boost in horsepower from 200 horsepower to 225 horsepower.

For 1987, Ford also did some serious axle ratio juggling. The five-speed cars retained their 3.08 ratio. However, the Mustang with a four-speed automatic dropped from 3.27 to 2.73. This slowed the quarter-mile performance slightly but greatly added to top speed.

With the stronger engines and taller gears, both the four-speed auto and the five-speed stick Mustangs exceeded 139 miles per hour. In fact, the 1987 5.0L HO Mustang LX with the five-speed set a record that is still unbroken after the 1997 model year tests. That 1987 Special Service package Mustang reached 139.6 miles per hour with two MSP troopers on board. This is an all-time, officially clocked, top speed record for any Ford-made police or Special Service package vehicle.

For 1987, Chevrolet bumped the horsepower on its 350-ci V-8 from 155 horsepower to 180 horsepower. The rest is Michigan State Police testing history, as the Caprice captured the road course, top speed, and acceleration to 100-miles-per-hour test phases. Engine development stagnated on the Diplomat and Gran Fury because Chrysler was focused on front-drive vehicles and had announced the exit from rear-drive cars in previous

For 1987, the 5.0L V-8 used in this Boswell, Indiana, Police unit gained even more power. This fuel-injected engine would remain at 160 horsepower through 1991. *Cindy Sanow*

years. In 1987, Ford also had plans for the V-8-powered Crown Vic only through 1989. The 351-ci HO was not further developed. Even once the decision to extend the life of the Crown Vic, it was the 4.6L SOHC engine that got attention, not the 351-ci HO.

In 1988, the Ford police package was available for the LTD Crown Victoria "S" four-door sedan. By 1988, the two-door Crown Vic was not even available to retail buyers. A Special Service package was available for the Mustang LX.

For 1988, the Crown Vic was available with the 160-horsepower, 302-ci SEFI V-8 and the 180-horsepower, 351-ci HO 2-VV V-8. These were unchanged from 1987. The 302-ci engine had been teamed with a 3.08 axle ratio. To help improve responsiveness for city patrol, a 3.27 ratio was optional in 1988.

In 1988, Ford made five specially modified Thunderbirds and sent them to the Arizona Highway Patrol for testing. These experimental cruisers were powered by the 210-horsepower, 3.8L supercharged V-6 engine. This was a forerunner of the 1989 retail Thunderbird Super Coupe. At the time, the top T-bird engine was the 155-horsepower 302-ci V-8. The 104.2-inch wheelbase T-bird was extremely fast. Ford and the Arizona Highway Patrol teamed up again in 1991 to conduct hot weather durability tests. This time it was a Thunderbird Super Coupe, again with a supercharged 3.8L V-6.

Nothing ever became of either study for police officers. The Thunderbird was never a police nor special service vehicle. The supercharged 3.8L V-8 was never a police nor special service engine. In fact, no police package from Ford, GM, or Chrysler has ever included a supercharged or turbocharged engine.

For 1988, the Crown Vic was significantly restyled. It went from the abruptly square front end like a Dodge

A 1987 Florida Highway Patrol Mustang. The police Mustangs with automatic transmissions got lower numeric gear ratios and now reached top speeds of 139 miles per hour. *Darryl Lindsay*

The 1987 police five-speed Mustang, like this Nevada Highway Patrol unit, set an all-time, Ford top speed record at 139.6 miles per hour. *Darryl Lindsay*

Diplomat to a smoothly rounded look. The grille, hood, and trunk lid were all new, including wraparound tail-lamps. The front bumper was aerodynamically blended into the body with shrouding. The 114.3-inch wheelbase was retained.

The 1988 Crown Vic is visually different from the 1989 to 1991 models only by the door chrome strip. The 1988 Crown Vic has a wide chrome strip at the bottom of the doors and quarter panels. The later versions of this body style have a thin chrome strip running along the rocker and quarter panels but below the doors, not attached to them.

The 1988 Special Service package Mustang was basically unchanged from 1987. Cops got the 225-horse-power, 5.0L HO V-8 bolted with either the four-speed overdrive automatic and 2.73 or 3.27 gears, or the five-speed stick and 2.73 or 3.08 gears.

In spite of the much sleeker body lines for the Crown Vic, the overall performance during the annual Michigan State Police tests was nearly unchanged for both the 5.0L and 5.8L HO versions. The road course lap time is the ultimate measure of police car performance. Around the 1.63-mile course, the 1988 351-ci HO Crown Vic took 88.59 seconds compared to 88.60 seconds for the 1988 version.

Performance from the four-speed auto and five-speed stick Mustang was also unchanged. With two MSP troopers on board, the five-speed Mustang ran the quarter-mile in 15.48 seconds at 91.1 miles per hour.

The 1989 model year was one of change and transition. In midyear, Chrysler Corporation discontinued the Dodge Diplomat and Plymouth Gran Fury. And then there were two : Ford LTD Crown Victoria and Chevrolet Caprice.

For its part, Chevrolet had a nasty surprise in order for Ford. The 1989 version of its 350-ci/5.7L V-8 now

For 1987, Ford boosted the power of 5.0L V-8 in Mustangs, like this Texas Highway Patrol pursuit, from 200 horsepower to 225 horsepower.

had throttle body fuel injection. Chrysler had fuel-injection on its compact K-cars. Ford had it on the midsize LTD. Chevrolet had it on the-V-6-powered Celebrity and Impala. However, Chevrolet became the first police car-maker to offer fuel-injection on the full-size police sedan with the large, pursuit-oriented V-8.

In a year of mass transition "from" Dodge and Plymouth "to" something else, fuel injection on the Chevrolet 350-ci really hurt Ford. Police fleet managers had been begging for a large, fuel-injected V-8 since the mid-1980s.

For 1989, the Ford 55A police package was available for the LTD Crown Victoria "S" and LX four-door sedan. The Mustang LX was again available with a Special Service package. The powertrains for both the 114.3-

In 1987, the police Mustang like this California Highway Patrol unit, was restyled from recessed quad headlights to flush-bezel dual headlights. This was the first major styling change since 1979. *CHP*

inch wheelbase Crown Vic and the 100.5-inch wheelbase Mustang were unchanged from 1988.

At the annual Michigan State Police tests, the 5.8L HO Crown Vic came in second to the 5.7L TBI Caprice. Somehow, the Caprice was able to run 3.42 rear gears and still achieve both the highest top speed and the best EPA city fuel rating. It was clearly the strongest running four-door sedan of the year. The 5.0L Mustang, however, was the highest performing police vehicle with top speeds of 138 miles per hour and road course times a full 4 seconds faster than any four-door sedan.

In 1982, Ford police cars were used by the Oklahoma Highway Patrol, Missouri State Highway Patrol, and the Chicago Police. The severe service package version of the 1982 Mustang was only used by the California Highway Patrol. The 1983 Fords were used by the South Dakota Highway Patrol; Chicago Police; Iowa State Patrol; Cook County, Illinois, Sheriff; Minnesota State Patrol; South Carolina Highway Patrol; and Suffolk County, New

York, Police. In addition to the CHP, 1983 Mustangs were used by the Texas Highway Patrol and Georgia State Patrol.

In 1984, Ford police cars were used by the California Highway Patrol, Missouri State Highway Patrol, South Dakota Highway Patrol, and Indiana State Police. The Washington State Patrol; Cook County, Illinois, Sheriff; Los Angeles County Sheriff; and Florida Highway Patrol were among those who drove the midsize LTD in 1984, while the Oklahoma Highway Patrol joined the growing number of states who used the Mustang.

In 1985, Fords were used by the Indiana State Police, Tennessee Highway Patrol, Rhode Island State Police, and South Carolina Highway Patrol. The Baby LTD saw service with the Oregon State Police; Cook County, Illinois, Sheriff; Washington State Patrol; and Florida Highway Patrol. The Idaho State Police, Texas Highway Patrol, Georgia State Patrol, Nevada Highway Patrol, and California Highway Patrol were among 15 states that used the 1985 Mustang.

To improve the low-end performance for city and urban county police units, like this 1988 San Diego County Sheriffs Crown Vic, this year Ford offered a 3.27 rear gear ratio. *Bill Hattersley*

The 1988 Crown Vic, like this Georgia State Patrol unit, is different from the 1989 to 1991 versions. The 1988 models have a wide chrome strip at the bottom of the doors. *Greg Reynolds*

A 1988 5.0L Mustang in service with the Florida Highway Patrol. These pony pursuits had a 135-miles-per-hour top end. *Darryl Lindsay*

RIGHT: A 1989 New Hampshire State Police Crown Vic. With a 351-ci HO V-8, these sedans reached top speeds of 119 miles per hour. *Darryl Lindsay*

Fords were widely used in 1986. Agencies that used them included the North Carolina Highway Patrol, Pennsylvania State Police, Nebraska State Patrol, New Mexico State Police, Maryland State Police, Florida Highway Patrol, Iowa State Patrol, Kentucky State Police, Alabama State Troopers, Connecticut State Police, Missouri State Highway Patrol, Rhode Island State Police, and the Washington State Patrol.

In 1987, the list of police agencies using the Ford included the Wyoming Highway Patrol, South Dakota Highway Patrol, New Jersey State Police, Indiana State Police, Iowa State Patrol, Kansas Highway Patrol, and Arizona Highway Patrol. By 1987, more than half of the state police and highway patrols were using the Special Service package Mustang.

Police departments using the restyled 1988 Ford included the San Diego County Sheriff, Georgia State Patrol, North Carolina Highway Patrol, and Kansas Highway Patrol. In 1989, those driving Fords included North Dakota State Patrol, Indiana State Police, Nebraska State Patrol, Massachusetts State Police, Delaware State Police, Connecticut State Police, Washington State Patrol, New Hampshire State Police, and the Seattle Police.

In 1989, after more than 20 years of Dodge and Plymouth police cars, the Seattle, Washington, Police adopted this Crown Vic. *Bill Hattersley*

101

A 1989 South Carolina Highway Patrol Mustang. From 1987 to 1989, black wheels were standard and brushed aluminum wheels were optional. After 1989, black wheels were not available.

Here is a beautiful example of a 1986 Crown Vic. The Missouri State Highway Patrol dressed their cruisers with full wheel covers.

A 1984 Crown Vic in service with the Missouri State Highway Patrol. This 351-ci HO V-8 produced 180 horsepower, which was the most of any police sedan.

In 1988 and again in 1991, Ford sent the Thunderbird Super Coupe to the Arizona Highway Patrol for durability testing. These were powered by the supercharged 3.8L V-6.—*Greg Reynolds*

1982 Ford Police Drivetrains

Layout	cid/liter	carb	comp	hp	axle	model
V-8	255/4.2L	2-bbl	8.2	122	3.08	LTD
V-8	302/5.0L	2-bbl	8.4	132	3.08	LTD
V-8	351W/5.8L-HO	2-VV	8.3	165	2.73	LTD
I-4	140/2.3L	2-bbl	9.0	92	3.08	Fairmont
V-6	200/3.3L	1-bbl	8.6	87	2.73	Fairmont
V-8	255/4.2L	2-bbl	8.2	115	2.73	Fairmont
V-8	302/5.0L-HO	2-bbl	8.3	157	3.08	Mustang

1983 Ford Police Drivetrains

Layout	cid/liter	carb	comp	hp	axle	model
V-8	302/5.0L	CFI	8.4	130	3.08	LTD C. Vic
V-8	351W/5.8L-HO	2-VV	8.3	165	2.73	LTD C. Vic
I-4	140/2.3L	1-bbl	9.0	90	3.08	Fairmont
I-6	200/3.3L	1-bbl	8.6	92	2.73	Fairmont
V-8	302/5.0L-HO	4-bbl	8.4	175	3.08	Mustang

1984 and 1985 Ford Police Drivetrains

Layout	cid/liter	carb	comp	hp	axle	model
V-8	302/5.0L	CFI	8.4	140	3.55	Crown Vic
V-8	351W/5.8L-HO	2-VV	8.3	180	2.73	Crown Vic
I-4	140/2.3L	1-bbl	9.0***	88	3.45	LTD
V-8	302/5.0L-HO	CFI	8.4	165	3.08	LTD
V-8	302/5.0L-HO	CFI	8.4	165*	3.27	Mustang

Layout	cid/liter	carb	comp	hp	axle	model
V-8	302/5.0L-HO	4-bbl	8.3	205**	3.27	Mustang

*180 hp in 1985
**210 hp in 1985
***9.5:1 in 1985

1986 Ford Police Drivetrains

Layout	cid/liter	carb	comp	hp	axle	model
V-8	302/5.0L	EFI	8.9	150	3.08	Crown Vic
V-8	351/5.8L-HO	2-VV	8.3	180	2.73	Crown Vic
V-8	302/5.0L-HO	EFI	9.2	200	3.08, 3.27	Mustang

1987 to 1989 Ford Police Drivetrains

Layout	cid/liter	carb	comp	hp	axle	model
V-8	302/5.0LS	EFI	8.9	160	*3.08	Crown Vic
V-8	351/5.8L-HO	2-VV	8.3	180	2.73	Crown Vic
V-8	302/5.0L-HO	SEFI	9.2	225	3.08, 2.73	Mustang

*3.27 optional in 1988

1982 Michigan State Police Patrol Vehicle Test Results
(four- and six-cylinder cars)

Make	Ford	Plymouth	Chevrolet	Ford	Dodge
Model	Fairmont	Gran Fury	Malibu	Fairmont	Aries K
Engine, ci & carb	200, 1-bbl	225, 1-bbl	229,2-bbl	140,2-bbl	135,2-bbl
HP, SAE	87	90	110	92	84
Axle ratio	2.73	2.94	2.41	3.08	2.78
Weight, test, lb	3,038	3,706	3,376	2,926	2,444
Wheelbase, in	105.5	112.7	108.1	105.5	99.9
0–60 mph, sec	18.72	20.36	17.99	17.26	17.58
Top speed, mph	97.3	96.2	100.6	103.4	97.4
1/4-mile ET, sec	22.00	22.53	21.85	21.85	21.55
1/4-mile speed, mph	64.86	2.3	65.3	67.5	66.3
EPA city mpg	19.7	17.9	20.8	20.5	25.0

1982 Michigan State Police Patrol Vehicle Test Results
(V-8-powered cars)

Make	Ford	Chevrolet	Dodge	Ford	Plymouth	Chevrolet
Model	LTD	Impala	Diplomat	Fairmont	Gran Fury	Malibu
Engine, ci & carb	351,2VV	350,4-bbl	318,4-bbl	255,2-bbl	318,4-bbl	305, 4-bbl
HP, SAE	165	150	165	115	165	145
Axle ratio	2.73	3.08	2.94	2.73	2.94	2.73
Weight, test, lb	4,086	3,996	3,875	3,200	3,863	3,672
Wheelbase, in	114.3	116.0	112.7	105.5	112.7	108.1
Road course lap time, sec	91.99	92.04	92.57	94.16	92.63	92.61
0–100 mph, sec	42.54	45.79	39.95	57.04	39.36	49.73
Top speed, mph	115.8	107.8	115.4	107.0	116.3	110.0
1/4-mile ET, sec	19.15	19.40	19.20	19.88	19.08	19.53
1/4-mile speed, sec	75.5	73.0	75.3	72.0	76.5	72.5
Braking, ft/sec^2	22.6	24.0	23.7	23.2	24.3	24.6
EPA city mpg	13.9	14.3	13.8	18.6	13.8	16.6

1983 Michigan State Police Patrol Vehicle Test Results
(four- and six-cylinder cars)

Make	Chevrolet	Dodge	Ford	Ford	Plymouth
Model	Impala	Diplomat	Fairmont	Fairmont	Reliant K
Engine, ci & carb	229, 2-bbl	225, 1-bbl	200, 1-bbl	140, 1-bbl	156, 2-bbl
HP, SAE	110	90	92	90	93
Axle ratio	2.73	2.94	2.73	3.08	3.02
Weight, test, lb	3,713	3,688	2,872	2,979	2,659
Wheelbase, in	116.0	112.7	105.5	105.5	100.1
Road course lap time, sec	na	na	na	97.68	94.58
0–60 mph, sec	17.4	18.8	17.7	18.4	15.5
Top speed, mph	104.3	96.5	97.7	95.8	102.8

1/4-mile ET, sec	21.50	22.03	21.93	21.8	19.7
1/4-mile speed, mph	67.0	63.5	66.3	65.0	68.0
Braking, ft/sec^2	na	na	na	24.2	24.0
EPA city mpg	18.6	18.7	18.6	20.9	23.6

1983 Michigan State Police Patrol Vehicle Test Results
(V-8-powered cars)

Make	Chevrolet	Dodge	Ford	Chevrolet	Plymouth	Ford	Ford
Model	Impala	Diplomat	LTD-CV	Malibu	Gran Fury	LTD-CV	Mustang
Engine, ci & carb	350, 4-bbl	318, 4-bbl	351, 2VV	305, 4-bbl	318, 4-bbl	302, cfi	302, 4-bbl
HP, SAE	155	165	165	145	165	130	175
Axle ratio	3.08	2.94	2.73	2.73	2.94	3.08	3.08
Weight, test, lb	3,993	3,887	4,059	3,516	3,881	3,892	2,970
Wheelbase, in	116.0	112.7	114.3	108.1	112.7	114.3	100.4
Road course lap time, sec	92.21	93.54	90.59	92.13	92.64	na	88.31
0–100 mph, sec	42.51	40.46	39.81	40.73	39.68	69.01	22.71
Top speed, mph	115.0	118.8	117.9	116.3	120.0	104.4	132.0
1/4-mile ET, sec	18.55	19.30	18.83	10.3?	18. 86	19.93	16.68
1/4-mile speed, mph	73.5	75.5	75.3	75.0	76.5	71.3	78.19
Braking, ft/sec^2	23.2	24.3	24.0	24.5	24.9	na	25.0
EPA city mpg	14.8	14.0	14.0	17.8	14.0	16.6	17.0
Adjusted bid, $	no bid	8,259.77	8,534.60	8,069.60	7,918.96	DQ	na

1984 Michigan State Police Patrol Vehicle Test Results
(midsize and pursuit cars)

Make	Chevrolet	Ford	Plymouth	Ford	Ford	Dodge
Model	Celebrity	LTD	Reliant K	Mustang	Mustang	Aires K
Engine, ci & carb	173, 2-bbl	302, cfi	156, 2-bbl	302, cfi	302, 4-bbl	135, 2-bbl
HP, SAE	112	165	101	165	205	96
Axle Ratio	3.06	3.08	3.22	3.27	3.27	3.02
Weight, test, lb	3,056	3,429	2,674	3,129	3,015	2,617
Wheelbase, in	104.9	105.5	100.3	100.5	100.5	100.3
Road course lap time, sec	93.15	88.41	92.88	86.81	na	na
0–100 mph, sec	61.54	29.89	na	25.99	20.77	na
Top speed, mph	110.7	122.6	105.3	118.3	129.6	101.9
1/4-mile ET, sec	19.95	17.76	19.51	16.88	15.90	21.5
1/4-mile speed, mph	71.8	79.5	71.0	83.5	89.0	71.0
Braking, ft/sec^2	24.3	24.4	23.6	24.6	na	na
EPA city mpg	21.1	18.0	23.2	18.0	15.9	25.6

1984 Michigan State Police Patrol Vehicle Test Results
(fullsize cars)

Make	Chevrolet	Dodge	Ford	Plymouth	Plymouth	Ford	Chevrolet
Model	Impala	Diplomat	Crown Vic	Gran Fury	Gran Fury	Crown Vic	Impala
Engine, ci & carb	350, 4-bbl	318, 4-bbl	351, 2VV	318, 4-bbl	318, 2-bbl	302, cfi	229, 2-bbl
HP, SAE	155	165	180	165	130	140	110
Axle ratio	3.08	2.94	2.73	2.94	2.94	3.55	2.73
Weight, test, lb	3,920	3,879	4,084	3,888	3,853	3,961	3,752
Wheelbase, in	116.0	112.7	114.3	112.7	112.7	114.3	116.0
Road course lap time, sec	89.97	90.40	90.07	90.01	na	88.41	na
0–100 mph, sec	37.18	34.57	40.36	34.43	60.75	na	na
Top speed, mph	116.4	118.8	118.1	121.4	106.2	100.5	101.0
1/4-mile ET, sec	17.80	18.23	19.25	18.20	19.5	19.8	21.9
1/4-mile speed, mph	76.0	76.8	76.5	77.5	71.8	69.8	64.8
Braking, ft/sec^2	26.4	23.4	26.3	25.6	na	na	na
EPA city mpg	14.6	14.6	14.0	14.6	16.5	16.5	19.0

1985 Michigan State Police Patrol Vehicle Test Results
(compact and pursuit cars)

Make	Chevrolet	Chevrolet	Dodge	Plymouth	Ford	Ford	Ford
Model	Celebrity	Celebrity	Aries K	Reliant K	LTD	Mustang	Mustang
Engine, ci & carb	173, 2-bbl	173, pfi	135, 2-bbl	156, 2-bbl	302, cfi	302, cfi	302, 4-bbl
HP, SAE	112	130	96	101	165	180	210
Axle ratio	3.06	3.18	3.02	3.22	3.08	3.27	3.27
Weight, test, lb	3,047	3,076	2,652	2,706	3,414	3,108	3,101
Wheelbase, in	104.9	104.9	100.3	100.3	105.5	100.5	100.5
Road course lap time, sec	na	92.78	na	94.11	89.07	86.36	85.59
0–100 mph, sec	55.31	42.26	na	na	30.74	26.07	21.72
Top speed, mph	116.1	115.3	97.0	100.2	120.6	122.8	135.5
1/4-mile ET, sec	19.7	18.7	21.03	19.98	17.98	17.13	16.08
1/4-mile speed, mph	71.5	75.0	67.75	69.0	79.0	83.00	87.0
Braking, ft/sec^2	na	25.56	na	25.81	26.47	25.05	25.66
EPA city mpg	20.1	19.5	24.2	20.4	16.1	16.1	16.4

1985 Michigan State Police Patrol Vehicle Test Results
(fullsize cars)

Make	Chevrolet	Dodge	Ford	Plymouth	Ford	Plymouth
Model	Impala	Diplomat	Crown Vic	Gran Fury	Crown Vic	Gran Fury
Engine, ci & carb	350, 4-bbl	318, 4-bbl	351, 2VV	318, 4-bbl	302, cfi	318, 2-bbl
HP,SAE	155	175	180	175	140	140
Axle ratio	3.08	.94	2.73	2.94	3.55	2.24
Weight, test, lb	3,906	3,998	4,095	3,902	4,182	3,771
Wheelbase, in	116.0	112.7	114.3	112.7	114.3	112.7
Road course lap time, sec	90.82	90.83	89.67	90.69	na	na
0–100 mph, sec	42.24	40.15	39.78	42.00	59.14	53.27
Top speed, mph	114.3	117.6	116.9	119.4	104.4	116.1
1/4-mile ET, sec	18.85	19.10	18.80	19.23	19.53	20.05
1/4-mile speed, mph	74.8	74.5	75.5	73.8	71.00	71.8
Braking, ft/sec^2	25.92	27.11	26.34	26.6	na	na
EPA city mpg	13.3	12.6	12.6	12.6	15.6	16.1

1986 Michigan State Police Patrol Vehicle Test Results
(midsize cars)

Make	Ford	Ford	Dodge	Plymouth	Chevrolet	Chevrolet
Model	Mustang	Mustang	Aries K	Reliant K	Celebrity	Celebrity
Engine, ci & carb	302, pfi	302, pfi	135, tbi	153, tbi	173, pfi	173, 2-bbl
HP,SAE	200	200	97	100	125	112
Axle ratio	3.27	3.083.02	3.22	3.18	3.06	
Weight, test, lb	3,238	3,216	2,615	2,692	3,075	3,034
Wheelbase, in	100.5	100.5	100.3	100.3	104.9	104.9
Road course laptime, sec	84.22	85.49	na	91.79	89.76	na
0–100 mph, sec	20.55	19.81	na	na	38.06	48.86
Top speed, mph	126.1	137.2	101.0	103.0	113.8	113.6
1/4-mile ET, sec	15.8	15.5	20.7	19.7	18.3	19.5
1/4-mile speed, mph	88.5	90.5	69.0	70.5	76.0	73.7
Braking, ft/sec^2	24.31	26.43	na	26.42	26.43	26.43
Ergonomics, pts	147.9	147.9	na	165.0	164.0	164.0
EPA city mpg	17.5	17.3	23.3	19.6	18.1	16.8

1986 Michigan State Police Patrol Vehicle Test Results
(fullsize cars)

Make	Dodge	Ford	Plymouth	Chevrolet	Plymouth	Ford	Chevrolet
Model	Diplomat	Crown Vic	Gran Fury	Caprice	Gran Fury	Crown Vic	Caprice
Engine, ci & carb	318,4-bbl	351, 2VV	318,4-bbl	350, 4-bbl	318,2-bbl	302,pfi	262,tbi
HP, SAE	175	180	175	155	140	150	140
Axle ratio	2.94	2.73	2.94	3.08	2.94	3.08	3.08
Weight, test, lb	3,897	4,092	3,929	3,956	3,871	3,934	3,792
Wheelbase, in	112.7	114.3	112.7	116.0	112.7	114.3	116.0
Road course lap time, sec	89.46	89.37	89.43	89.73	na	na	na

Make	Dodge	Ford	Plymouth	Chevrolet	Plymouth	Ford	Chevrolet
0–100 mph, sec	36.07	38.49	36.58	37.96	43.11	46.57	55.40
Top speed, mph	121.5	115.1	119.4	117.0	110.1	106.1	107.8
1/4-mile ET, sec	18.53	18.53	18.70	18.25	18.88	18.80	19.53
1/4-mile speed, mph	76.5	76.5	76.3	76.0	73.8	72.3	70.3
Braking, ft/sec^2	25.95	24.68	26.71	24.20	na	na	na
EPA city mpg	12.2	12.6	12.2	13.4	14.8	17.7	17.6

1987 Michigan State Police Patrol Vehicle Test Results (fullsize cars)

Make	Dodge	Ford	Plymouth	Chevrolet	Chevrolet	Plymouth	Ford
Model	Diplomat	Crown Vic	Gran Fury	Caprice	Caprice	Gran Fury	Crown Vic
Engine, ci & carb	318, 4-bbl	351, VV	318, 4-bbl	351, 4-bbl	262, tbi	318, 2-bbl	302, pfi
HP, SAE	175	180	175	180	140	140	160
Axle ratio	2.94	2.73	2.94	3.08	3.08	2.24	3.08
Weight, test, lb	3,885	4,079	3,924	3,948	3,803	3,895	4,051
Wheelbase, in	112.7	114.3	112.7	116.0	116.0	112.7	114.3
Road course lap time, sec	89.95	88.59	89.77	8.22	na	na	na
0–100 mph, sec	40.53	39.30	38.64	34.62	59.22	52.44	43.47
Top speed, mph	116.9	115.2	117.5	118.0	106.0	113.3	109.2
1/4-mile ET, sec	19.35	18.93	19.18	17.85	19.90	20.63	18.55
1/4-mile speed, mph	73.5	76.3	75.0	77.8	71.0	71.8	74.0
Braking, ft/sec^2	27.2	25.7	27.4	26.12	na	na	na
EPA city mpg	12.7	12.9	12.7	13.9	18.3	14.8	17.5
Ranking	disqual.	third	second	first	disqual.	disqual.	disqual.

1988 Michigan State Police Patrol Vehicle Test Results

Make	Dodge	Ford	Plymouth	Chevrolet	Chevrolet	Plymouth	Ford
Model	Diplomat	Crown Vic	Gran Fury	Caprice	Caprice	Gran Fury	Crown Vic
Engine, ci & carb	318, 4-bbl	351, VV	318, 4-bbl	350, 4-bbl	262, tbi	318, 2-bbl	302, efi
HP, SAE	175	180	175	180	140	140	160
Axle ratio	2.94	2.73	2.94	3.08	3.08	2.24	3.08
Weight, test, lb	3,930	3,965	3,910	3,982	3,827	3,873	3,982
Wheelbase, in	112.7	114.3	112.7	116.0	116.0	112.7	114.3
Road course lap time, sec	89.27	88.60	89.43	88.60	na	na	na
0–100 mph, sec	38.76	37.67	40.13	34.91	52.44	57.84	40.62
Top speed, mph	117	117	117	116	109	110	108
1/4-mile ET, sec	18.59	18.84	19.01	18.03	19.90	20.18	18.35
1/4-mile speed, mph	75.4	76.4	74.8	77.6	70.3	71.8	75.3
Braking, ft/sec^2	24.92	26.79	23.74	25.55	na	na	na
EPA city mpg	12.7	12.4	12.7	13.5	19.0	14.6	17.3
Ranking	third	second	fourth	first	disqual.	disqual.	disqual.

1987 to 1989 Michigan State Police Patrol Vehicle Test Results—Mustang

Make	Ford		
Model	Mustang		
Engine, ci & carb	302, HO		
HP, SAE	225		
Trans	5-spd		
Axle ratio	3.08		
Weight, test, lb	3,198		
Wheelbase, in	100.5		
Year	**1987**	**1988**	**1989**
Road course lap time, sec	82.02	82.57	81.56
10–100 mph, sec	20.42	19.07	19.24
Top speed, mph	139.6	134.0	138.0
1/4-mile ET, sec	16.00	15.48	na
1/4-mile speed, mph	89.75	91.10	na
Braking, ft/sec^2	23.99	25.69	24.45
EPA city mpg	16.4	16.5	16.9

Make	**Ford**		
Model	Mustang		
Engine, ci & carb	302, HO		
HP, SAE	225		
Trans	4-spd AOT		
Axle ratio	2.73		
Weight, test, lb	3,270		
Wheelbase, in	100.5		
Year	**1987**	**1988**	**1989**
Road course			
lap time, sec	83.78	83.79	82.5
10–100 mph , sec	21.73	21.78	22.89
Top speed, mph	139.1	135.0	137.2
1/4-mile ET, sec	16.33	16.16	16.59
1/4-mile speed, mph	86.75	87.78	87.03
Braking, ft/sec^2	23.14	25.69	24.45
EPA city mpg	17.6	18.2	16.8

1989 Michigan State Police Patrol Vehicle Test Results (pursuit-class)

Make	**Dodge**	**Ford**	**Plymouth**	**Chevrolet**
Model	Diplomat	Crown Vic	Gran Fury	Caprice
Engine, ci & carb	318, 4-bbl	351, VV	318, 4-bbl	350, tbi
HP, SAE	175	180	175	190
Axle ratio	2.94	2.73	2.94	3.42
Weight, test, lb	3,894	4,091	3,885	3,965
Wheelbase, in	112.7	114.3	112.7	116.0
Road course				
lap time, sec	88.66	88.24	88.63	86.20
0–100 mph, sec	38.95	36.55	38.02	29.35
Top speed, mph	119.1	119.1	120.2	122.0
1/4-mile ET, sec	18.79	18.86	18.63	17.62
1/4-mile speed, sec	75.5	77.1	76.2	79.8
Braking, sec	26.32	26.09	26.01	26.03
EPA city mpg	12.7	13.1	12.7	14.3
Ranking	fourth	second	third	first

1989 Michigan State Police Patrol Vehicle Test Results (urban patrol-class)

Make	**Chevrolet**	**Chevrolet**	**Ford**	**Plymouth**	**Dodge**
Model	Caprice	Caprice	Crown Vic	Gran Fury	Diplomat
Engine, ci & carb	262, tbi	305, tbi	302, pfi	318, 2-bbl	318, 2-bbl
HP, SAE	140	170	160	140	140
Axle ratio	3.08	3.08	3.08	2.24	2.24
Weight, test, lb	3,872	3,960	4,132	3,895	3,876
Wheelbase, in	116.0	116.0	114.3	112.7	112.7
Road course					
lap time, sec	92.51	88.83	89.49	na	na
0–100 mph, sec	58.16	42.88	42.14	58.13	55.58
Top speed, mph	109.0	114.1	110.0	111.2	113.6
1/4-mile ET, sec	20.50	19.01	18.77	na	20.23
1/4-mile speed, mph	69.5	73.4	74.3	na	71.6
EPA city mpg	19.0	17.2	17.4	14.2	14.2

Chapter Thirteen

1990-1991
The Front-Wheel-Drive Taurus

In 1990, the 55A police package was available for the full-size, 114.3-inch wheelbase LTD Crown Victoria "S" and LX four-door sedan. The 55H police package was available for the midsize, 106-inch wheelbase Taurus "L" four-door sedan. A Special Service package was available for the 5.0L HO Mustang LX. The only real change to the Mustang was the standard equipment driver's side air bag and rear shoulder belts.

The big news for 1990 was Ford's first front-wheel-drive police car, the Taurus. Chrysler was the first police carmaker with a front-drive police car in 1982. The Dodge Aries K and Plymouth Reliant K were available with a "scout" package (special service) from 1982 through 1987. Chevrolet was next with its special service Celebrity from 1984 through 1986. None of these

Pentastar nor Bowtie vehicles were anywhere near successful, even for light-duty police use.

The Taurus was different. Ford learned many lessons from the failings of the K-cars and Celebrity. They beefed up the Taurus to the point where it met Ford's durability standards for a "police package." In this regard, the first true front-drive police package car was the 1990 Taurus.

The front-drive, 3.8L V-6 powered Taurus was introduced to the retail market in 1986. This was Ford's replacement for the midsize LTD. The Baby LTD had a wheelbase of 105.5 inches compared to 106 inches for the Taurus.

The Taurus was a startling stylistic statement in the mid-1980s. It had no grille and flush-mounted glass all

New for 1990 was Ford's first front-wheel-drive police car, the 3.8L V-6 Taurus, shown here with the Wayne County, Michigan, Sheriff. Note the cooling slits in the grille. *Ford Division*

The first Ford police car with a four-wheel independent suspension and the option of ABS brakes was the 1990 Taurus, like this Texas DPS Capital Police cruiser. *Terry Fiene*

A 1990 New York State Police Crown Vic powered by the 351-ci HO. For the first time in 10 years, the full-size Ford had a top speed of over 120 miles per hour. *Greg Reynolds*

around. The aerodynamic styling gave the Taurus a drag coefficient of just .33, very low for a four-door sedan.

The Taurus had a fully independent, four-wheel, MacPherson strut suspension. This was a first for a Ford police car. It also had four-wheel disc brakes. The last series of Ford police cars available with four-wheel discs was the 1976 to 1978 Custom 500 and LTD. By 1990, the antilock braking system (ABS) was an option on the Taurus.

This was also the first year for the driver's side air bag on the Taurus, which was standard with tilt steering. The 1990 Crown Vic and Mustang also came standard with a driver's side air bag. Chrysler was the first with an air bag on the midyear 1988 Diplomat and Gran Fury. Full-size Mopars never had four-wheel discs and never got ABS. Chevrolet's first air bag and ABS car was the 1991 Caprice. The Caprice did not get four-wheel discs until 1994, two years after the Crown Vic got them.

The 1990 police Taurus was only available with the 3.8L overhead-valve V-6 with 140 horsepower. The 3.0L overhead-cam SHO engine was never available with a police package. The Taurus only came with a four-speed automatic overdrive transaxle.

The 1990 Crown Vic continued to be powered by either a 160-horsepower 5.0L V-8 or a 180-horsepower 5.8L HO V-8. The Mustang's 5.0L HO was again rated at 225 horsepower. Except for the air bag, these cars were all carried over from 1989.

The 1990 model year was a strange one for vehicle tests. For the first time since organized police car tests were conducted by the Los Angeles Police Department in 1956, no Chrysler Corporation vehicle was tested. This was especially awkward since the top speed, acceleration, and braking phases of the Michigan State Police tests were done at Chrysler's Chelsea Proving Ground.

During the MSP testing, the 5.0L and 5.8L Crown Vic and 5.0L Mustang performed about the same as in previous years. The 5.8L HO Crown Vic broke the 120-miles-per-hour top speed. The last full-size Ford to break

120 miles per hour was 10 years previous with the 1980 351-ci LTD.

The real shock at the 1990 MSP tests was the Taurus. Most cops expected it to run like other six-cylinder front-drive police cars. Not so. The 3.8L Taurus beat the 5.8L Crown Vic to 60 miles per hour and tied it to 100 miles per hour. The 3.8L V-6 Taurus also outdragged the 302-ci V-8 Crown Vic and the 305-ci V-8 Caprice. While the 5.8L Crown Vic had a higher top end, the Taurus had better braking performance.

On the all-important road course, the 5.7L Caprice took top honors; however, the 3.8L Taurus was just 0.5 second behind. The 3.8L Taurus outran the 5.8L HO Crown Vic, 5.0L Crown Vic, and 5.0L Caprice. This was just a warning shot from the Taurus. It would do better in 1991 when it gained 15 horsepower.

In 1990, and for only the second time since the mid-1950s, the California Highway Patrol adopted the full-size Ford. The Mercury Monterey had won the bid in 1970 while the Ford LTD captured the 1984 contract.

In 1991, the 55A police package was available for the LTD Crown Victoria "S," Standard, and LX. This full-size, 114.3-inch wheelbase four-door sedan was powered by either the 160-horsepower 302-ci SEFI V-8 or the 180-horsepower 351-ci HO 2-VV V-8. The California Highway Patrol was among hundreds of police departments to use the Crown Vic in 1991.

The 55A police package was also available for the Taurus "L" midsize four-door sedan. This front-drive, 106-inch wheelbase squad car was powered by the 155-horsepower 3.8L V-6. For 1991, Ford engineers bumped the output of the 3.8L V-6 from 140 horsepower to 155 horsepower. That was what it needed to make its mark on law enforcement. The quickest way to spot a police package Taurus was the cooling slots in the grille on either side of the Ford blue oval emblem.

The Special Service package was also available for the Mustang LX powered by the 5.0L HO V-8. The

In 1990, for only the second time since the mid-1950s, the CHP selected a Ford-marque police car, this LTD Crown Victoria, as its Enforcement-class vehicle.

The Mustang was the only high-performance police car for nearly a decade. It literally re-invented the term "pursuit" car. In the 1950s and 1960s, a pursuit car was a four-door sedan with a 122-inch wheelbase, tipping the scales at 3,800 pounds, powered by a 300-horsepower big-block V-8. In the 1980s it was a 100-inch wheelbase, two-door pony car weighing 3,200 pounds, powered by a 200-horsepower small-block V-8.

All things come to an end, especially if continuous improvements are not made. For the Mustang, that end happened in 1991 with the introduction of the special service Camaro RS. The Mustang was still everything it used to be, however, the Camaro was more of everything the Mustang was. The Camaro reached 150 miles per hour and had faster lap times, quicker acceleration, and better brakes, which were a longtime weak spot on the Mustang.

The Mustang was a much better police car than a comparison on paper to the Camaro might indicate, but the paper success of the Camaro did indeed hurt the Mustang. However, the reality is the 130-miles-per-hour Caprice hurt the Mustang more than the Camaro ever could.

The original reason for the Special Service Mustang was the sluggish performance from the 360-ci and 318-ci Dodges used by the California Highway Patrol from 1979 to 1981. With four-door sedans back up to 130 miles per hour, the drawbacks of a single-purpose traffic vehicle like the Mustang and Camaro were less tolerated.

Mustang was again available with either a four-speed automatic overdrive or a five-speed manual shift.

The Special Service Mustang had been the cock of the walk since 1982. It stood in stark contrast to the pitiful police sedan performance for the rest of the 1980s. Those four-door sedans ran the quarter-mile in 19 seconds with top speeds around 118 miles per hour. The Mustang, full of cop gear, ran the quarter-mile in 15 to 16 seconds and had top speeds over 135 miles per hour.

A 1990 5.0L CHP Mustang. The car that reinvented the meaning of pursuit vehicle was still going strong eight years later. *Matt Campbell*

The Special Service package 5.0L Mustang, like this 1990 Michigan State Police pursuit car, was the highest performing police vehicle of any kind for eight years straight. *Greg Reynolds*

For 1991, the 3.8L V-6 used in the Taurus, like this Montgomery County, MD Police unit was bumped from 140 horsepower to 155 horsepower. This made the Taurus the fastest four-door police sedan of any make around the MIS road course. *Dave Dotson*

To put this in perspective, the full-size Caprice in 1994 had the same road course lap times as the 1993 Special Service Mustang. The Mustang and the Camaro were no longer needed. Ford dropped the Special Service Mustang after 1993.

The 1991 model year will be remembered by cops for two reasons. First, this was the year the Chevrolet Caprice was remodeled. It now looked like a Hudson, turtle, bathtub, or whale, depending upon the beholder. The laughter, however, stopped when the aero-Caprice hit 130 miles per hour. The last full-size four-door sedan to reach 130 miles per hour was the 1978 Plymouth Fury powered by a 440-ci, the last year of the big-block V-8.

Second, this was the year the police Taurus stole the show at the Michigan State Police tests. The 3.8L Taurus had the fastest road course lap time of all four-door sedans. It was a full second quicker than the aero-Caprice. That performance was felt from coast to coast. Of all the four-door police cars available in 1991, the most successful around a pursuit course was a V-6 powered, front-drive, midsize car. This gave every cop in the country something to think about.

The 3.8L Taurus was just a half second slower to 100 miles per hour than the 5.7L Caprice and a full 5 seconds quicker than the 5.8L Crown Vic. It was over 11 seconds quicker to 100 miles per hour than the 302-ci and 305-ci four-door sedans that were geared to urban patrol duties like the Taurus. The final triumph for the 1991 Taurus was the top speed phase. The 5.7L Caprice reached 130 miles per hour, but the 3.8L Taurus reached 129.4 miles per hour. The 5.8L Crown Vic ran just 121 miles per hour. This was certainly the year of the Taurus.

The California Highway Patrol used the 351-ci HO Crown Vic in 1990 and 1991. They soon faced the reality of the somewhat sluggish acceleration from the 5.8L V-8. The big Ford took 11.4 seconds to reach 60 miles per hour and ran an 18.5 second quarter-mile. The 5.7L

Caprice got to 60 miles per hour in 9.9 seconds, ran a 17.5 second quarter-mile, and the CHP and all their traffic officers knew it.

Being the original hot-rodding cops, the CHP experimented with supercharging the 5.8L V-8 engine. The CHP had a Paxton supercharger installed on one 5.8L Crown Vic. If the experiment worked, Paxton offered to install superchargers on the entire CHP fleet of Crown Vics for just $1 each. They figured the press they would get by outfitting the CHP would more than make up the cost in retail sales.

Supercharging lowered the 0 to 60-miles-per-hour time by 2.5 seconds to 8.9 seconds, or about a second faster than the 5.7L Caprice.

For what had to be a combination of reasons, the CHP officially stated, "The improvement was hardly noticeable at all." More likely, however, the CHP figured the improved acceleration would be more than offset by worse gas mileage, more engine wear, and increased maintenance costs. To be sure, Ford would void any drivetrain warranty claims even remotely related to the supercharger.

Before the official CHP decision, however, Paxton made a press release to the enthusiast magazines on the hot-rod project. One magazine reported that Paxton had a contract to outfit 250 CHP cruisers. Another reported the Paxton supercharger improved the 0 to 60-miles-per-hour times by over 6 seconds.

Paxton jumped the gun with the press release and the enthusiast magazines read more into the release than was reality. Paxton and the magazines made formal retractions. The answer to the question "Didn't the CHP supercharge a bunch of their 351-ci Crown Victorias?" is no.

The Los Angeles County Sheriff's Department had good things to say about the police Taurus and Special Service Mustang. (The Crown Vic was not tested.)

3.8L Taurus: Very good handling vehicle, very good ABS brakes, top speed on longest straight was

In 1991, the Minnesota State Patrol used the Crown Victoria. The Ohio State Highway Patrol, Kansas Highway Patrol, and Massachusetts State Police also patrolled in the full-size Ford. *Greg Reynolds*

By 1991, the 351-ci HO Crown Vic, like this San Francisco Police cruiser, was pretty slow compared to the competition. The CHP even supercharged one Crown Vic to help its performance. *Bill Hattersley*

A sharp looking 1991 West Virginia State Police LTD Crown Victoria. This was the last year for this body style but the 114.4-inch wheelbase would be retained. *A. W. Robinson*

The Texas Highway Patrol was close behind the California Highway Patrol in their widespread use of the Mustang as a special traffic enforcement vehicle. A 1991 5.0L Mustang is shown.

controllable, overall a good vehicle, very fast, slight oversteer under hard acceleration at exit of turn, very good handling in turns, needs four-wheel disc brakes for maximum braking, otherwise very good overall, top speed of 110 miles per hour on the longest straight, steering ratio was very quick, vehicle shifted well and pulled strong in both second and third gears.

In 1990, Ford police cars were used by the Texas Highway Patrol; Washington, D.C., Police; Montgomery County, Maryland, Police; Ohio State Highway Patrol; South Carolina Highway Patrol; New York State Police; Mississippi Highway Safety Patrol; Indiana State Police; Iowa State Patrol; Louisiana State Police; Arizona Highway Patrol; San Diego Police; West Virginia State Police; and California Highway Patrol.

Police departments using the Taurus for uniformed patrol included San Diego County Sheriff's Department; Wayne County, Detroit, Michigan Sheriff's Department; Utah Highway Patrol; and Baltimore, Maryland, Police.

Police departments using the 1991 Ford included San Francisco Police, Minnesota State Patrol, California Highway Patrol, Kansas Highway Patrol, Ohio State Highway Patrol, Pennsylvania State Police, Massachusetts State Police, and Georgia State Patrol.

100 miles per hour (equal to 5.7L Caprice), vehicle displayed slight understeer but was very controllable, ABS system worked well, excellent handling vehicle, stable in turns, good steering ratio, very predictable, excellent vehicle overall.

5.0L Mustang five-speed: Very fast vehicle out of the turns, brakes and tires excellent, predictable and easily

1990 and 1991 Ford Police Drivetrains

Layout	cid/liter	carb	comp	hp	axle	model
V-8	302/5.0L	SEFI	8.9	160	3.08,3.27	Crown Vic
V-8	351/5.8L-HO	2-VV	8.3	180	2.73	Crown Vic
V-8	302/5.0L-HO	SEFI	9.0	225	2.73,3.08	Mustang
V-6	232/3.8L	SEFI	9.0	140*	3.37	Taurus

*increased to 155 horsepower in 1991

1990 Michigan State Police Patrol Vehicle Test Results

Make	Chevrolet	Ford	Chevrolet	Ford	Chevrolet	Ford
Model	Caprice	Crown Vic	Caprice	CrownVic	Caprice	Taurus
Engine, ci & carb	350, tbi	351, VV	305, tbi	302, pfi	262, tbi	232, pfi
HP, SAE	190	180	170	160	140	140
Axle ratio	3.42	2.73	3.08	3.08	3.08	3.37
Weight, test, lb	3,893	4,152	3,958	3,899	3,812	3,323
Wheelbase, in	116.0	114.3	116.0	114.3	116.0	106.0
Road course						
lap time, sec	86.75	88.58	89.74	88.77	90.65	87.31
0–100 mph, sec	29.71	34.02	42.60	38.67	53.09	34.00
Top speed, mph	122.1	121.0	113.0	107.3	110.2	114.0
Braking, ft/sec^2	24.23	22.96	24.23	22.96	24.23	23.30
EPA city mpg	14.0	13.1	16.4	17.4	19.0	18.5

1990 Michigan State Police Patrol Vehicle Tests Results—Mustang

Make	Ford	Ford
Model	Mustang	Mustang
Engine, ci & carb	302, HO	302, HO
HP, SAE	225	225
Trans	5-speed	4-speed AOT
Axle ratio	3.08	2.73
Weight, test, lb	3,168	3,250
Wheelbase, in	100.5	100.5
Road course		
lap time, sec	82.18	82.55
0–100 mph , sec	18.66	21.25
Top speed, mph	135.4	136.0
1/4-mile ET, sec	na	na
1/4-mile speed, mph	na	na
Braking, ft/sec^2	26.19	26.19
EPA city mpg	16.9	16.8

1991 Michigan State Police Patrol Vehicle Test Results

Make	Chevrolet	Ford	Chevrolet	Ford
Model	Camaro	Mustang	Camaro	Mustang
Engine, ci & carb	350, pfi	302, pfi	305, pfi	302, pfi
HP, SAE	245	225	230	225
Axle ratio	3.23	2.73	3.42	3.08
Transmission	4-speed auto	4-speed auto	5-speed stick	5-speed stick
Test weight, lb	3,463	3,251	3,393	3,185
Wheelbase, in	101.0	100.5	101.0	100.5
Road course				
lap time, sec	81.08	83.80	82.45	83.06
0–100 mph, sec	17.31	22.80	19.98	18.84
Top speed, mph	150.0	136.1	149.1	135.5
1/4-mile ET, sec	15.05	16.54	15.84	15.33
1/4-mile speed, mph	93.4	87.2	88.6	91.8
Braking, ft/sec^2	26.63	21.68	25.17	na
EPA city mpg	16.4	16.8	16.5	16.9

1991 Michigan State Police Patrol Vehicle Test Results

Make	Chevrolet	Ford	Chevrolet	Ford	Ford	Chevrolet
Model	Caprice	CrownVic	Caprice	CrownVic	Taurus	Wagon
Engine, ci & carb	350, tbi	351, VV	305, tbi	302, pfi	232, pfi	305, tbi
HP, SAE	195	180	170	160	155	170
Axle ratio	3.42	2.73	2.56	3.08	3.37	2.73
Weight, test, lb	4,134	4,136	4,138	4,080	3,307	4,477
Wheelbase, in	115.9	114.3	115.9	114.3	106.0	115.9
Road course						
lap time, sec	88.07	89.20	90.66	90.56	87.05	92.11
0–100 mph, sec	29.24	34.54	41.84	40.98	29.62	42.23
Top speed, mph	130.0	121.3	124.1	107.6	129.4	109.0
1/4-mile ET, sec	117.5	118.47	19.00	18.56	17.58	19.06
1/4-mile speed, mph	79.6	78.1	74.3	74.7	79.7	71.09
Braking ft/sec^2	24.88	23.86	na	na	23.54	25.09
EPA city mpg	13.9	13.1	17.1	17.4	18.0	16.2

Chapter Fourteen

1992-1997
The 4.6L SOHC Crown Victoria

In 1992, the 55A police package was available for the 106-inch wheelbase, midsize, front-drive Taurus. This proven four-door sedan was powered by the 3.8L overhead-cam V-6.

The Taurus was restyled for 1992. The front end was more rounded. It now had a drag coefficient of just .32. The police Taurus no longer had cooling slots in the grille. The rear trunk lid had the appearance of having a tiny ducktail spoiler. All the sheet metal, except the doors, was new for 1992. The passenger side air bag was an option.

The Special Service package was once again available for the 1992 Mustang LX. The Mustang was powered by a 225-horsepower, 5.0L HO V-8 teamed with either a five-speed manual and 3.08 rear gears or a four-speed overdrive automatic and 2.73 rear gears. The Special Service Mustang was almost unchanged for 1992.

Ford did not have a police package for the full-size Crown Vic at the beginning of the 1992 model year. The big police news for 1992, of course, was the February 1992 introduction of the newly restyled Crown Vic. This was close to a totally new vehicle. The new Crown Vic had sleek, aerodynamic styling with a .34 coefficient of drag. Also new for 1992 1/2 were four-wheel disc brakes, speed-sensitive power steering, a passenger-side airbag option, and a 114.4-inch wheelbase.

Antilock brakes were a new option. This included the ABS-based Traction Assist. Traction Assist used the reverse of ABS logic to pulse the rear brakes when it sensed they were spinning faster than the front wheels. It worked at speeds under 35 miles per hour. Since the combination of ABS and Traction Assist was a $600 option and ABS was new to so many cops, many police departments just went with the straight four-wheel discs without ABS. By 1993, only half of the Crown Vics were ordered with ABS/TA. By 1997, this increased to only 75 percent of the police Crown Vics. Chevrolet never offered a traction control option for the police Caprice, but ABS was standard in 1991.

Of course, the really big news was the Crown Vic's drivetrain: 4.6L single overhead-cam (SOHC) "modular" V-8 and electronic four-speed overdrive automatic. This was the first overhead-cam engine ever used in a full-size

police sedan. The 4.6L V-8 weighed 40 pounds less than the 5.0L overhead-valve V-8. The 4.6L V-8 was rated at 210 horsepower. This is a full 50 horsepower more than the 5.0L V-8 and 30 horsepower more than the 5.8L HO V-8.

The 4.6L V-8 was the first of Ford's new family of modular V-8 engines. It was built at Ford's Romeo, Michigan, Engine Plant. With the new engine design, it was possible to build an entire family of engines on a single assembly line in several different configurations and different displacements. The family of engines used similar combustion chambers, pistons, and valvetrains so that components could be interchanged easily. The modular design also allows sharing a number of similar components within engine families such as cylinder blocks, aluminum cylinder heads, camshafts, connecting rods, and water and oil pumps.

Most important, the engine design can be easily adapted to future designs such as dual overhead-cams with four valves per cylinder, variable cam timing and dual induction. The 4.6L SOHC engine was later expanded to a DOHC configuration for the Lincoln and 5.4L displacement for the Expedition and F-series truck.

A 1992 Taurus in service with the North Carolina Highway Patrol. The newly styled Taurus no longer had front grille cooling slots. *M. K. Holcomb*

The 1992 5.0L Mustang, like this Utah Highway Patrol pursuit car, had a 136-miles-per-hour top end. *Bill Hattersley*

A 1992 Los Angeles County Sheriff Taurus. Police departments large and small and from coast to coast gave the front-drive, heavy-duty police package a try. *Bill Hattersley*

Ford engine enthusiasts were quick to compare the 4.6L SOHC V-8 to Ford's successful engines of the past. The 4.6L engine uses cross-bolted mains like the 427-ci NASCAR engines of the 1960s for maximum crank stability. It also uses the deep-skirt block design from the FE-series of big-blocks for maximum block rigidity.

The SOHC design, of course, eliminates the pushrods. Instead of one camshaft located over the crankshaft, the SOHC engine has two camshafts. One cam is located in each head, one per bank of cylinders. The overhead-cam design greatly reduces valvetrain friction. It also allows a straighter intake port design that flows more air at Wide Open Throttle. The 5.0L and 5.8L overhead-valve engines produced an average of 31.5 horsepower per liter. The 4.6L and 5.4L single overhead-cam engines average 44.1 horsepower per liter. The non-police 4.6L double overhead-cam engine produces 65 horsepower per liter.

The 4.6L SOHC engine used SEFI induction, the EEC-IV Electronic Engine Control computer, hydraulic timing chain tensioner, interchangeable aluminum cylinder heads, roller cam followers, and cross-bolted main bearing caps. The new AOD-E four-speed transmission used electronic shift control with a fourth gear overdrive and fourth gear torque converter lockup.

The 1992 Michigan State Police tests had the makings of the match race of the decade. The 4.6L Crown Vic was rated at 210 horsepower and 270 ft-lbs of torque. The 5.7L Caprice was rated at 205 horsepower with 300 ft-lbs of torque. The Crown Vic weighed 100 pounds less than the Caprice and 100 pounds less than the 1991 Crown Vic. Chevrolet Fleet officials were indeed concerned about the high revving and better breathing characteristics of the 4.6L SOHC engine. Would more torque win the day? Or more horsepower and lighter weight?

The 4.6L Crown Vic turned in the best braking performance of any four-door sedan. The volumetric efficient, low-friction 4.6L V-8 also produced better gas mileage than the 5.7L Chevy engine by 4.5 miles per gallon. However, the 5.7L Caprice took the road course, acceleration, and top speed honors.

The 1992 4.6L Crown Vic was, however, an improvement over the 1991 5.8L Crown Vic. It reached 100 miles per hour 6 seconds faster and was 3 miles per hour faster on the top end. Actually, the 124-miles-per-hour top end was a disappointment to Ford engineers. This same test car had run 130 miles per hour-plus earlier that week at the Romeo Proving Ground.

The Los Angeles County Sheriff's Department does not conduct top speed tests. However, they do perform quarter-mile tests on the famous Pomona drag strip. Any questions about whether the Crown Vic was running properly were settled in Los Angeles a month later after Ford Fleet checked out the vehicle numerous times. The 4.6L Crown Vic ran a 17.48 second quarter during MSP tests and a 17.45 second quarter during LASD tests.

A 123-miles-per-hour top end a year later during 1993 MSP tests confirmed the worst. As great an engine as the 4.6L SOHC V-8 was, it was not a 5.7L Caprice-killer. The 4.6L Romeo was instead a powerful and economical replacement for both the 302-ci and 351-ci Windsor. It gave slightly better performance and much better fuel economy. That, of course, was Ford's goal.

The 1992 special service 5.7L Camaro was pretty hard on the 5.0L Mustang in a repeat of the 1991 test results. The 3.8L Taurus, however, evened the score by completely outclassing the 3.1L Lumina. In the Taurus-versus-Lumina match race, the Taurus would win five to six out of six test phases every year.

The 1992 1/2 Crown Vic was ordered by the state police and highway patrol in 32 states, including the California Highway Patrol. The new 4.6L Crown Vic was apparently worth the 15-month wait!

The 1992 1/2 to 1997 Crown Victorias can be hard to tell apart. However, the late-model Crown Vic has three distinct styles. The half model year in 1992 stands

The wedge-shaped 1992 Crown Vic, like this factory test mule, had four-wheel discs, speed-sensitive steering, and ABS as a first-time option.

This single overhead cam (SOHC) modular V-8 caused quite a stir in 1992. This was the first SOHC engine ever used in a full-size police sedan. At 210 horsepower, this 4.6L V-8 had 30 horsepower more than the 5.8L HO V-8.

alone as its own style. The 1992 1/2 is "grille-less." The blue oval is in the center of a curved nose panel between the headlights. At the rear, there is a chrome strip but no reflector between the taillights. The license plate is recessed into the bumper. The 1993 and 1994 models form the second styling. These have a fine mesh chrome grille with two crossbars. The blue oval is suspended between these two crossbars. At the rear, a narrow reflector strip is at the bottom of the trunk lid between the taillights. The 1995 and later models have an open mesh, chrome front grille with a single crossbar that holds the blue oval. At the rear, the license plate has been moved from the bumper to a recess in the trunk lid. A wide reflector panel is on each side of the license plate between the taillights.

For 1993, Ford released four police and Special Service package vehicles. First, the 55H police package was on the full-size Crown Victoria. Powered by the 4.6L SOHC V-8, the 114.4-inch four-door sedan was unchanged from its mid-1992 debut.

Second, the 55A police package was available for the midsize, front-drive Taurus L. For 1993, the horsepower from the 3.8L V-6 was bumped from 155 horsepower to 160 horsepower, however, the overall vehicle performance was unchanged.

Third, the 5.0L Mustang was available with a Special Service package. In what would be its last year in the police fleet, the Mustang was unchanged from 1992. Ford engineers, instead, were busy with the next generation Mustang.

Fourth, as a midyear release, the Explorer 4x4 was available with a Special Service package. By now, these sport/utes were catching on with police and retail buyers alike. Ford had the first 4x4 available to cops with the

The 4.6L SOHC V-8 powering this 1992 Los Angeles County Sheriff Crown Vic produces 40 percent more horsepower than the same size overhead-valve V-8. *Bill Hattersley*

The mid-1992 Crown Vic, like this CHP unit, had a styling all its own. This is the only year for the blue oval in a grilleless front end. *Bill Hattersley*

This 1993 Crown Vic is on duty with the Royal Canadian Mounted Police. The 1993 and 1994 models have a fine mesh grille with the blue oval suspended between two crossbars. *Bill Hattersley*

A 1993 California Highway Patrol Enforcement-class Crown Vic. These 4.6L police cars had a top speed of 123 miles per hour. *Bill Hattersley*

1967 Bronco. This was dropped after 1987. By 1997, fully half of the vehicles tested by the Michigan State Police were sport/utes.

The Explorer was powered by the 4.0L overhead-valve V-6 rated at 160 horsepower. It came with either a 4x4 or 4x2 layout. Transmissions included the five-speed stick and four-speed automatic overdrive. It had rear drum brakes, but ABS was standard. The 1993 Explorer used the Twin I-Beam front axle made famous on Ford's F-series pickups.

For 1993, the horsepower rating on the Mustang's 5.0L HO V-8 dropped from 225 horsepower to a mere 205 horsepower. The reason was a change in the way the horsepower was rated. No change in the engine took place for 1993. Since the 225-horsepower rating, which took place in 1987, the 5.0L V-8 was not tested until 1993. Subtle changes had taken place with the induction, timing, and exhaust to lower the official SAE rating. However, the actual performance was not changed. The 5.0L Mustang still ran 135 to 137 miles per hour with exactly the same 15-second (five-speed) and 16 second (four-speed) quarter-mile times as in the past.

The special service 5.0L Mustang LX was available from 1982 through 1993. It completely changed the way cops thought about pursuit cars. It remains Ford's most important and most influential police car. It did the job when nothing else could.

The 1993 5.0L HO Mustang went out in style. The quarter-mile run from the 1993 five-speed Mustang was the best performance ever turned in by a Special Service package Mustang. It ran the quarter in 15.22 seconds at 92.4 miles per hour.

The 1993 Michigan State Police vehicle tests held good and bad news for Ford enthusiasts. The good news was the runaway victory of the 3.8L Taurus over the 3.1L Lumina. The Taurus captured all six test phases to literally define the ideal midsize, front-drive police car. The bad news was the equally lopsided showdown between both the Camaro and Mustang and the Caprice and Crown Vic.

By 1993, Ford Fleet was aware that cops wanted more performance from the 4.6L Crown Vic. Many jurisdictions had adopted nonpursuit policies, making the

What this 1993 Suffolk County, New York, Police 4.6L Crown Vic lacks in torque it makes up in high-revving horsepower. This year, Ford talked about 3.73 gears to make the most of the drivetrain on city patrol. *Bob Rice*

California Highway Patrol actually used this car in 1980. It may not have been as slow as it was represented, but it was indeed slower than the CHP's 1979 360-ci, 4-bbl St. Regis and much slower than the CHP's 1978 440-ci, 4-bbl Monaco.

In the early and mid-1980s, even the best full-size, four-door police sedans ran 19 second quarter-miles and had top speeds around 115 miles per hour. By the mid-1990s, however, the full-size, four-door police sedans were very much improved. They had acceleration, top speeds, and road course times comparable to the 5.0L HO Mustang.

The rough ride and lack of prisoner space in the pony pursuits were drawbacks the cops no longer had to tolerate. The last time cops had true pursuit car performance in a traditional-size, four-door sedan was 1976 for

Year	1980	1993	1994	1996
Make	Dodge	Ford	Chevy	Ford
Model	St. Regis	Mustang	Caprice	Crown Vic
Engine, ci & carb	318, 4-bbl	302, pfi	350 LT1	4.6L SOHC
0–60 mph, sec	13.14	7.98	8.30	9.10
0–100 mph, sec	45.7	222.34	21.64	25.18
Top speed, mph	114.7	135.1	141.2	135.0
1/4-mile ET, sec	19.63	16.24	16.18	16.89
1/4-mile speed, mph	74.50	87.6	86.8	83.8
Road course, sec	93.9	83.4	83.8	84.8

ability of the police car to reach top speeds over 130 miles per hour less important. However, the need for quicker acceleration to close the gap with the violator in less time was becoming a more serious issue. In 1993, Ford Fleet openly discussed a "highway" police package with 3.27 rear gears and a "city" police package with 3.73 rear gears. The 3.73 gears would give up top speed and fuel economy but gain acceleration from the same 210-horsepower 4.6L engine. No action, however, was taken. That was a shame. In 1994 the Caprice would get the Corvette's LT1 engine. The Caprice would continue to outrun the Crown Vic just as the LT1 Camaro outran the Mustang.

While the retail Mustang enthusiasts anxiously looked forward to the next generation Mustang in 1994, cops bid farewell to the 1993 Mustang. A Special Service package would not be offered on the 1994 Mustang. The 5.0L Mustang, the Ford that chases Porsches for a living, had served its purpose. The Mustang bridged the performance gap from the 1980s. The full-size four-door sedans were now running well enough that the Mustang was no longer needed for traffic enforcement. Full-size sedans could now do that once again.

This comparison shows why the Mustang, and for that matter, Camaro, is no longer needed. The pursuit pony was desperately needed in the early and mid-1980s. The car that got this all started was the small-block-powered, full-size Dodge St. Regis. The

Chevrolet and 1978 for Ford, Dodge, and Plymouth. The Mustang bridged the gap.

Here are the subjective evaluations from the LA Sheriff's EVOC instructors about the 1993 Fords:

4.6L Crown Vic ABS: good handling, very good brakes overall but slight fade under hard braking on last (of four) laps, predictable handling when accelerating through turns, minimal bounce and body lean, constant brake pedal, no extreme fade, slight but controlled understeer.

3.8L Taurus ABS: vehicle handled well with minimal bounce or body lean, predictable and consistent, slight understeer but controllable, mid-range acceleration was lacking.

5.0L Mustang 5-speed: slight understeer but controllable, slight brake fade, outstanding acceleration, very smooth transmission, consistent and predictable handling characteristics, good brakes.

4.0L Explorer 4x4: good handling for van/truck-type vehicle, minimal lean and bounce, handled well for its size and shape, adequate acceleration, slight to moderate understeer but predictable.

For 1994, Ford fielded three police vehicles. As in 1993, Ford called the cop gear for the Crown Victoria its Interceptor Police Package. The full-size 114.4-inch wheelbase four-door sedan was powered again by the 4.6L SOHC V-8 rated at 210 horsepower. New for 1994 were heavier brake rotors with

A King County, Washington, Sheriff' Department 1993 Mustang. This was the best year for the famous special service package. *Bill Hattersley*

For 1993, the 5.0L HO V-8 was down-rated to 205 horsepower due to a change in test methods. Mustangs, like this Ford fleet test mule, still ran 137 miles per hour. *Cindy Sanow*

The special service Mustang, like this 1993 CHP unit, was available from 1982 to 1993. It completely changed the way cops thought about pursuit cars. *Bill Hattersley*

The 1993 3.8L Taurus like this Salt Lake City, Utah, Police unit, has a top speed of 123 miles per hour and runs the quarter-mile in 17 seconds. *Bill Hattersley*

angled internal vents. Bucket seats were now standard, and so were dual air bags.

The 55A police package was available for the 106-inch wheelbase front-drive Taurus. This four-door sedan was again powered by the 3.8L V-6 producing 160 horsepower. Dual air bags were now standard. For 1994, the Taurus got larger disc brake rotors and larger brake pads. Also new for 1994 were 15-inch diameter wheels to accommodate the larger brakes. Up to this point, the police Taurus used 14-inch wheels.

The 1985 Special Service Mustang was the first police car of any make to be fitted with unidirectional tires, the Goodyear Eagle "Gatorbacks." Unidirectional tires have a V-pattern and can only rotate in one direction. The 1994 police Taurus was the first police car of any make to come with asymmetrical tires, the General XP-2000 V4. Asymmetrical tires have a different tread pattern on the outside edge of the tire than on the inside edge. They can rotate in any direction, but a certain sidewall must be mounted facing out. Asymmetrical tires have better wet and dry performance along with better tread wear. All police cars except the Lumina came with asymmetrical tires in 1995.

The Special Service package was available for the 1994 4.0L Explorer. Again, this was available in 4x4 and 4x2. The Explorer was the only 1994 Ford police vehicle available with a five-speed stick. The four-speed auto overdrive was an option. The 111.9-inch wheelbase, four-door Explorer was a complete carryover from its mid-1993 introduction. It was again powered by the 160-horsepower V-6.

By 1994, Chevrolet had two versions of its LT1-technology pushrod V-8 in the Caprice. One was the 260-horsepower, 5.7L engine geared for state police and rural sheriffs departments. The other was the 200-horsepower 4.3L engine geared for city police and urban sheriffs departments. The 4.6L SOHC V-8 in the Crown Vic offered performance exactly in the middle of these two Bowtie police engines. The 5.7L Caprice reached 141 miles per hour while the 4.6L Crown Vic got to 128 miles

per hour. The 3.8L Taurus reached 129 miles per hour. The 4.0L Explorer was speed limited to 110 miles per hour. Chevrolet did not field a police Lumina in 1994.

Ford Fleet discounted the need for a 140-miles-per-hour four-door sedan like the 5.7L Caprice. However, many

New for mid-1993 was a Special Service package for the 4.0L V-6 four-door Explorer, like this Taylor, MI Police K-9 unit. Ford invented police sport/utes with its 1967 Bronco. *Ford Division*

police departments like the California Highway Patrol adopted the Caprice specifically for the performance from the 260-horsepower engine. This, in turn, caused speculation at Ford Fleet about the use of the upcoming 5.4L SOHC "modular" V-8, a 230-horsepower stroked version of the 4.6L engine. Again, no action was taken.

The 1994 4.0L Explorer was logically grouped with the 4.0L Cherokee however, these were two very different vehicles. The Explorer was larger and heavier than the short-wheelbase Cherokee. By 1994, Ford Fleet had become embroiled in two serious police car problems, or at least allegations of problems. One was a power steering failure under a special set of circumstances on the 4.6L Crown Vic. The other was transaxle failures during general patrol duties on the 3.8L Taurus.

All carmakers have had serious problems with their police cars. Chrysler suffered sagging suspensions and cracked K-members on the Diplomat and Gran Fury in the early 1980s. This led to excessive front tire wear for the entire fleet and to brakes that would lock and suddenly pull to one side or another. Chevrolet took heat from the Heat for the failure of door-mounted seat belt anchors in 1990, which resulted in a fatality. Its ABS brakes became the center of intense controversy in 1991,

also alleged to have caused a fatality, until the departments trained officers in their use.

Ford had avoided serious problems until a fatal accident with a 1992 Crown Victoria involving a Paramus, New Jersey, police officer. In responding to a shooting, the officer weaved in and out of traffic, got into an oversteer skid during braking, and slid sideways into a telephone pole. The correction for an oversteer is to steer in the direction of the slide. Tests conducted by the Bergen County, New Jersey, Prosecutor's Office confirmed that "the Crown Vic had a tendency to lose power steering assist when the vehicle underwent hard braking and rapid turns. The assist loss for periods up to 1.5 seconds is caused by the engine speed dropping below its normal idle setting." The officer was apparently not able to correct the slide due to the loss of power steering.

Law and Order's Tom Yates did a follow-up investigation:

Ford Motor Company spokesperson said the power steering problem/situation has been described as "low idle tip-off." Ford explained, "The concern that we have had is when someone is in a hard braking maneuver, as you get down to the bot-

121

This 1994 Crown Vic is on duty with the Spokane, Washington, Police. These 210-horsepower patrol cars run a 17-second quarter-mile. *Bill Hattersley*

tom of the stop, maybe a couple of miles per hour, the engine speed on some cars would have a tendency to drop below idle." At that point, if a driver tried to make an abrupt turn they might feel a higher steering effort. The low power assist lasts about 1.5 seconds at the most. The increased steering effort depends on how low the vehicle's idle drops.

There's been a total of 19 complaints out of total sales of 60,000 police vehicles. This is no way to predict if the low-idle situation is going to occur in a particular police car. Ford's position is the low idle situation is not a defect, problem or safety issue.

Ford dismissed the Crown Vic power steering problem as a design idiosyncrasy. Neither Ford nor the NHTSA made a recall. Since the problem was subtle, intermittent, and nonrepeatable, it is difficult to determine if it was ever fixed.

The transaxle reliability issue with the Taurus was far from subtle. Both the Baltimore, Maryland, Police and *The Baltimore Sun* newspaper made a national scandal out of the issue. As an indirect result, Ford dropped the police package for the Taurus after 1995. Ford continued to use the Taurus as a "fleet" car but not for the rugged demands of a "police" fleet.

The Baltimore Police experience with the Taurus has proven to be typical of many large urban departments across the country. What makes the Baltimore events so unique and eye-brow raising are formal statements by high-ranking Ford Customer Service Division and Ford Fleet Division officials that are in direct contrast to one another on the fitness-for-use of the police Taurus.

In early 1992, the Baltimore Police purchased 170 front-drive Taurus police cars. Taurus would eventually account for 42 percent of the police fleet but 63 percent of the downtime.

The Baltimore Police found the transaxles would not hold up under round-the-clock patrol use. The Taurus became a lightening rod for the problems all fleets have with front-drive vehicles. The lighter frames could not take the pounding from an inner-city patrol. Alignment problems became tire wear problems. The pursuit radials needed replacement after just 3,000 miles. Worst of all, front end accidents, which are what police tend to have, almost always ended up damaging the transaxle. On a rear-drive car, the same impact would damage the front sheet metal and radiator. These front-end collisions ended up bending the Taurus' unibody frame, which was difficult to straighten.

In fairness, all of these problems, with the possible exception of the transaxle failures, would have happened to the Lumina had it been as widely used as the Taurus.

Amid widely published problems with the Taurus, police departments from across the country that had experience with the Taurus confirmed that there was a right way and a wrong way to use the Taurus. From the Omaha, Nebraska, Police to the Hillsborough County, Florida, Sheriff to the Michigan State Police, the message was clear. Use the front-drive, midsize cars for detective, investigator, and administration use. Do not use front-drive, midsize cars for 24-hour uniformed patrol use, even if they have a "Police package."

The Baltimore Police experience with the Taurus would have been chalked up as normal fleet maintenance woes compounded by city politics and in-fighting as usual. What made this issue a problem from coast to coast were conflicting and confusing statements made by Ford officials about the Taurus. Quoting from news accounts:

Representatives of Ford Motor Co. in Detroit said Friday that they were astounded to learn from *The Sun* that the department had purchased their car from local dealers for use as a police cruiser because the Taurus was never designed or marketed for that purpose. "If they had called us in 1992 and told us they planned to use the Taurus as a police squad car, we would have been the first ones to tell them not to," said Joy Wolfe of the Ford Customer Service Division. "It was never intended to be driven as a primary police vehicle. It sounds to me like the department misunderstood the purpose that the car was sold for. It's the No. 1-selling family sedan in America, but it is most certainly not a police car.

"I think that is generally understood in every major police department in the country," said Ms. Wolfe of Ford. "It is certainly true that any front-wheel-drive car would be more expensive and difficult to maintain if you subjected it to the kind of hard use they get in police departments. That's why no one uses them for patrol cars."

New for the 1994 Crown Vic, like this New York City Transit Police unit, was dual side air bags and beefier brake rotors. *Neal Kemp*

A plain-looking 1994 Montana Highway Patrol Crown Vic. This 4.6L SOHC V-8-powered cruiser reached 128 miles per hour. *Bill Hattersley*

The Wyoming Highway Patrol used this 1994 4.6L Crown Vic. This was the year bucket seats and dual air bags were standard. *Bill Hattersley*

A week later, *The Baltimore Sun* report was picked up by the wire service where it eventually made *USA Today*. Ford responded by sending a team of technicians to Baltimore to resolve their complaints. This time it was Ford Fleet, not Ford Customer Service, who spoke with the press.

Amid such assessments–and lingering questions about the way Baltimore went about purchasing 140 of the cars—Ford has issued conflicting statements about the Taurus' fitness for police work.

The company's customer service division in Detroit has said in recent weeks that Ford engineers never designed the Taurus—the nation's top-selling family sedan–for use as a police cruiser. But Ford's government sales manager said this week that the car was beefed up so that it could be sold to police.

"It has been fully tested as a police vehicle," said Jack LaBelle of Ford. "Believe me, as the government sales manager I would know. And I think you'll find if you contact some of our customers that they are fully satisfied."

"We test a lot of vehicles for Ford so there's a lot of goodwill there," said Dan Riley auto repair foreman for the city of Omaha which bought about 140 Tauruses for its police. "But I can't say the car is something it's not. And it's not a good police car."

Regardless of official statements, the police package Taurus had become a real liability for Ford. The company produced the police version for just one more year, then used the major restyling for 1996 as an opportunity to make a clean break. Few questions were asked. Police officers still strongly prefer the V-8-powered, full-size, rear-drive four-door sedan. Ford, Chevrolet, and Chrysler have tried since 1982 to change the way cops and police fleet managers felt about the front-drive police car. People mover for detectives, yes. Police car for uniformed patrol, no. Long live the Crown Victoria.

In spite of the Crown Vic power steering controversy earlier in the year, here is what the Los Angeles County Sheriff EVOC instructors observed about the 1994 Ford police vehicles:

4.6L Crown Vic: The vehicles displayed moderate understeer, bounce and body lean was minimal, slight wheel hop on hard braking applications, good acceleration out of turns, predictable neutral steering.

3.8L Taurus: Acceleration was very good out of the turns, only slight understeer, body lean minimal with light to moderate bounce, good acceleration with some torque steer, overall handling of this vehicle was predictable.

4.0L Explorer: Good acceleration out of turns but under-powered at top end, slight understeer, lots of body lean in turns.

For 1995, Ford offered its Interceptor Police Package on the 4.6L SOHC V-8, full-size Crown Victoria. The 55A police package was available on the 3.8L V-6, midsize Taurus. As a late 1995 release, a Special Service package was available for the newly restyled four-door Explorer.

The big news for the Crown Vic was an upgrade to the EEC-V engine control computer. The EEC-IV dates back to at least 1984! The big Ford's 4.6L V-8 was still

A 1994 police package Taurus in service with the Utah Highway Patrol. These 160-horsepower, front-drive patrol cars have a top speed of 129 miles per hour. *Bill Hattersley*

A 1994 Pierce County, Washington, Sheriffs Taurus. With a full-size lightbar, drivers side spotlight, and front pusher bars, this front-drive car was worked hard. *Bill Hattersley*

rated at 210 horsepower, however, the peak dropped from 4600 rpm to 4250 rpm. The torque remained at 270 pounds per foot, except the peak dropped from 3400 rpm to 3250 rpm.

By all accounts, Ford engineers had figured out how to make the most from its 4.6L engine. The Crown Vic still ran a low 17-second quarter-mile. However, for the first time since the 1970 428-ci Cobra Jet, the big Ford cruiser broke the 130-miles-per-hour top speed barrier. Its top end of 132 miles per hour was just 3-miles-per-hour slower than the 260-horsepower, 5.7L LT1 Caprice. The 4.6L Crown Vic had steadily improved its performance each year since its mid-1992 introduction. The decision to stay with the 4.6L engine, instead of rushing the development of the 5.4L SOHC V-8, seemed justified.

The 3.8L Taurus held up its end of the Ford police banner against a much sleeker and 20 horsepower more

powerful Lumina. The 3.8L Taurus and 3.1L Lumina now both produced 160 horsepower. However, the larger Taurus engine still produced 225 pounds per foot of torque, 40 pounds per foot more than the Lumina. Torque wins drag races, not horsepower. Ironically, in its last appearance at the MSP tests, the police Taurus captured all six of the six test phases.

The Explorer was completely redesigned for mid-1995. This included all new, and much rounded, sheet-metal. It also had an entirely new suspension. The Twin I-Beam (4x2) and Twin Traction Beam (4x4) coil spring front suspension was replaced by an independent Short Long Arm (SLA) suspension using torsion springs. The 1995 Special Service package was only available on the 4x4 version of the Explorer. The 4.0L V-6 and the rest of the drivetrain remained unchanged for 1995. The Explorer was released too late in the model year to be tested by either the Michigan State Police in

This 1995 Crown Vic is in service with the Indiana State Police. The 1995 through 1997 models have an open-mesh chrome grille with the blue oval in a single crossbar.

The 1995 and later Crown Vics, like this Chicago Police unit, have a wide reflector between the taillights and a trunk lid-mounted license plate. *Greg Reynolds*

New for 1995, the Crown Vic, like this San Francisco Police unit, was upgraded to the EEC-V engine control computer.

August–September or the Los Angeles County Sheriff in November–December.

For their part, the Los Angeles County Sheriffs Dept. EVOC instructors were satisfied with the 1995 Crown Vic and Taurus:

4.6L Crown Vic: good handling vehicle, good and consistent brake pedal, acceleration was good coming out of the turns, suspension displayed predictable neutral steering with minimal lean and bounce, steering was very responsive, positive steering characteristics with slight oversteer during aggressive throttle use.

3.8L Taurus: very predictable vehicle but could be a little more responsive between brake application and return to throttle, vehicle displayed slight to moderate understeer, bounce and body lean was moderate without any control problems.

For 1996, Ford fielded just two police vehicles. One was the full-size 4.6L V-8 Crown Vic. The other was the 4x4, 4.0L V-6 Explorer. Both vehicles were strict carryovers from 1995.

New for 1996 was a dedicated Natural Gas Vehicle (NGV) intended for departments pushed by legislation or local governments to adopt this lower emissions powerplant. The NGV was powered by the 4.6L SOHC V-8 converted to use only natural gas. The 4.6L V-8 was bumped from 9:1 to 10:1 in compression for natural gas use. Chevrolet had developed a bi-fuel option for its 4.3L V-8 in 1994. In 1996, Ford became the first to offer a police car exclusively powered by natural gas.

The NGV Crown Vic had a 178-horsepower rating and 2.73 rear gears. It was almost as slow as the slowest full-size sedans from the early 1980s.

The 1996 Michigan State Police tests held a late-entry surprise for both Chevrolet and Ford. Volvo showed up with its 850 Turbo police sedan. The 850 Turbo is a midsize, front-drive sedan with a wheelbase and weight close to the Lumina. However, Volvo was

clearly at the MSP tests to knock off the LT1 Caprice in its last year. Volvo knew this was a year of transition. Cops would be looking to see what would be available to compete against the Crown Vic after 1996.

Volvo first splashed on the police fleet scene during the fuel crisis of the mid-1970s. *Motor Trend* magazine pushed the Volvo 164E in a series of articles as the ideal police car for the times. Volvo tried the police market again in the mid-1980s with its baseline 240 turbo equipped with a taxi package. This, too, resulted in only a limited market penetration, and the police package was not pursued. For 1996, Volvo was back in the police market with an 850 Turbo police sedan powered by a transverse-mounted, in-line five-cylinder engine fitted with a single turbo. No domestic automaker has ever released a police package on a car powered by a turbo-charged engine.

Of course, Ford had a point to prove at the 1996 MSP tests also. The closer the 4.6L Crown Vic ran to the 5.7L LT1 Caprice, the easier the transition from Chevy to Ford for 1997. Against the nine-year winning streak of the Caprice and the smug arrogance of the Volvo team, the 4.6L Crown Vic turned in the best performance since its introduction.

For the first time, the 4.6L Crown Vic ran the quarter-mile in the 16-second bracket. For the first time, it got to 100 miles per hour in the 25-second bracket. And for the first time, it equaled the top speed of the 5.0L HO Mustangs by running 135 miles per hour. The 5.7L LT1 Caprice extended its MSP record to 10 straight, the most of any police car. However, the 4.6L Crown Vic did as well as any 281-ci full-size car could be expected to do. It had a higher top end than the Volvo 850 Turbo, had far better brakes and, in a coupe de grace, beat the smaller, more powerful Volvo around the MIS road course. And the people said, Who needs a 5.4L V-8?

A 1995 Missouri State Highway Patrol Crown Vic. In 1995, and for the first time since the 1970 428-ci Cobra Jet sedans, the Crown Vic broke the 130-miles-per-hour top speed barrier.

A 1995 Taurus on patrol with the Cassia County, Idaho, Sheriff's Department. Plagued by transaxle problems and lack of acceptance by cops, this was the last year the police package was offered. *Mark Boatwright*

The special service package Explorer was completely redesigned for late 1995. The rugged 4x4 got new sheet metal and a new suspension but retained its 4.0L V-6 engine.

For the first time, the 1996 Crown Vic, like this Oregon State Police unit, equaled the top speed of the Mustang with 135-miles-per-hour runs. *Bill Hattersley*

A 1996 4.6L SOHC Crown Vic on duty with the Los Angeles Police Department. For the first time with this engine, the 1996 Crown ran the quarter-mile in 16 seconds. *Bill Hattersley*

For 1997, Ford released an Interceptor Police package for its 4.6L Crown Vic. Again, the powerplants were a 210-horsepower gasoline engine and a 178-horsepower natural gas engine. Both vehicles were strict carryovers from 1996.

Ford also released a Special Service package for the four-door Explorer 4x4. This popular sport/ute had big changes to the drivetrain. In fact, both Special Service package Explorer engines were new for 1997.

The long-promised 5.0L pushrod V-8 was finally available. The retail Mustang had been converted from the 5.0L V-8 to the 4.6L SOHC V-8. This freed-up the 5.0L V-8, now rated at 210 horsepower, to be used in the Explorer. Except for the three years from 1994 to 1996 and two years from 1975 to 1976, this 302-ci pushrod-activated, overhead-valve engine has been in constant police car or special service sedan use since 1968. The 5.0L V-8 was teamed with a four-speed overdrive automatic.

Brand new for 1997 is a 4.0L V-6. This can be very confusing because the Explorer had used a 4.0L V-6 since its 1993 introduction. The old 160-horsepower 4.0L V-6 was an overhead-valve engine. The 205-horsepower new 4.0L V-6 is an overhead-cam engine, but not a part of the Romeo "modular" engine family.

To make the 4.0L SOHC V-6, Ford designers started with the block from the pushrod V-6. The iron blocks for both engines are cast in Ford's Windsor, Ontario, engine plant. The overhead-cam blocks are then sent to Cologne, Germany, for finishing. To the SOHC block, Ford adds a balance shaft to reduce vibration, aluminum cylinder heads, counterweighted crankshaft, forged connecting rods, knock sensor, and a special split intake manifold. At low engine speeds, a valve closes to split the intake plenum in half. This forms a long intake tract for the air that enhances low-speed torque. At high engine speeds, this valve opens, which shortens the intake path. The engine can pull in more air which increases high speed power.

The 205-horsepower, 4.0L SOHC V-6 is the standard engine for the special service Explorer. It uses an EEC-V electronic engine control system.

The only transmission available with the SOHC V-6 is a brand-new "five" speed automatic overdrive. The new transmission is basically Ford's 4R55E electronically controlled four-speed overdrive automatic. Ford electronically added a fifth gear without having to physically add another gear to the transmission. The "new" 1.86:1 second gear is designed to improve acceleration and towing capabilities. Again, the four-speed transmission has been electronically, not mechanically, modified to gain the "fifth" gear.

The sophisticated split intake system, high-revving capability of the overhead-cam engine, and addition of the pseudo-fifth gear all added up to a 4.0L Explorer that had more straight-line acceleration than the 5.0L Explorer. In the quarter-mile, the 4.0L SOHC V-6 version was .8 second quicker and 4 miles per hour faster. It was 13 seconds faster to 100 miles per hour than the 5.0L OHV V-8, even though the V-8 version had lower rear gears. In fact, the only sport/utes to beat the 4.0L SOHC V-6 Explorer to 100 miles per hour were the 5.7L V-8 Tahoe and 5.2L V-8 Grand Cherokee.

While 1996 was a great year for the Crown Vic at the Michigan State Police tests, 1997 was the worst possible year. The full-size Dodge and Plymouth four-door police sedans were discontinued after 1989. The full-size Chevrolet four-door police sedan was dropped after 1996. The 1997 Crown Vic literally had no competition.

The pesky Volvo 850 Turbo was back. This time it ran much faster, but it was still priced way out of the reach of police fleets. The 5.7L Chevy Tahoe two-wheel-drive ran well, but that was no substitute for a full-size four-door sedan. All the 4.6L Crown Vic had to do was show up. Well, not quite.

In 1978, the Michigan State Police had established minimum acceleration and top speed standards for their full-size police sedans. These standards varied each year based on the previous year's performance. As a general statement, the acceleration standards for the upcoming year are 10 percent tougher than the *average* actual performance from the previous year. This forces a general but gradual improvement each year. For 1997, Ford and the Michigan State Police agreed to keep the standard the same as 1996.

Each year since 1978, the MSP has disqualified full-size cars for failing to meet their minimum acceleration and top speed standards. The 1978 Buick LeSabre 350-ci 4-bbl and Ford LTD II 400-ci, 2-bbl were the first to get the black flag. In 1979, the Ford LTD 351-ci Windsor and Ford LTD II 351-ci Modified got the axe.

In 1980, the Buick LeSabre 350-ci, 4-bbl and Chevy Impala 350-ci, 4-bbl failed to make the cut.

Nearly every year one of the bona fide police package sedans with a top-of-the-line pursuit engine was flatly

The Montana Highway Patrol used the Crown Vic in 1996. So did the Indiana State Police, Ohio State Highway Patrol, and Utah Highway Patrol. *Bill Hattersley*

A sharp-looking 1996 Royal Canadian Mounted Police Crown Vic powered by the 4.6L V-8. These cars get about 16 miles per gallon. *Bill Hattersley*

This 1996 Los Angeles County Sheriffs Crown Vic has the traditional black body with white doors and roof. This is clearly recognized as a police car. *Bill Hattersley*

127

New for 1997, the Explorer, shown here at the MSP test track, is available with either a 4.0L SOHC V-6 or a 5.0L OHV V-8. The V-6 is actually faster.

A 1997 Utah Highway Patrol Crown Vic powered by the 210-horsepower 4.6L V-8. With an average quarter-mile and road course time the same as a sport/ute, the Crown Vic really needs the 245-horsepower, 5.4L V-8. *Bill Hattersley*

disqualified by the humorless MSP troopers. The strictest example was the 1987 Dodge Diplomat. It was disqualified for failing to meet 0 to 80-miles-per-hour acceleration standards even though it met the 0 to 60 miles per hour and 0 to 100-miles-per-hour standards. Since the beginning of the MSP tests, the only marque *not* to be black flagged was Plymouth.

By now, it should be painfully obvious that the unthinkable happened. The 1997 4.6L Crown Vic was disqualified by the MSP for failing to meet all three acceleration standards. The year that should have been a cake-walk turned out to be a plank-walk.

Test phase	MSP standards	1997 Crown Vic
0–60 mph	10.00 sec.	10.50 sec.
0–80 mph	17.20 sec.	17.63 sec.
0–100 mph	28.20 sec.	28.99 sec.

After its run, the Crown Vic displayed a steady "check engine" warning light. Ford was unable to correct the problem at the track. The MSP times became official. Ford later determined the problem to be a faulty EGR sensor, possibly indicating an unfavorable change in the air-to-fuel mixture. Clearly, this particular test vehicle was not representative of all 4.6L Crown Vics. The 1996 MSP results show how strong the 4.6L Crown Vic can run. The 1997 MSP results show that sophisticated electronic engine control systems can be a two-edged sword!

For 1997, Ford gave a glimpse of what could be a full-size 1998 Special Service package sport/ute, its Expedition. This would be Ford's answer to the 5.7L Tahoe.

The 1997 Expedition is a 119-inch wheelbase sport/ute that draws heavily from Ford's F-series pickup truck. The Expedition was *not* available with a police or a Special Service package for 1997. The MSP, instead, were

The police Crown Vic could really use the torque of this 5.4L SOHC Triton V-8 for quicker "catch" times and to be sure it meets widely accepted acceleration standards.

asked to test a retail 5.4L Expedition 4x2 to give Ford an idea of how suitable the Expedition might be for police work.

The retail version of the 1997 Expedition is available as a 4x2 with a coil spring front suspension and as a 4x4 with a torsion bar front suspension. In either layout the rear suspension uses coil springs. The retail Expedition is available with either the 210-horsepower 4.6L V-8 or the 5.4L V-8. The 4.6L-powered sport/ute gets a four-speed automatic overdrive trans and 3.31 or 3.55 rear gears. The 5.4L-powered Expedition uses an electronic four-speed AOT and 3.31 or 3.73 gears.

The 5.4L SOHC V-8 is a stroked version of the 4.6L SOHC "modular" V-8. At 230-horsepower, this new Triton engine is either underrated or underdeveloped. Using the same horsepower per liter as the 4.6L SOHC, the 5.4L SOHC should be cranking out 245 horsepower.

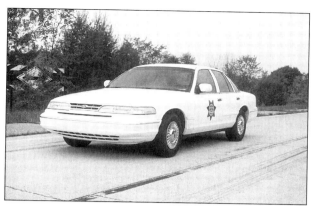

Here is the slick-top, 1997 police package, 4.6L Crown Vic during annual tests by the Michigan State Police. Ford Fleet assured cops the rear-drive V-8 full-size sedan will be available through 2001.

Exactly as it is, the 1997 4.6L Crown Vic, like this Seattle, Washington, Police unit, makes a great city and urban county patrol car. It has nimble handling around town for a full-size four-door sedan. *Bill Hattersley*

By 1998, the 119-inch wheelbase Expedition, shown here during MSP testing, will be available with a Special Service package. This heavy but 5.4L SOHC sport/ute was quicker around a road racing course than either Explorer.

For the first time in many decades, the Michigan State Police selected this 1997 Crown Vic as their patrol vehicle. Note the traditional hood-mounted STOP sign. *Matt Campbell*

At any rate, the 5.4L Expedition made a very respectable showing at the 1997 MSP tests. The full-size, 4,850-pound sport/ute negotiated the 1.63-mile road racing course more than a second ahead of both the 4.0L SOHC and 5.0L OHV Explorer. It has a 0 to 100-miles-per-hour time similar to the 4.0L Cherokee, and a road course time right behind Chevy's 255-horsepower 5.7L Tahoe.

As of the 1997 model year, the Ford Crown Victoria is the only full-size, rear-drive, V-8-powered police car available. The Crown Vic has outlasted the best police cars from Dodge, Plymouth, Pontiac, Buick, Oldsmobile, Chevrolet, Mercury, and Chrysler. It truly is the last of a breed. We really are back to where we were 65 years ago: Ford, with no real competition.

The obvious question at this point is, How long will the Crown Vic remain a full-size, rear-drive police car? To this question, we have a very encouraging answer.

The Crown Vic will be slightly restyled for 1998 1/4. This is good news on several fronts. First, it will remain a V-8-powered, rear-drive, four-door sedan and the changes will not affect the full-size 114.4-inch wheelbase. Second, it will extend the life of the Crown Vic as we know it through the year 2001.

Ford officials indicated the Crown Vic will get a different braking package when the chassis is redesigned in 1998. The front discs will get larger diameter pads. Most important, the Crown Vic will be able to have both a limited slip (locking) axle and ABS/Traction Assist. Right now, police cars with ABS cannot have a limited slip rear end.

With its longevity assured, the next question becomes one of more power for the Crown Vic. When, if ever, will the Crown Vic get the 5.4L SOHC V-8? This 230 to 245-horsepower 5.4L engine is exactly the same physical size as the existing 210-horsepower 4.6L V-8. It will literally drop right in. The larger engine, of course, also produces more torque, and that means faster overtake times in police use.

Does the police Crown Vic really need more power and torque than what the 4.6L engine produces? Decide for yourself.

The average quarter-mile time for the 4.6L Crown Vic over the six years since its introduction is 17.3 seconds. The average quarter-mile time for the 4.0L Cherokee, 5.7L Tahoe, 5.0L Explorer, and 4.0L Explorer is 17.4 seconds. The average road course time for the 4.6L Crown Vic is 86.2 seconds. The average road course time for the seven 4x2 and 4x4 vehicles tested in 1997 is 87.1 seconds.

That's right. Ford's heavy-duty Police Interceptor accelerates like the average sport/ute and is less than a second quicker around a pursuit-oriented, high-speed road racing course.

With the 5.4L SOHC V-8 producing 245 horsepower, the Crown Vic would perform more like the 5.7L LT1 Caprice, which is to say, more like the 5.0L HO Mustang. Ford Fleet stated the 5.4L V-8 was not scheduled for the 1998 1/4 Crown Vic. Of course, those statements were made before the fateful 1997 MSP tests. If ASC can drop a 4-valve, 4.6L DOHC V-8 into a Crown Victoria and call it a Crown Sport, the least Ford could do is drop a 5.4L SOHC V-8 into a Crown Victoria and call it a Police Interceptor.

1992 Ford Police Drivetrains

Layout	cid/liter	carb	comp	hp	axle	model
V-6	232/3.8L	SEFI	9.0	155	3.37	Taurus L
V-8	302/5.0L-HO	SEFI	9.0	225	2.73, 3.08	Mustang LX
V-8	281/4.6L-SOHC	SEFI	9.0	210	3.27	Crown Vic

1993 Ford Police Drivetrains

Layout	cid/liter	carb	comp	hp	axle	model
V-6	232/3.8L	SEFI	9.0	160	3.37	Taurus L
V-8	302/5.0L-HO	SEFI	9.0	205	2.73, 3.08	Mustang LX
V-8	281/4.6L-SOHC	SEFI	9.0	210	3.27	Crown Vic
V-6	245/4.0L	SEFI	9.0	160	3.73	Explorer

1994 and 1995 Ford Police Drivetrains

Layout	cid/liter	carb	comp	hp	axle	model
V-6	232/3.8L	SEFI	9.0	160	3.37	Taurus L
V-6	245/4.0L	SEFI	9.0	160	3.73	Explorer
V-8	281/4.6L-SOHC	SEFI	9.0	210	.27	Crown Vic

1996 Ford Police Drivetrains

Layout	cid/liter	carb	comp	hp	axle	model
V-8	281/4.6L-SOHC	SEFI	9.0	210	3.27	Crown Vic
V-8	281/4.6L-SOHC	CNG	10.0	178	2.73	Crown Vic NGV
V-6	245/4.0L	SEFI	9.0	160	3.55	Explorer 4x4

1997 Ford Police Drivetrains

Layout	cid/liter	carb	comp	hp	axle	model
V-8	281/4.6L-SOHC	SEFI	9.0	210	3.27	Crown Vic
V-8	281/4.6L-SOHC	CNG	10.0	178	2.73	Crown Vic NGV
V-6	245/4.0L-SOHC	SEFI	9.7	205	3.73	Explorer 4x4
V-8	302/5.0L-OHV	SEFI	9.0	210	3.73	Explorer 4x4
V-8	330/5.4L-SOHC	SEFI	9.0	230	3.31	Expedition 4x2**

**Fleet Special Package, not police nor special service

1992 Michigan State Police Patrol Vehicle Test Results

Make	Chevrolet	Ford	Chevrolet	Chevrolet	Chevrolet	Ford
Model	Caprice	Crown Vic	Caprice	Caprice	Lumina	Taurus
Engine, L & carb	5.7, tbi	4.6, pfi	5.0, tbi	5.0, tbi	3.1, pfi	3.8, pfi
HP, SAE	205	210	170	170	140	155
Axle ratio	3.42	3.27	3.08	2.56	3.33	3.37
Weight, test, lb	4,444	4,032	4,121	4,121	3,263	3,339
Wheelbase, in	115.9	114.4	115.9	115.9	107.5	106.0
Road course						
lap time, sec	86.40	87.63	89.23	na	91.78	87.11
0–100 mph, sec	25.87	28.58	35.53	36.40	41.87	30.29
Top speed, mph	133.0	124.1	114.0	128.1	111.0	128.0
1/4-mile ET, sec	16.89	17.48	18.44	18.43	18.67	17.66
1/4-mile speed, mph	82.9	81.3	75.4	76.7	74.1	78.8
Braking, ft/sec^2	21.38	26.41	na	na	23.10	24.62
EPA city mpg	14.0	18.5	17.4	17.4	18.6	17.1

1992 Michigan State Police Patrol Vehicle Test Results

Make	Chevrolet	Ford	Chevrolet	Ford
Model	Camaro	Mustang	Camaro	Mustang
Engine, L & carb	5.7, pfi	5.0, pfi	5.0, pfi	5.0, pfi
HP, SAE	245	225	230	225
Trans	4-speed auto	4-speed auto	5-speed stick	5-speed stick
Axle ratio	3.23	2.73	3.42	3.08
Weight, test, lb	3,458	3,221	3,390	3,183
Road course				
lap time, sec	80.56	82.54	81.56	82.69
0–100 mph, sec	17.29	21.92	18.40	18.99
Top speed, mph	152.0	136.1	150.0	136.0
1/4-mile ET, sec	15.10	16.25	15.49	15.41
1/4-mile top speed, mph	93.4	88.2	91.8	91.6
Braking, ft/sec^2	26.74	22.45	26.32	na
EPA city mpg	16.8	17.6	16.5	16.7

1993 Michigan State Police Patrol Vehicle Test Results

Make	Chevrolet	Ford	Chevrolet	Chevrolet	Chevrolet	Ford
Model	Caprice	Crown Vic	Caprice	Caprice	Lumina	Taurus
Engine, L & carb	5.7, tbi	4.6, pfi	5.0, tbi	5.0, tbi	3.1, mpfi	3.8, pfi
HP, SAE	205	210	170	170	140	155
Axle ratio	3.42	3.27	3.08	2.56	3.33	3.37
Weight, test, lb	4,141	4,053	4,087	4,131	3,372	3,333
Wheelbase, in	115.9	114.4	115.9	115.9	107.5	106.0
Road course						
lap time, sec	85.87	87.57	88.91	na	89.95	86.86
0–100 mph, sec	25.86	27.91	35.28	41.56	38.23	29.89
Top speed, mph	132.0	123.0	110.1 (L)	121.0	115.0 (L)	123.0
1/4-mile ET, sec	16.75	17.29	18.25	18.70	18.21	17.28
1/4-mile speed, mph	82.9	81.8	76.1	75.1	75.8	80.2
Braking, ft/sec^2	27.69	27.21	na	na	24.16	25.08
EPA city mpg	14.0	16.7	17.4	17.3	18.6	18.8

1993 Michigan State Police Patrol Vehicle Test Results

Make	Chevrolet	Ford	Chevrolet	Ford
Model	Camaro	Mustang	Camaro	Mustang
Engine, ci & carb	350, pfi	302, pfi	350, pfi	302, pfi
HP, SAE	275	205	275	205
Axle ratio	3.23	2.73	3.23	3.08
Trans	4-speed auto	4-speed auto	6-speed stick	5-speed stick
Weight, test, lb	3,475	3,243	3,461	3,164
Wheelbase, in	101.1	100.5	101.1	100.5
Road course				
lap time, sec	79.52	83.39	80.12	82.28
0–100 mph, sec	15.82	22.34	16.12	18.45
Top speed, mph	154.0	135.1	147.1	137.0
1/4-mile ET, sec	14.69	16.24	14.82	15.22
1/4-mile speed, mph	95.8	87.6	95.7	92.4
Braking, ft/sec^2	30.34	23.76	na	na
EPA city mpg	16.6	17.3	16.7	16.6

1994 Michigan State Police Patrol Vehicle Test Results

Make	Chevrolet	Ford	Chevrolet	Chevrolet	Chevrolet	Ford
Model	Caprice	Crown Vic	Caprice	Camaro	Camaro	Taurus
Engine, ci & carb	350, pfi	281, pfi	265, pfi	350, tpi	350, tpi	232, pfi
HP, SAE	260	210	200	275	275	160
Trans	4-speed AOD	4-speed AOD	4-speed AOD	4-speed AOD	6-speed man	4-speed AOD
Axle ratio	3.08	3.27	3.23	3.23	3.42	3.37
Weight, test, lb	4,244	3,997	4,178	3,463	3,463	3,348
Wheelbase, in	115.9	114.4	115.9	101.0	101.0	106.0
Road course						
lap time, sec	83.80	85.79	86.76	79.38	79.95	86.69
0–100 mph, sec	21.642	6.32	30.18	17.37	17.00	31.82
Top speed, mph	141.2	128.2	122.1	152.8	153.5	129.0

Make	Chevrolet	Ford	Chevrolet	Chevrolet	Chevrolet	Ford
1/4-mile ET, sec	16.18	17.25	18.11	15.02	15.53	17.81
Braking, ft/sec^2	25.98	27.27	27.03	29.75	na	26.07
EPA city mpg	16.7	16.7	17.6	16.6	16.8	18.8

1994 and 1996 Michigan State Police Patrol Vehicle Test Results—4x4 Sport/Ute

Make	Ford			Make	Jeep	
Model	Explorer 4x4			Model	Cherokee 4x4	
Engine, ci & carb	245, pfi			Engine, ci & carb	242, pfi	
HP, SAE	160			HP, SAE	190	
Trans	4-speed AOT			Trans	4-speed AOT	
Axle	3.73			Axle	3.55	
Weight, lb	4,306			Weight, lb	3,554	
Wheelbase, in	111.9			Wheelbase, in	101.4	
Year	**1994**	**1996**		Year	**1994**	**1996**
Road course, sec	92.16	91.28		Road course, sec	86.26	86.35
0–100 mph, sec	44.28	49.23		0–100 mph, sec	34.99	35.84
Top speed, mph	110	106		Top speed, mph	114	112
1/4-mile ET, sec	18.36	18.64		1/4-mile ET, sec	17.67	17.78
Braking, sec	24.68	25.17		Braking, sec	26.97	25.97
EPA city mpg	15.3	14.9		EPA city mpg	14.8	15.0

1995 Michigan State Police Patrol Vehicle Test Results

Make	Chevrolet	Ford	Chevrolet	Chevrolet	Chevrolet	Ford	Chevrolet
Model	Caprice	Crown Vic	Caprice	Camaro	Camaro	Taurus	Lumina
Engine, ci & carb	350, pfi	281, pfi	265, pfi	350, tpi	350, tpi	232, pfi	191, pfi
HP SAE	260	210	200	275	275	160	160
Trans	4-speed AOD	4-speed AOD	4-speed AOD	4-speed AOD	6-speed man	4-speed AOD	4-speed AOD
Axle ratio	3.08	3.27	3.23	3.23	3.42	3.37	3.33
Weight, test, lb	4,248	4,005	4,201	3,468	3,445	3,340	3,415
Wheelbase, in	115.9	114.4	115.9	101.0	101.0	106.0	107.5
Road course lap time, sec	83.07	85.14	86.31	79.20	80.19	87.08	88.30
0–100 mph, sec	22.43	26.71	33.121	6.48	16.463	3.58	34.04
Top speed, mph	135	132	120 (L)	155	152	128	118
1/4-mile ET, sec	16.29	17.32	18.46	14.95	15.11	18.15	18.24
1/4-mile speed, mph	86.8	82.6	79.4	95.18	95.80	77.9	77.8
Braking ft/sec^2	28.4	26.5	28.4	29.6	na	26.4	24.4
EPA city mpg	16.7	16.7	17.6	16.6	16.8	18.8	18.7

1996 Michigan State Police Patrol Vehicle Test Results

Make	Chevrolet	Ford	Chevrolet	Volvo	Chevrolet	Chevrolet	Chevrolet
Model	Caprice	CrownVic	Caprice	850-T	Lumina	Camaro	Camaro
Engine, ci & carb	350, pfi	281, pfi	265 pfi	142, turbo	191, pfi	350, tpi	350, tpi
HP, SAE	260	210	200	222	160	285	285
Trans	4-speed AOD	4-speed AOD	4-speed AOD	4-speed AOD	4-speed AOD	4-speed AOD	6-speed man
Axle ratio	3.08	3.27	3.23	na	3.33	3.23	3.42
Weight, test, lb	4,249	3,974	4,180	3,399	3,426	3,480	3,457
Wheelbase, in	115.9	114.4	115.9	104.9	107.5	101.0	101.0
Road course lap time, sec	83.35	84.79	87.20	84.97	88.03	79.21	80.57
0–100 mph, sec	21.47	25.18	32.00	24.14	32.19	16.65	15.99
Top speed, mph	139	135	120	126	122	159	157
1/4-mile ET, sec	16.14	16.89	18.05	16.65	17.90	14.98	14.99
1/4-mile speed, mph	88.0	83.8	80.2	86.1	79.37	94.9	96.
Braking, ft/sec^2	29.10	29.02	28.41	26.90	25.03	28.10	na
EPA city mpg	16.8	16.7	18.0	19.1	18.7	17.0	16.4

1997 and Prototype Michigan State Police Patrol Vehicle Test Results—Sport/Utes

Make	Jeep	Jeep*	Jeep	Chevy	Ford*	Ford	Ford
Model	Cherokee	Gr. Cherokee	Cherokee	Tahoe	Expedition	Explorer	Explorer
Drive	4x2	4x2	4x4	4x2	4x2	4x4	4x4
Engine, L & carb	4.0, I-6	5.2, V-8	4.0, I-6	5.7, V-8	5.4, V-8	5.0, V-8	4.0, V-6
HP, SAE	190	220	190	255	230	210	205
Trans	4-speed	4-speed	4-speed	4-speed	4-speed	4-speed	5-speed
Axle	3.55	3.55	3.55	4.10	3.31	3.73	3.55
Wheelbase, in	101.4	104.0	101.4	117.5	119.0	111.5	111.5
Road course, sec	84.84	85.55	85.95	86.25	88.19	89.35	89.46
0–100 mph, sec	31.37	26.52	35.53	28.90	37.56	43.13	30.15
Top speed, mph	111	120	111	121	107	113	106
1/4-mile ET, sec	17.31	na	17.53	17.20	na	18.02	17.23
1/4-mile speed, mph	79.7	na	78.2	81.5	na	77.8	82.0
Braking, ft/sec^2	27.21	na	26.02	23.99	na	25.63	24.23
EPA city mpg	15.5	na	14.9	13.5	na	13.5	15.1

*prototype or retail but not police nor special service package

1997 Michigan State Police Patrol Vehicle Test Results—Sedans

Make	Ford	Ford	Chevy	Volvo	Chevy	Chevy
Model	Crown Vic	Crown NGV	Lumina	850 Turbo	Camaro	Camaro
Engine, L & carb	4.6, SOHC	4.6, CNG	3.1, V-6	2.3, DOHC	5.7, LT1	5.7, LT1
HP, SAE	210	178	160	222	285	285
Axle	3.27	2.73	3.33	2.54	3.23	3.42
Weight, lb	3,986	3,278	3,442	3,232	3,488	3,475
Wheelbase, in	114.4	114.4	107.5	104.9	101.1	101.1
Road course, sec	85.97	89.44	90.06	83.41	79.75	80.36
0–100 mph, sec	28.99	37.70	36.11	20.64	16.21	16.33
Top speed, mph	129	107	113	145	156	157
1/4-mile ET, sec	17.63	19.18	18.16	16.18	14.87	15.07
1/4-mile speed, mph	80.00	76.58	77.65	88.88	95.88	95.90
Braking, ft/sec^2	28.42	25.45	24.96	27.26	28.18	28.18
EPA city mpg	16.2	17.3	19.6	19.2	17.0	16.4

4.6L SOHC V-8 Crown Vic Performance Summary

Year	1992	1993	1994	1995	1996	1997	Average
0–100 mph, sec	28.58	27.91	26.32	26.71	25.18	28.99	27.28
Top speed, mph	124.1	123.0	128.2	132.0	135.0	129.0	128.6
1/4-mile ET, sec	17.48	17.29	17.25	17.32	16.89	17.63	17.31
1/4-mile speed, mph	81.3	81.8	83.9	82.6	83.8	80.0	82.2
MIS road course, sec	87.63	87.57	85.79	85.14	84.79	85.97	86.15

Chapter Fifteen

Severe Service Package Mustang
by Matt Campbell

The target speed window on the MPH S-80 radar unit flashes "77" as Missouri State Highway Patrol Sergeant Larry L. Varner hits his left turn signal and begins his descent into the deep, grassy median dividing the eastbound and westbound sides of Interstate 70 just outside of Boonville, Missouri. In a few seconds, Varner's 1990 Special Service Mustang is climbing the incline on the opposite side of the median. Varner lets out the clutch and hits the gas, and in an instant, the rear end of the Mustang snaps around to face the rapidly disappearing taillights of the offending motorist. With a slight squeal of the tires, the car lurches forward. In about 15 seconds, the Mustang is approaching 100 miles

per hour and the motorist is already pulling over to the shoulder. Varner hits the overhead lights and pulls in behind the car on the shoulder.

The entire episode took just over a minute and the offending motorist was stopped in less than 2 miles. That distance would have been greatly increased were it not for the nimble agility and rapid acceleration of one of the most well-known Ford police vehicles of all time, the Special Service Mustang.

The Special Service Mustang was produced by the Ford Motor Company for 11 years: 1982 through 1993. By its final year, the Special Service Mustang was in use by hundreds of police and sheriff's departments as well

The Severe Service package Mustang was adopted by the CHP in 1982. This is the Ford that chased Porsches for a living. *Jim Dingell*

The 1982 police Mustang, like this CHP pursuit, was powered by a 157-horsepower, 5.0L HO 2-bbl engine. It got a 4-bbl in 1983. The 2-bbl Mustang reached 126 miles per hour. *Jim Dingell*

If there were one reason for the existence of the Special Service Mustang, it would be the failure of the 1980 CHP Dodge St. Regis to perform like the CHP Dodges of the past. In 1978, the California Highway Patrol initiated a plan to examine the feasibility of a police fleet being divided into vehicles purchased for specific purposes. As federal emissions standards and, even more so, California emission standards began to affect the performance of vehicles being produced in Detroit, the CHP realized that an alternative to the rapidly declining performance of police vehicles must be found.

The CHP chose four vehicles to be a part of their Special Purpose Vehicle Study: the 302-ci Ford Fairmont classified as a compact sedan, the 318-ci Plymouth Volare classified as a station wagon, the 305-ci Chevy Malibu classified as a compact sedan, and the 350-ci Chevy Camaro classified as a sport coupe.

New for 1986 police Mustangs was multiport fuel injection. This system on the 200-horsepower 5.0L HO V-8 replaced both central fuel injection and 4-bbl carb versions.

as federal agencies all over the United States. Even in 1997, Mustangs are still in service with agencies like the California Highway Patrol and Michigan State Police. The cars still turn heads and gather crowds. Many agencies have retired the cars from active road patrol duties but still retain the cars for use in public relations and recruiting duties.

As the CHP test progressed, the patrol car situation in the United States became more bleak. In 1980, only three cars met the California Air Resources Board (CARB) emission standards for squad cars. In 1981, not a single American squad car had a top speed of over 120 miles per hour.

For their part, the Camaros suffered repeated engine problems, usually due to piston failures. They had an

A 1987 Special Service Mustang exactly as it was used by the Texas Highway Patrol. For 1987 dual composite headlights replaced the quad light front end. *Robert Booth*

The 1982 Mustang featured a new look with a new grille and a large hood scoop. The car was also equipped with a new engine: a 302-ci HO, 2-bbl V-8 rated at 157 horsepower. The vehicle was tested by the Michigan State Police in its annual vehicle tests at the request of Ford. The car was tested with a full load of CHP equipment already installed. The Mustang recorded a 0 to 60 time of 8.35 seconds, completed the quarter-mile in 15.96 seconds, and reached a top speed of 126.4 miles per hour.

In 1983, 10 more states added the Mustang to their fleets as traffic enforcement pursuit cars. The Mustang's engine was upgraded to a 4-bbl carb, which increased the power rating to 175 horsepower. The Mustang also received a new front end with a more rounded look. Gone was the large hood scoop. The Mustang's 0 to 60-miles-per-hour time improved to 8.32 seconds. More

The Special Service Mustang was so fast in comparison to the cars of the 1980s that special training was required for all cops who drove them. The Hall County, Georgia, Sheriff's STEP team is shown at Road Atlanta. *Dave Moon*

The Hall County, Georgia, Sheriff's deputies assigned to Special Traffic Enforcement Patrol, like all officers driving the powerful 5.0L HO Mustang, got training on wet and dry skid pads. *Dave Moon*

unusually high operating cost and downtime compared to other test vehicles and the St. Regis, which was used as a baseline for the study. In spite of this, the CHP approved the overall concept of a sport coupe for use as a special, single-purpose, traffic-enforcement vehicle.

In order to be considered for bid and purchase by the CHP in 1982, a pursuit vehicle had to attain 60 miles per hour in a maximum of 10 seconds and had to attain a minimum top speed of 120 miles per hour. Two vehicles met these requirements, the 1982 350-ci Chevy Camaro Z28 and the 1982 Severe Service 302-ci Mustang GL. Considering the Camaro's terrible mechanical history during the 18-month study and the fact that Chevy's bid price for the Camaro was $11,445 versus Ford's $6,868 per car, the CHP purchased 406 of the Mustangs. A new era in law enforcement vehicle history began.

important, the Mustang attained a top speed of 132 miles per hour, the first time in five years that a police vehicle had recorded a top speed of over 130 miles per hour. The last car to attain that speed was the 1978 440-ci Plymouth Fury.

By 1984, the Special Service Mustang had begun to achieve the recognition and respect from law enforcement only garnered previously by the likes of the 440-ci Dodges. For 1984, although the Mustang did not change much externally, the car received two major internal changes. The 1984 Special Service Mustang was offered in either a four-speed automatic with overdrive or a five-speed stick. All previous Special Service Mustangs had been equipped with four-speed sticks only.

Another major change for the 1984 Special Service Mustang was the availability of either a 205-horsepower, 302-ci HO 4-bbl V-8 or a 165-horsepower, 302-ci central

Here are two Missouri State Highway Patrol Mustangs, one unmarked and one fully marked. The 5.0L HO Mustang is the most specialized car to ever wear a lightbar. *Matt Campbell*

fuel-injected V-8. The fuel-injected version of the Mustang recorded a 0 to 60-miles-per-hour time of 9 seconds flat, while the carbureted version traversed 0 to 60 miles per hour in 7.43 seconds. Less than a second separated the two versions on the quarter-mile, with the carbureted version still holding the edge at 15.9 seconds compared to the fuel-injected version's 16.88 seconds. Top end, however, varied greatly. The fuel-injected version only reached 118.3 miles per hour compared to the carbureted version which, once again, reached 130 miles per hour. According to Ford, the 1984 Mustang police car was now in use by 15 states. Ford touted the success of the Mustang with an advertising campaign, one ad from which appeared in the September 1984 issue of *Motor Trend* magazine.

In 1985, the Special Service Mustang came in two configurations: a 180-horsepower central fuel-injected 302-ci V-8 with a four-speed auto or a 210 horsepower 302-ci 4-bbl V-8 with a five-speed stick. Performance changed only slightly from 1984 except for one category. Times for 0 to 60 miles per hour remained close with the fuel-injected version recording a time of 9.13 seconds and the carbureted version covering the distance in 7.92 seconds. In the quarter-mile, the carbureted version once again beat out the injected version by a second with times of 16.0 seconds and 17.13 seconds, respectively.

The difference came in the top end category. The fuel-injected version reached 122.8 miles per hour, a slight improvement over the 1984 speed. The carbureted version, however, reached 135.5 miles per hour, improving by more than 5 miles per hour. This top speed of 135 miles per hour was not topped by any Ford police sedan until 1995, ten years later, when the 1995 Ford Crown Victoria attained 135 miles per hour.

Herein lies one of the reasons for the discontinuation of the Special Service Mustang. As performance of the standard-duty police vehicle has continued to improve over time, the necessity of a specific purpose police vehicle has virtually disappeared. One will note that the purpose of the CHP Special Purpose Vehicle Study was to examine the possibility of utilizing certain vehicles for specific purposes because of the lack of one police vehicle that could do it all. With the appearance of the 4.6L modular V-8 in the Crown Victoria in 1992, and the appearance of Chevrolet's 5.7L LT1-equipped Caprice in 1994, the standard full-size patrol car was now attaining speed and performance which paralleled that of the limited use traffic enforcement pursuit vehicle. With the ability to carry much more equipment and transport prisoners while still maintaining performance similar to that of the pursuit vehicles, the full-size squads had become the only logical choice.

For two reasons 1986 was a very big year for the Special Service Mustang. The first big change for 1986 was that Ford introduced the new 200-horsepower multiport, fuel-injected, 302-ci V-8. This engine replaced both the carbureted and central fuel-injected versions of the 302-ci. The police car was now available with either a five-speed stick or a four-speed automatic. The MSP performance times for the 1986 Mustang are basically standards that the car maintained with little derivation until its final year of production in 1993. The auto reached 0 to 60 miles per hour in 7.59 seconds while the stick reached 60 miles per hour in 7.3 seconds. In the quarter-mile, the Mustangs completed the distance in 15.8 seconds for the auto and 15.5 seconds for the stick. Top end was 126.1 miles per hour for the auto and 137.2 miles per hour for the stick.

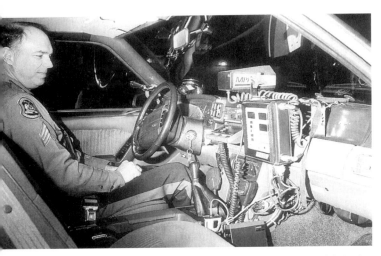

MSHP Sgt. Larry Varner is shown inside his 1990 Special Service Mustang. Note the lack of an armrest. *Matt Campbell*

The second big change was 1986 became the first year for many major equipment additions specific to the Special Service package. Through the 1985 model year, the Special Service Mustang varied little from the standard production civilian version. Before 1986 most

Special Service package equipment additions were related to durability and convenience. These included a relocated decklid release to the driver's side of the dash from the inside of the glovebox, 14x6 inch, then in 1985, 15x7-inch heavy-duty steel wheels with plain or dog-dish center caps, a full-size spare tire, performance tires, and 140-miles-per-hour certified calibration speedometer. Essentially, these were the only additions to a standard production Mustang for the Special Service package.

By 1986, the reputation of the Mustang had cemented itself among the law enforcement community. States such as Texas, Florida, Georgia, and Oregon added large orders in the hundreds for Mustangs. The CHP, of course, continued to utilize the car with orders reaching into the 600 range. The General Services Administration of the federal government also began ordering the car for agencies such as the DEA and the FBI.

The majority of special equipment manufactured and added specifically to the Special Service Mustang began in 1986. In addition to the standard convenience and durability items listed above, which were already part of the Special Service Package, many new items were now included and essentially constituted the Special Service Package from 1986 until the final year of Special

MSHP Trooper Brian Berry is shown inside his 1993 Mustang. Yep, that is a real speeding ticket he is writing. Note that this is a four-speed auto car. Most had five-speed sticks. *Matt Campbell*

Service Production in 1993. These items for the Special Service package included: silicone-impregnated radiator hoses with "aircraft-style" hose clamps, an engine oil cooler, an external automatic transmission cooler, a heater hose inlet restrictor, VASCAR two-piece speedometer cables, radio noise suppression package, 135-amp Lestek alternator with an external transistorized voltage regulator (this was replaced for the 1992 and 1993 model years with a 130-amp Motorcraft internally regulated alternator), the availability of door bodyside molding and pinstripe deletion to facilitate the application of the special paint and markings of a police car, a recalibrated cooling fan clutch, 140 miles per hour, and, from 1990 to 1993, a 160-miles-per-hour certified calibration speedometer, inoperative door courtesy lamp switches, single key locking system, heavy-duty low-back front bucket seats, underhood sound insulation deleted, and a reinforced floor pan.

Although some of these parts were carried over from Ford's other police package vehicles, many were designed specifically for the Mustang. This was an indication of the huge increase in interest in the car by the law enforcement community.

For 1987, the multiport fuel-injected 302-ci V-8 Mustang's power rating was increased to 225 horsepower. The 1987 Mustang also featured new front and rear ends. Gone were the four-beam headlights, replaced with a pair of new composite headlights. The performance stayed essentially the same from 1986 until its demise in 1993. Acceleration from 0 to 60 miles per hour was 7.64 seconds for the five-speed stick and 8.16 seconds for the four-speed automatic. The quarter-mile times were 16 seconds flat for the five-speed stick and 16.33 seconds for the automatic. Top end speeds for the

two versions were slightly higher than 1986. The four-speed automatic with a 2.73 rear-end gear reached 139.1 miles per hour and the five-speed stick equipped with a 3.08 rear-end gear reached 139.6 miles per hour. This set an all-time, top speed record for any Ford-made police or Special Service package car that still stands as of the 1997 model police cars.

For 1988, the Mustang remained unchanged from 1987. The Mustang recorded 0-to-60-miles-per-hour times of 7.99 seconds and 6.9 seconds for the automatic and five-speed, respectively. In the quarter-mile the times were 16.16 seconds and 15.48 seconds for the auto and stick, respectively. The top end dropped slightly with the auto and stick recording speeds of 135 miles per hour and 134 miles per hour, respectively.

In 1989, the Mustang again remained essentially the same. Acceleration to 60 miles per hour was 8.6 seconds for the auto and 7.04 seconds for the stick. The quarter-mile time was only recorded for the auto at 16.59 seconds. Top speeds increased slightly to 137.1 miles per hour for the auto and 138 miles per hour for the stick.

The 1990 model year featured two minor interior changes to the Mustang. In order to conform with Corporate Average Fuel Economy (CAFE) standards for 1990, Ford dropped the center console armrest. The reaction from the public at the removal of this Mustang standard was so strong Ford had put the armrest back into production before the end of the model year. Unfortunately, most Special Service Mustangs were built early in the model year and do not have the armrest (see photo of Missouri State Highway Patrol Sergeant Larry L. Varner inside his 1990 Special Service Mustang). Also in 1990, Ford added shoulder seatbelts to the two rear seat positions.

The Michigan State Police used the 1993 Mustang for traffic enforcement. It has the same acceleration and top speed as big-block pursuit cars of old, yet handles much better. *Matt Campbell*

A 1993 Missouri State Highway Patrol Mustang. This was the last year the Special Service package was produced.

From 1987 through 1989, the Special Service Mustang's 10-hole aluminum alloy wheels came standard from Ford with a black powder finish. Only the small 5-inch wide center caps were unpainted, creating an unmistakable "cop" look. Departments could order the cars with all-silver wheels but had to do so with a special order. In 1990, Ford made it a standard option to have the wheels all silver, the blacked-out wheels were no longer offered. Mustang MSP test result scores continued to remain essentially unchanged. Times for 0 to 60 were 7.97 seconds and 6.64 seconds for the auto and stick. Top speeds were essentially identical at 135.4 for the stick and 136 for the auto.

The Mustang's top speed was the highest speed recorded by the MSP for any vehicle tested in 1990. The Mustang claimed this title every year from its inception in 1982 until 1990 with a gap ranging from a low of 7 miles per hour to a high of 28 miles per hour faster than any other vehicle tested. This, however, would be the last time the Mustang had the highest top speed.

In 1991, with the introduction of the Special Service Camaro, the Mustang no longer cruised the highways of America as the lone specially prepared police pursuit vehicle. For 1991, all retail 5.0L Mustangs received new 5-spoke aluminum alloy wheels. In order to maintain the business-like appearance of the Mustang, Ford chose to continue using the 10-hole aluminum alloy wheels that had been standard on all 5.0L Mustang LXs since 1987. The Special Service Mustang was the only Mustang produced by Ford from 1991 to 1993 to come with these wheels.

The Mustang's 0-to-60-miles-per-hour times again remained constant with the five-speed stick reaching the mark in 6.72 seconds and the four-speed auto hitting the mark at 8.41 seconds. The quarter-mile times were 16.54 seconds and 15.33 seconds for the auto and stick, respectively, and the top speeds were 136.1 miles per hour and 135.5 miles per hour. In comparison, the Camaro's 0-to-60-miles-per-hour time was 6.51 seconds, the quarter-mile time was 15.05 seconds and top speed was a remarkable 150 miles per hour. Although the Camaro continues through 1997 to record remarkable performance times and speeds, the police Camaro never came close to being a real competitor to the police Mustang. In 1992, production of the Special Service package Camaro was just under 600 units. The California Highway Patrol order for Mustangs that year alone surpassed the entire production of B4C Camaros. By 1991, the Mustang was used extensively in both the United States and Canada. By most estimates, somewhere between 60 and 70 state, federal, and provincial agencies were using the Mustang. The number of police and sheriff's departments using the cars was well into the hundreds.

In 1992, a small change was made to the Special Service Mustang upper rear control arm bushings. This part was differentiated with a small blue dot painted on the control arm. This marked essentially the only change ever made to a Special Service Mustang engine, transmission, or suspension component as compared to a retail 5.0L Mustang. The fact that most of the Special Service Mustang was identical to its assembly-line civilian brother says mountains about the strength and reliability of the Mustang. For 1992, the Mustang recorded 0-to-60-miles-per-hour times of 8.08 seconds for the auto and 6.78 seconds for the stick. The quarter-mile times were 16.25 seconds and 15.41 seconds and top speeds were 136 miles per hour and 136.1 miles per hour, respectively.

The final year of production for the Special Service Mustang was 1993. This was also the final year of the third-generation Mustang design that was replaced with a radically re-designed pony for 1994. For the first time in 1993, Special Service Mustang came standard with Eagle GT+4 tires instead of the Eagle Gatorbacks that had been standard for many years. The Mustang's horsepower rating was also dropped from 225 horsepower to 205 horsepower, which was actually more a result of a change in the testing procedure than a change in the drivetrain. The 1993 was a virtual carryover from 1992. For 1993, the Mustang recorded 0 to 60-miles-per-hour in 7.98 seconds for the auto and 6.59 seconds for the stick. Once again, the times were nearly unchanged from 1986. In the quarter-mile, the auto crossed the finish line in 16.24 seconds and the stick in 15.22 seconds. Top end was once again nearly even at 135.1 miles per hour for the auto and 137 miles per hour for the stick. Although production of the Special Service Mustang ceased in August 1993, there are still many police Mustangs in use on U.S. highways in mid-1997.

One misconception by many people is that the Special Service Mustang comes with special engines, rear disc brakes, specially calibrated performance chips, special suspensions, and so on. One of the most remarkable things about the Special Service Mustang is its similarity to the civilian version of the car. They are more alike than they are different. This is made even more evident by the fact that many 1994 and newer retail Mustangs have made their way into law enforcement fleets around the country. A recent news program featured a video of an unmarked 1994 Mustang stopping a motorist in Louisiana. Similar 1994 and newer Mustangs have been spotted in South Carolina and California. Without question these are nothing more than standard Mustangs placed into law enforcement duty. It is not surprising to see Mustangs making it into service once again.

Even during the time Ford produced the Special Service package Mustang, many departments placed standard issue Mustangs or Mustang GTs into service. It must be stressed that simply because a department places a vehicle into service and puts police markings on it, that does not make it a police package car. The Wayne County, Michigan, Sheriff's Department, which does quite a bit of vehicle testing for Ford, had two 1993 retail Mustang LX sedans in police service. These fully marked Mustangs had been "enhanced" by Ford for testing purposes. They were powered by the dual-overhead-cam 32-valve V-8, which eventually was put into the 1996 Mustang Cobra. Although this was a police car built by Ford, it was not a true police package car.

Although the Special Service Mustang is no longer being produced, it has left an indelible mark on the police car market and will continue to do so for many years to come. It single-handedly forged a totally new class of police car. The 1982 to 1993 Severe Service and Special Service package Mustang will forever be the baseline against that which all police pursuit cars in the future will be compared.

Chapter Sixteen

Experiences of the Washington State Patrol
by Bill Hattersley

The Washington State Patrol (WSP) was established in 1921. The department consisted of six troopers, each equipped with a new Indian motorcycle. In 1921, motorcycles made a lot of sense as patrol vehicles. Most roads were dirt or gravel, garages widely scattered, and car tires of the time were very fragile. As the size of the patrol grew, Harley-Davidson cycles replaced the Indian.

In about 1933, the decision was made to convert the patrol vehicles from cycles to panel trucks. Besides trooper safety and comfort, the trucks could carry more equipment, and could even transport accident victims to the hospital in rural areas. Also, two-way radios started to become more practical. Radios of that period were bulky and heavy and had antennas that ran horizontally around the rooftop. The patrol bought Ford half-ton panels, powered by the standard 85-horsepower flathead V-8, weighing about 3,200 pounds. Ford was the obvious choice as it had the only V-8 engine available in a light truck. The early trucks were painted two-tone silver and black.

In 1938, Ford introduced the passenger car-based sedan delivery. Smaller and lighter than the earlier panel trucks, the sedan deliverys also cornered better due to a much lower center of gravity. In 1939, Ford coupes were bought for the Safety Education Division. During the war, the WSP got their money's worth from the Fords. One trooper in Ellensburg reported getting an incredible 450,000 miles out of his 1941 Ford, albeit with at least one engine rebuild. Sergeants and captains of the period used a variety of coupes and two-door sedans, including 1940 Buicks, 1942 Dodges, and various years of Ford and Mercury.

The Ford sedan-delivery body style continued to serve faithfully through the late 1940s. More compact radios and other equipment, along with increasing emphasis on speed enforcement prompted a gradual switch to four-door sedans. Troopers on the high mountain passes continued to use the wagons until the late 1950s.

In 1949, with the first general issue of sedans, Ford was still the obvious choice. It was the only car in the "Low-Priced Three" that offered a V-8 engine. The WSP Fords were powered by 100-horsepower, 239-ci flathead. In 1951, police cars were available with the 112-horsepower Mercury 255-ci engine. For some reason, the WSP also experimented with some six-cylinder Ford coupes in 1951. Reliable, they were. Fast, they weren't! In the early 1950s, patrol cars had black trunks, roofs, and hoods with the sides painted white. A red spotlight and under-hood siren were the only warning equipment.

In 1952, Ford went to a new, tighter body and the WSP slightly modified their paint scheme with a scallop of paint at the forward end of the front fenders. The 1952 and 1953 patrol cars continued to be powered by

From 1933 to 1938, WSP troopers patrolled in Ford half-ton panel trucks like this 1937 model. It was powered by an 85-horsepower flat-head V-8. *WSP*

From 1938 to 1949, WSP troopers used Ford's passenger-car-based sedan delivery like this restored 1940 Ford. *Bill Hattersley*

the Mercury 255-ci flathead V-8, now bumped up to 125 horsepower. Six of the 1953 Fords were ordered with two-speed Fordomatic transmissions as an experiment. Along with the Fords, a few 1953 Chevys were bought with manual transmissions. As with the 1951 Ford six-cylinder coupes, the Chevy six-cylinder engines were underpowered for pursuit work. Sergeants were now driving 1952 Mercurys. The 1954 Ford was the first Ford to ever come with an overhead-valve V-8 engine. As before, the Mercury engine was again available as a "Police Only" option. The new 256-ci engine was nearly the same displacement as the old 255-ci Mercury flathead, but the power was now up to 160 horsepower. As one central Washington trooper put it, "That car would go faster than I wanted to drive it." With a ball-joint front end, 1954 Fords had a reputation for excellent handling. The black-and-white 1951 to 1954 Fords were affectionately referred to as Holsteins, for obvious reasons!

Starting in 1955, the WSP started the practice of buying more than one make of car each year. This may have been to make it harder for speeders to spot the patrol cars. Also in 1955, the color scheme for patrol cars was changed. Now cars were painted a solid blue, which varied in shade by year and make of car. Some cars had white front doors; others had the door badge with a white lightning bolt on a blue door. During this period, cars were still equipped with three-speed sticks. A few cars each year were ordered with the Warner gear three-speed with overdrive. The overdrive cars had faster acceleration due to a lower rear end ratio, which was 3.78, 3.89, or 3.92 to 1.

The overdrive cars were a little trickier to drive due to overdrives free-wheeling at speeds under 28 miles per hour and were issued to troopers who earned top scores in academy driver training courses. Cars delivered in 1955 were a mixture of light blue Fords powered by 292-ci engines with 188 horsepower, together with all-new medium blue-gray Chevys powered by the hot new 265-ci

The other Ford police car used by the WSP in 1951 was this two-door sedan powered by a 95-horsepower 226-ci Six. It was slow. *WSP*

V-8. Emergency warning equipment was still limited to a red spotlight and underhood siren and a heater was the only factory option. A few 1955 Plymouth sedans were also tried out, the first Mopars bought by the WSP since the 1942 Dodge coupe sergeant's cars. As Plymouth had no police package yet, the 1955s did not handle as well as the Fords.

For 1956, the WSP again bought a mix of Fords and Chevys. This time, there were more Chevys ordered. Only three had overdrive. Two body styles of 1956 Fords were delivered. Most were four-door sedans, while others were the last sedan deliveries bought by the WSP. Called "Couriers" by Ford, the wagons were used until about 1960 to patrol the high mountain pass highways. All of the 1956 Fords were powered by the Thunderbird 312-ci V-8. One trooper assigned to Stevens Pass recalled how the patrol-issue, walnut-shell-impregnated snow tires would start shedding their walnut shells at about 100 miles per hour. Captains in 1956 were issued Pontiac sedans.

A major equipment change took place for 1957. According to most sources, automatic transmissions became standard issue for the WSP. Again in 1957, a mix of cars was purchased. Reportedly, most of the cars were Fords, powered by 245-horsepower 312-ci V-8s, with two-speed Fordomatic automatic transmissions. About six of the 1957 Fords were painted white and carried small beacon-ray roof lights. Called the "gray ghosts," the white cars were tried out in patrol use all over the state. Along with the 312-ci Fords, a smaller number of Chevy 150 sedans with the 283-ci V-8 and two-speed

A 1954 WSP Ford. With the new 256-ci overhead-valve Mercury V-8, this cruiser would go faster than some troopers wanted to drive it. *WSP*

This 1957 WSP Ford is powered by the 245-horsepower 312-ci V-8 and has an unusual option for that era of police car: the two-speed Fordomatic automatic transmission. *WSP*

This 1963 WSP Ford has a 330-horsepower, 390-ci FE-block V-8. This was one of Ford's most popular and durable police engines. *WSP*

Powerglide were used. Reportedly, a handful of 1957 Plymouth patrol cars were also used.

Again in 1958, a mix of cars was purchased. Most of the new cars were Ford sedans powered by the brand-new "FE" block 300 horsepower 352-ci V-8. The new Cruise-O-Matic three-speed automatic was much more flexible than the older two-speed automatics. A smaller number of 1958 Plymouths were also delivered. A small number of 1958 Pontiacs were bought for issue to captains. The 1959 bid was split between equal numbers of Ford Custom 300s and Plymouth Savoys. The Plymouths were powered by a potent combination of the 305 horsepower 361-ci V-8, with the brand-new three-speed TorqueFlite automatic. The 1959 Fords used the carryover 352-ci V-8 with Cruise-O-Matic. One retired trooper reported that his 1959 Ford would top out at about 114 miles per hour. The Plymouths were several miles per hour faster.

In 1960, all three members of the Low Priced Three shared the WSP bid. The newly restyled, wider Ford Fairlanes were equipped identically to the 1958s and 1959s. For the first time, new patrol cars were now equipped with two alternate flashing red lights behind the front grille. The left post mounted spotlight now had a clear bulb in place of the previous red one. Additional 361-ci V-8 powered Plymouths went into service as well. Also purchased in 1960 were a number of 1960 Chevys equipped with the trouble-prone Turboglide automatic. These transmissions were so often broken down that the 1960 Chevys were sold off early. The WSP bought no more Chevy patrol cars until eight years later when the TurboHydraMatic three-speed was available.

Chrysler Corporation won the primary bids for the next two years. The 1961 Savoys with the unusual jet-tube taillights were followed in 1962 by midsize Dodge Darts. Both cars were powered by the strong 361-ci V-8s. Some of the 1962 Dodges were equipped with French

Michelin radial tires as an experiment. Troopers liked the traction in snow and rain, but reported blowouts due to sidewall failure.

Perhaps influenced by the California Highway Patrol as well as several other state police agencies, in 1962 the WSP also purchased at least two models of medium-priced sedans. Reportedly, the patrol bought 10 1962 Chryslers, probably powered by the big-block 413-ci V-8. At the same time, 10 Pontiac Catalinas powered by 389-ci V-8s were also delivered. The larger cars were tried out in patrol detachments all over the state. Apparently, there were no advantages found as purchase of shorter wheelbase, lighter cars continued in 1963. Fords were delivered in 1961 and 1962 as sergeant's cars. Sergeants drove unmarked cars painted a variety of factory colors with only a single spotlight as a giveaway to the sharp-eyed speeders.

Ford was back in 1963 with a large delivery of dark blue Custom 300 sedans. Powered by the 330-horsepower 390-ci V-8, these cars were still a bit slower than the Mopars. More white patrol cars were purchased. These had large red roof–mounted rotators. The white cars were mostly assigned in the Seattle area where traffic was heaviest. The light-colored cars with roof lights were much more visible when blocking traffic at accident scenes.

The split bid of 1964 marked the last time that the WSP would buy two makes of standard patrol car in the same year with the notable exception of 1968. Ford Custom 500s delivered were equipped identically to the 1963 Fords. Also, a smaller number of 1964 Dodge sedans were purchased, powered by 330-horsepower 383-ci V-8s. Again, the Mopars were a little faster than the Fords.

In 1965, Plymouth won the bid with a large number of 383-ci powered Fury I's. As an experiment, some of the 1965s were delivered with Kelsey-Hayes four piston front disc brakes. The disc brake cars impressed troopers with

Due to an error when ordering the 1967 Fords, the WSP units came with the 345-horsepower, Thunderbird 428 V-8 instead of the 360-horsepower Interceptor V-8. Thirty years later these cars are still remembered as being slower than expected. *Trooper Don Ginter*

their fade resistance and lack of brake loss after running through deep puddles. The only drawback on the early four piston cars was occasional piston lockup after a hard series of stops. This was corrected on later cars.

The 1965 model year marked the end of an era for the WSP. Other than the 1962 Chryslers with 413-ci V-8s, all patrol cars from 1958 on had been powered by midsize V-8s ranging in size from 348-ci to 390-ci with horsepower ratings in the 300-horsepower to 330-horsepower range. Now that Chrysler and General Motors offered muscle cars on midsize platforms, the WSP felt the need for more power in its full size sedans. The patrol was about to enter the maximum displacement big-block period.

The high performance period at the WSP started with the purchase of 1966 Ford Custom four-doors powered by the new 360-horsepower 428-ci interceptor engine. These were the fastest cars bought by the WSP up to that time. As the last Ford police engine with solid lifters, they were higher revving than the later 428-ci mills. With the 1966 order, brakes were upgraded to match the higher horsepower. Front disc brakes with power assist were ordered from then on.

For 1967, Ford won the bid again. With the 1967 order, the WSP finally started ordering power steering and six-way power seats were added to the equipment list as well. Through an apparent error in ordering, the 1967 WSP Fords were equipped with the lower performing

345-horsepower Thunderbird 428-ci V-8 instead of the 360 horsepower Interceptor 428-ci V-8. Both were police engines. As a result, the 1967 Fords were quite a bit slower in acceleration than the 1966 360-horsepower Fords. The top speed was also down.

In 1968, the patrol bought its first air-conditioned cars. All cars ordered for the hotter eastern half of the state were 1968 Ford Customs with air conditioning. This time the error in ordering was corrected, and the 1968 Fords came with the 360-horsepower 428-ci V-8. Even with the extra weight and engine drag of the air conditioner, the 1968 cars were noticeably quicker than the 1967 Fords. All this in spite of the fact the 1968 360-horsepower 428-ci V-8 was only available with the tall 2.80 rear end! All three years of 428-ci Fords were tough, strong cars, well liked by troopers, as well as by the mechanics. Strong understeer at lower speeds was the only major complaint.

The other half of the 1968 bid for non-air conditioned western Washington cars was won by Chevy. For the first time, all Washington trooper cars were now painted white and carried a large red rotator on the roof. Sergeants' cars were still unmarked and painted in a variety of colors. The 1968 Chevys powered by the 390-horsepower, 427-ci V-8 and three-speed TurboHydraMatic. If the Fords tended to understeer in low-speed turns, the Chevys wanted to oversteer at higher speeds.

In 1974, the WSP ordered midsize police package cars like this unmarked Montego. Note the roll cage and spotlight. They were powered by the 351-ci Cleveland V-8. *WSP*

Starting in 1969, Mopar won a string of WSP bids with a hard-to-beat combination of hot 440-ci V-8s, tough TorqueFlite transmissions and perhaps most important of all, price bids that beat the competitors by several hundred dollars per car. Plymouth Fury was the chosen patrol car for 1969 and again in 1970. Dodge Polara was the winner in 1971, 1972, and 1973. The Monaco won the order in 1974. All of the 1969 to 1974 Mopars gave good service and were respected by troopers. Brakes were not quite as fade resistant as the 428-ci Fords, maybe because the Mopars were a bit faster.

In mid-1973, as a result of U.S. support for Israel in the Yom Kippur War, the Arab countries cut back on oil production and raised prices sharply. One result of the ensuing oil shortage was political pressure on police agencies, including the WSP, to cut back on fuel usage. One logical effort was to buy smaller, less thirsty patrol cars. So, in 1974, the WSP ordered a number of midsize Ford Torinos and Mercury Montegos along with the larger Monacos. Apparently, someone forgot to read the specification sheets carefully. At about 4,150 pounds, midsize Fords outweighed the full-size Dodges by about 100 pounds. With 351-ci V-8s, the Fords could have had better mileage than the 440-ci Dodges, but not enough

to outweigh trooper complaints of cramped interiors and small trunks. Acceleration and handling were both less than standard cars. For 1975, Ford returned to WSP service with the purchase of Custom 500 sedans. In the era of falling compression ratios and increasing weight, the 4,600-pound Ford was powered by the 460-ci V-8. A 3.00-to-1 axle ratio was standard in an attempt at fuel economy. Typical of Fords, the 1975s displayed strong understeer in tight curves. Similar to Mopars of that era, the Ford power steering was of the one-finger, ultra-low-effort type. A tough car, many of the big Customs held up through years of abuse at pursuit driving school. Service-wise, the big 460-ci engines were a standout as well. Broken valve springs were the only common engine failure. Surprisingly, for such a heavy car, the brakes were strong and resistant to fade.

As the low-performance years continued, with ever more stringent smog controls and reduced compression engines, many state police agencies started buying midsize cars, usually Dodge or Plymouth. So it was a little surprising when the WSP again bought 4,500-pound 1976 Chevy Impalas with 454-ci V-8s. Like the 1975 Fords, these Chevys were just a bit too much car with just a bit too few horsepower, and the handling suffered.

A 1975 WSP Ford Custom 500 complete with single blue rotator and front pusher bars. These four-door sedans were powered by the 460-ci V-8. *WSP*

In 1977, the WSP made another experiment with midsize cars. A large number of Pontiac LeMans with 400-ci engines were purchased for issue as unmarked cars to sergeants. Usually, painted dark metallic green, these cars suffered from the same weight problems as the 1974 Torinos and Montegos. Ironically, the new downsized 1977 Impala was about 400 pounds lighter than the midsize LeMans! The other half of the 1977 purchase was Dodge Royal Monacos with 440-ci V-8s. These would be the last truly large cars bought by the WSP. By this time, it was obvious to just about everyone that the era of the two-and-a-half-ton patrol car was at an end.

For 1978, Ford was the only automaker with a full-size, long wheelbase police car. The WSP bought the midsize 440-ci Plymouth Fury for the line troopers. Unfortunately, Mopar quality was at a low point. Fleet personnel remember the 1978 Furys as the worst built cars ever purchased by the WSP.

Chevy marked 1979 with an all-out assault on the police market. The WSP, along with many other large agencies, bought Impalas. Powered by 165-horsepower 350-ci engines, the 1979s were underpowered. Of course, all the other 1979 patrol cars were similarly handicapped. The Impalas were remembered as nimble handling cars

The WSP was quick to see the advantages of the 5.0L Mustang. They bought 30 of these Special Service cars in 1983, just one year after the package was developed for police. *WSP*

A 1989 WSP 5.0L Mustang fitted with a blue spotlight and an aerodynamic Jetsonic lightbar. These were all five-speed cars. *Bill Hattersley*

In 1988, the WSP used the Crown Vic with the standard door emblem as a general patrol vehicle. They also used this Crown Vic for commercial vehicle traffic enforcement. *Bill Hattersley*

that were comfortable to drive. The pursuit instructors recall them as absolutely unbreakable.

The 1980 model year marked the last Mopar that was popular with the WSP troopers. Dodge won the bid with the four-door 360-ci St. Regis. The St. Regis was remembered as being surprisingly fast, which has a lot to do with their 185-horsepower engines. While the CHP was going through tough times with their 318 ci St. Regis, the WSP found the 360-ci version to be perfectly acceptable.

Probably the most disliked cars in recent memory at the WSP were the 1981 and 1982 Dodge Diplomats. Slow acceleration together with driveability problems were the two most common complaints.

The WSP driving instruction program has steadily advanced since its inception in 1946. Unused sections of Shelton airport were used for many years. Starting in 1956, high-speed pursuit driving was added to the course. Expanded air traffic forced closure to the WSP in 1982, so a dedicated facility was designed, and built on the ground of the WSP Academy near the airport. A 1.1-mile basic course, including a vehicle placement section, was completed in 1982. A 1.6-mile advanced course, designed by head pursuit instructor Don Ginter, was added in 1989. The state-of-the-art road course was designed to include the actual types of curves and reduced visibility situations that most commonly contribute to trooper crashes. Some of the turns start out banked, leading downhill into a reducing radius section transitioning to reversed banking. These are designed to be as difficult as possible to negotiate at speed. Due to the climate, much of the training is conducted during rainy or foggy weather. A full program of night training is also included, as most pursuits take place at night. The driver training course includes 20 hours of classroom instruction and 50 hours of behind-the-wheel training. Over the years that the pursuit driving course has been taught, some vehicles proved to be outstanding at the track. According to Trooper Ginter, the 1975 Ford Custom 500 was one of the best cars to teach in.

Typical of state police agencies in the low-performance years of the late 1970s, the WSP had been having increasing difficulty in catching violators. The 1980 Dodge St. Regis with a 360-ci V-8 had been acceptable, but the 318-ci Diplomats were not fast enough, especially in hilly regions and the wide open stretches found in eastern Washington. Troopers were frustrated with the slow acceleration and poor driveability of the desmogged engines. Taking note of California's experiments with Z-28 Camaros and subsequent quantity purchase of 1982 Mustangs, the patrol took advantage of an opportunity to try out some pursuit-type vehicles.

The Alaska State troopers had purchased three (nonpolice package) 1981 Firebird Trans Am coupes to try out. Assigned to a borough with few paved roads, the low-slung Trans Ams were continually stuck in snow or mud. Only a few months old, the Trans Ams were offered to the WSP. Though not completely satisfactory, the Pontiacs did show that there was merit to the pursuit car concept. This experience led to the WSP use of the Special Service Mustang.

For 1983, no four-door sedans were purchased by the WSP. Instead, 30 Mustang coupes equipped with 302-ci engines and five-speed manual transmissions were acquired. Using some creative reasoning, the state legislature was sold on the Mustangs on the basis of their good gas mileage! Troopers who were issued the Mustangs received special training in pursuit driving with the light manual transmission cars. Fitting of rev limiters restrained the troopers who forgot to upshift at the appropriate moments.

The Fleet Division had a few unsolvable problems with the Mustangs. There was no way to fit a push bar to the unit body. There were no high-speed-rated winter tires available in a size that fit the cars. The dilemma of how to fit a prisoner cage never was satisfactorily solved. A makeshift solution was removal of the right front seat and fitting of a diagonal cage that ran from the right

Like most city, county, state, and federal police departments, the WSP gave the front-drive V-6-powered 1990 Taurus a try. Troopers complained of torque steer and high-speed instability. *WSP*

front A pillar to the left rear C pillar. A fold-down section was provided next to the driver for escape in case the vehicle was rolled over onto the driver's side door. Still, the driver's seat was not a place for troopers who suffered from claustrophobia. A structural problem also showed up soon on cars that were driven by bigger troopers. The floor pans under the driver's seat started cracking. Ford reinforced that area on later model Mustangs.

The WSP bought Mustangs every year from 1983 through 1990, although the number purchased gradually shrank. The later models were almost all painted darker colors, unmarked, and used primarily to catch sharp-eyed truckers who were very good at spotting standard patrol cars. In the final evaluation, it always seemed that the Mustangs were not where the speeders were, and the stronger performance of the late 1980s sedans finally made the little pony cars obsolete. In the early to mid-1980s though, they were the only high-performance car available at a low enough price to be attractive to the WSP and they did their task well. After the disappointing experience with the 1981 and 1982 Dodge Diplomats and the positive results with the 1983 Mustangs, the patrol decided to move a different direction for 1984. Ford introduced a police package on the midsize LTD. Powered by a throttle body injected version

of the Mustang's 302-ci V-8, this looked like the answer to WSP's search for a reasonably high-performance sedan for all around patrol duties.

With an empty weight of around 3,300 pounds and a fairly roomy interior, the LTD promised to be an economical patrol car. Problems began during delivery. A combination of worn wheel dies and flimsy aluminum hubcaps left a trail of discarded hubcaps from the delivering dealer in Spokane to patrol headquarters in Olympia. Ford responded by replacing the errant hubcaps with full wheel covers. The next difficulties appeared soon after the new LTDs went into service with line troopers. Brakes were fading completely and engines were melting pistons. Both problems were showing up during high-speed pursuits and were obvious safety hazards.

The brake problems were puzzling at first. The Mustangs, which shared the LTD's Fox-body platform, had trouble-free brakes. Several factors were found. First, the Mustangs had five-speed manual transmissions that could be downshifted for positive engine braking versus the LTDs automatics. Second, the weight difference turned out to be considerably more than the 400-pounds difference in curb weight. As fully equipped patrol cars, the LTDs carried several hundred pounds of equipment deleted on the pursuit Mustangs. With a top

The WSP bought these 1993 Crown Vics simply because the fuel economy of the 4.6L SOHC V-8 was so much better than the competition. A number of agencies bought Fords for that reason. *Bill Hattersley*

speed over 120 miles per hour and quicker acceleration than the previous Diplomats, the Mustang-size brakes would fade completely after only a few severe applications. There was no practical way to upgrade the brakes and several of the LTDs were totaled in accidents caused by brake failure.

The engine failure problem was harder to figure out. Several LTDs were forced to drop out of high speed pursuits when one or both of the front pistons failed. As it happened, Ford engineers finally concluded that the intake manifold tended to divert most of the air-fuel mixture from the throttle body toward the rear cylinders at full throttle. As the oxygen sensor was located at the rear of the manifold the computer would be fooled into progressively leaning out the mixture. The front cylinders would starve and overheat, and the result was holed pistons. There was no practical correction for this problem. However, it only showed up during long pursuits.

By the time these problems were analyzed, a second batch of 1985 LTDs had already been delivered. Aside from the above problems, the LTDs were reliable cars. Also, the LTDs turned in the best fuel mileage anyone at

the WSP had ever seen from a patrol car. Handling was typical Ford in that understeer was the predominant characteristic.

Due to the problems experienced with the small LTDs, WSP specified full-size patrol cars for 1986. Ford won the bid with the 351-ci Crown Victoria. The 1986s were the last of the standard equipment cars bought by the WSP. Rubber floormats, roll-up windows, manual locks, and dog-dish hubcaps disappeared in 1987. Several reasons combined to favor the upgrading. Rubber floormats had become flimsier. Power windows and locks were felt to be trooper safety items. Hubcaps were just plain ugly. All of the upgrades would result in higher resale values at auction. The 1986 Crown Victorias would prove to be comfortable and durable cars. The one sore point, however, was the lack of acceleration, especially at low speeds. Troopers reported difficulty in safely merging with freeway traffic after making traffic stops.

The 351-ci was well proven, but was handicapped by gearing and induction problems. An electronic fuel injection system was developed for 351-ci engines used in pickups and Broncos. Ford engineers intended to adapt the system for the police 351-ci. Unfortunately, no one noticed until too late that the truck intake manifold was too high to fit under the Crown Victoria's hood. Since the 351-ci was a police-only option on passenger cars, the low volume of police cars sales did not warrant the expense of a special manifold. All the way through the 1991 model year, police cars were stuck with the Variable Venturi carburetor, a late 1970s attempt at meeting emissions laws without the expense of developing fuel injection. The 2-VV carburetor was only able to pass emissions tests with lean mixtures and further would not pass per-mile emissions limits with anything lower than a tall 2.73 axle ratio. Despite the poor acceleration, the 1986 Ford was an acceptable patrol car. Low repair costs, reasonable top speed, good brakes, and decent handling all were strong points.

For 1987, Chrysler submitted the low bid for patrol cars. Anxious to avoid the difficulties with previous Mopar M-bodied cars, the WSP specified bench seats for 1987. Since all 1987 Dodge Diplomat and Plymouth Gran Fury police package cars had bucket seats, the competition was narrowed to Ford and Chevy. Chevy won the 1987 and 1988 bids with the 350-ci Caprice. Popular with troopers due to responsive performance, the Caprices suffered more transmission and rear-end failures than the Fords.

For 1989, Ford won the bid with Crown Victorias. Again powered by the 351-ci 2-VV engine, the 1989s were considerably plusher than the 1986 cars. Improvements in the Variable Venturi carburetor resulted in cars that usually ran 100,000 miles without the carburetor rebuild that nearly all of the 1986s required. The 1989 Crown Victorias were the subject of the same complaints of slow off-the-line acceleration that had plagued the 1986 cars.

In 1990, the WSP bought 275 Caprices, in no small part due to the superior fuel economy of GM's proven throttle-body fuel injection system. Chevy also won the 1991 bid for 195 cars and again in 1992 with 235 additional Caprices delivered. Following the demise of the Mustang, the WSP experimented once again with midsize cars. Several police package 1990 Taurus were purchased and put in regular patrol service. Trooper complaints of instability at high speeds and strong torque steer during acceleration caused them to be withdrawn from patrol use. All were repainted and found use as either detective cars or as truck chasers.

When the 1993 patrol car bids came in, even though Chevrolet's bid was several hundred dollars per car lower, the bid was awarded to Ford on the basis of the new Crown Victoria's superior fuel economy.

Troopers had been well satisfied with the Caprice's performance. Obviously, the modular 4.6 liter Ford V-8, even with the greater efficiency of overhead-camshafts, promised lower levels of performance than the race proven 5.7 liter Chevy engine. Also, there was no durability data on the new engine in extended heavy-duty service. Regardless of these unknowns, due to purchasing division rules, the WSP was forced to buy the 1993 Fords. A total of 170 1993 Crown Victorias were delivered. In spite of the smaller engines, the 1993 Fords have held up very well in WSP service. After three years of use, with 60,000 to 80,000 miles on typical units, only two engines and one transmission have failed. The Fords are a bit slower than recent Chevys, but are fast enough to do the job. Troopers also praise the Crown Victorias for their interior comfort, as well as better visibility to the rear and sides.

For 1994, Chevrolet underbid Ford by just enough to win the bid, despite the fuel economy advantage of the smaller Ford engine. A total of 80 LT-1-equipped Caprices were purchased, the last Chevy patrol cars bought by the patrol.

Again in 1995, the WSP was having trouble with semi-truck speed enforcement. By careful usage of their mirrors and CB radio communication, the truckers were pretty successful at avoiding tickets. As all of the Mustangs were now out of service, the WSP bought a quantity of 1995 Taurus sedans. Painted a variety of civilian colors with no insignia or visible emergency lights, these cars are assigned to troopers in areas of I-5 and I-90 where speeding truckers are prevalent. In that limited role, they are considered satisfactory.

For 1995, 1996, and 1997, the WSP used the 4.6L Crown Victoria. In 1997, of course, Chevy had discontinued the Caprice, eliminating the Crown Victoria's only remaining competition. The later Fords continued the 1993's reputation as strong, reliable, comfortable, relatively economical albeit moderately performing patrol cars.

Currently, the WSP operates 990 Enforcement-class vehicles. Each trooper and sergeant is assigned his or her own car, usually keeping the same car from new until it is retired. Currently, cars are sold at public auction after reaching 100,000 miles. All cars are sold with all service records in the car, which is an advantage to prospective buyers.

After all the makes and models of patrol cars used over the years, many troopers have a special affection for the Fords. As retired Trooper Jim Jordan, put it, " . . . over the years Fords were the most dependable, they always got me home."

Chapter Seventeen

Ford Cop Car Quiz

Q: What is the only year a Ford police engine came with dual Holley 4-bbl carbs?
A: 1957 on the 270-horsepower, 312-ci V-8.

Q: What does FE, as in FE-block, stand for?
A: Ford-Edsel.

Q: What year was the flathead, L-head V-8 introduced?
A: 1932 on the 221-ci V-8.

Q: What year was the Ford police V-8 converted to overhead-valves?
A: 1954 on the 239-ci V-8.

Q: What year was the Ford police V-8 converted to single over-head-cam?
A: 1992 1/2 on the 4.6L V-8.

Q: What year was the two-speed automatic transmission introduced to law enforcement?
A: 1951 with the Fordomatic.

Q: What year was the three-speed automatic transmission introduced to police work?
A: 1958 with the Cruise-O-Matic.

Q: What year was the four-speed overdrive automatic introduced to police cars?
A: 1980 standard with the California 5.8L Police Package, optional with 5.0L and other 5.8L V-8s.

Q: In terms of brake horsepower, what was the most powerful Ford-marque engine ever used in police cars?
A: The 429-ci, 4-bbl with 11.3:1 compression and dual exhaust rated at 370 horsepower. This was used on the 1970 Fairlane/Torino and 1971 Custom and Torino.

Q: What is the largest displacement engine ever used in a Ford police car?
A: The 460-ci/7.5L V-8 used from 1973 through 1978.

Q: What was the first year a Ford police engine was rated at 300 brake horsepower or above?
A: 1958 with the 300-horsepower, 352-ci V-8 and the 303-horsepower, 361-ci V-8.

Q: What was the first FoMoCo police engine to be rated at 400 brake horsepower or above?
A: The 1958, 400-horsepower, 430-ci, 3x2-bbl "Super Marauder" V-8 used only on Mercury police cars.

Q: What year was the limited slip differential introduced on Ford police cars?
A: 1959 with the Equa-Lock.

Q: What were the two series of big-block Ford police engines?
A: The FE-series with 4.63-inch bore centers introduced in 1958 and the 385-series with 4.90-inch bore centers introduced to police cars in 1969.

Q: What was the first Ford police car engine to produce 1 (brake) horsepower per cubic inch?
A: No official Ford police engine has ever had one horsepower per cid. Same for Dodge and Plymouth. Chevrolet did with its 290-horsepower, 283-ci V-8; 350-horsepower, 348-ci V-8; and 425-horsepower, 409-ci V-8.

Q: What was Ford's first compact police package car?
A: 1962 Fairlane with a 115.5-inch wheelbase.

Q: What year was the rear suspension on the full-size Ford changed from leaf spring to coil spring?
A: 1965 on the Custom.

Q: What was the first Ford small-block V-8 used in a police car?
A: The 145-horsepower, 221-ci, 2-bbl designed for the 1962 Fairlane.

Q: What year did the full-size Ford get front disc brakes?
A: 1966.

Q: What popular retail engines were never used in Ford police cars?

A: 289-ci Hi-Po, Boss 302, Boss 351, Boss 429, any 406-ci V-8, any 427-ci V-8.

Q: In what year were rear disc brakes first available on a Ford police car?

A: 1976 through 1978, then re-introduced in 1992 1/2.

Q: The "7-litre" V-8 is the retail version of what police engine?

A: 428-ci V-8.

Q: Solid valve lifters were used on the highest performance police engines through what year and engine?

A: The 1966 428-ci Police Interceptor with 360 horsepower. The same 360-horsepower engine in 1967 used hydraulic lifters.

Q: When were radial tires first used on a Ford police package car?

A: 1967, but restricted to the 240-ci I-6 and 289-ci V-8 versions of the full-size Custom.

Q: What was the first police package four-wheel-drive vehicle?

A: The 1967 Ford Bronco.

Q: What famous police and retail small-block V-8 was introduced in 1968?

A: The 302-ci in both the 210-horsepower, 2-bbl police and retail version and the retail-only 230-horsepower, 4-bbl version.

Q: What was the first of the lightweight, 385-series big-blocks used in police cars?

A: 1969 429-ci V-8.

Q: What happened to the wheelbase on the full-size Ford for 1969?

A: Increased from 119 to 121 inches, the longest it would ever be.

Q: The 351-ci Windsor and 351-ci Cleveland had the same bore and stroke. Which one had the canted valvetrain?

A: The 351-ci Cleveland.

Q: Between the 351-ci Cleveland and 351-ci Windsor, which was generally available in the full-size Ford?

A: As a rule, the full-size cars got the Windsor, the midsize cars got the Cleveland.

Q: In what year were both the 360-horsepower, 428-ci and the 360-horsepower, 429-ci used as police engines?

A: 1970. The 428-ci was restricted to the full-size Custom while this 429-ci mill was restricted to the midsize Fairlane 500.

Q: In some years, Ford's midsize police car had an engine more powerful than its full-size police car. What years and what engines?

A: In 1970, the 370-horsepower, 429-ci in the Fairlane outpowered the 360-horsepower, 428-ci in the Custom. In 1972, the 248-horsepower, 351-ci in the Torino had more power than the 212-horsepower, 429-ci in the Custom. In 1973, the 266-horsepower, 351-ci in the Torino had a higher rating than the 219-horsepower, 460-ci in the Custom.

Q: What new 385-series big-block was released for police cars in 1973?

A: The 219-horsepower 460-ci Police Interceptor V-8.

Q: Put the confusing line of 335-series Cleveland big-block police engines in chronological order.

A: The original 351-ci Cleveland from 1970 to 1974, then the stroked and raised block 400-ci from 1971 to 1978, then the destroked, raised block 351-ci Modified from 1975 to 1980. The 351-ci Windsor is not in this family of engines.

Q: What year did Ford police car engines get converted to unleaded gasoline requiring catalytic converters?

A: 1975.

Q: In 1974, a product to lower maintenance and improve fuel economy was optional on all Ford police cars. What was it?

A: Steel-belted radial tires.

Q: Was the "midsize" LTD II ever larger than the "full-size" LTD?

A: Yes, in 1979. The LTD had just been reduced from a 121-inch wheelbase to a 114.4-inch wheelbase. The LTD II kept its 118-inch wheelbase for a half model year before being discontinued in police work.

Q: What new induction system was introduced on 1979 Ford police cars?

A: The 2-bbl Variable Venturi carb made by Motorcraft for the 351-ci Windsor V-8.

Q: What Ford was a part of the 1979 CHP Special Purpose Vehicle Study?

A: The 302-ci, 2-bbl Fairmont 105.5-inch wheelbase four-door sedan.

Q: What new police engine was released in the 1980 Fairmont?

A: The 255-ci V-8, a debored 302-ci.

Q: During what one year, after the mid-1950s, was overall police car performance so bleak that no police car of any kind reached 120 miles per hour?

A: 1981, when the fastest police car was the 351-ci HO LTD at 116.4 miles per hour.

Q: In 1982, Ford introduced what police vehicle?

A: The Special Service package Mustang, Ford's most famous police car.

Q: In 1983, what change took place to the 302-ci V-8?

A: The change from a 2-bbl or 2-VV carburetor to central fuel injection.

Q: Between 1959 and 1989, the California Highway Patrol selected FoMoCo cars as Enforcement-Class vehicles just twice. What were the years and cars?

A: 1970 Mercury Monterey with 428-ci V-8, 1984 Ford Crown Victoria with 351-ci HO V-8.

Q: What was significant about the 302-ci HO engines in the 1984 and 1985 Special Service Mustang?

A: They were available with either a 4-bbl carb or central fuel injection. The 4-bbl version was 40 horsepower more powerful.

Q: What year did the Crown Victoria and Mustang get sequential multi-port fuel injection?

A: 1986 on the 302-ci engines replacing both central fuel injection and 4-bbl carburetion.

Q: What is the highest top speed ever officially timed by the Michigan State Police for the Special Service Mustang?

A: 139.6 miles per hour from the 1987 5.0L HO Mustang with five-speed stick and 3.08 rear gears.

Q: When in the 1980s was the Crown Vic restyled from the abruptly square, Diplomat-look to the rounded-look that cased in the front bumper?

A: 1988, the first major styling change since 1979.

Q: According to the Michigan State Police test method, which includes a driver and passenger for all acceleration, braking, and top speed tests, what is the best quarter-mile performance from a Special Service package Mustang?

A: In 1993, the 5.0L HO five-speed Mustang with 3.08 gears ran the quarter in 15.22 seconds at 92.4 miles per hour.

Q: What totally new kind of police vehicle was introduced by Ford in 1990?

A: Ford's first front-wheel-drive police car, the 3.8L Taurus, with a heavy-duty police package.

Q: In the history of Ford police cars, which ones had four-wheel disc brakes?

A: 1976 to 1978 Custom 500 and LTD, 1990 to 1995 Taurus, 1992 1/2 to current Crown Victoria.

Q: In 1991, which four-door Ford sedan had the fastest MSP road course time, quickest 0 to 100-miles-per-hour acceleration, best brakes and highest top speed?

A: The 3.8L Taurus with the 55A police package.

Q: What is the quickest way to spot a 1990 or 1991 police package Taurus?

A: The grille has cooling slots on either side of the Ford blue oval emblem.

Q: What were at least two things new about the 1992 1/2 Crown Vic?

A: 4.6L SOHC V-8, electronic four-speed automatic overdrive trans, four-wheel discs, ABS with Traction Assist, speed-sensitive power steering, aerodynamic styling, 0.1 inch longer wheelbase, passenger side air bag.

Q: What Ford police car was discontinued after 1993, having served since 1982?

A: Special service package 5.0L Mustang LX.

Q: The change to the EEC-V engine control computer for the Crown Vic in 1995 resulted in what record-setting performance?

A: Breaking the 130-miles-per-hour top speed barrier for the first time since the 428-ci Cobra Jet engine.

Q: Did the full-size, 4.6L Crown Vic ever equal the top speed of the 5.0L HO Mustang?

A: Yes, 135 miles per hour in 1996.

Q: What is the 5.4L V-8?

A: A stroked version of the 4.6L SOHC "modular" V-8, rated at 230 horsepower, developed for the 1997 Expedition, and long hoped as an optional engine for the Crown Vic.

Grading Scale

Give yourself one point for each question you answer correctly.

55 to 58 correct: *Excellent*; genuine Ford historian status.

50 to 54 correct: *Very Good*; consider writing a Ford column for one of the police car clubs.

45 to 49 correct: *Good*; you know Fords but probably have your mind cluttered with Chevy stuff too.

40 to 44 correct: *Fair*; is that a front-wheel drive, four-cylinder in your garage?

0 to 39 correct: *Poor*; an obvious Volvo-lover.

Appendix A
Contributors

Benton County, Indiana, Sheriff Butch Pritchett
Boatwright, Mark, Idaho photo
Booth, Robert, 1987 Texas DPS Mustang
Bryant, Shane, 1971 SCHP Custom 500
Bujosa, John, EVOOA president and founder
Carroll, John, Canadian photos
Color Tech, Gene Coffing and staff
Dingell, Jim, Mustang Special Service Registry founder
Donohoe, James, Louisiana photos
Fay, Michael, Canadian and New England photos
Fellenzer, Jack, 1965 Mayberry Custom
Ford Division, government sales manager Robert Williams
Ford Division General Fleet Office, Jack LaBelle
Ford Division police and taxi design engineer Thomas Stevens
Ford Division General Fleet Office, Anthony Gratson
Ford Division Crown Vic platform engineer Lee Smith
Ford Division General Fleet Office, Mary Spitery
Ford Division Public Affairs, Thomas Hoxie
Ford Division Public Affairs, William O'Neil
Ford Division Taurus platform engineer Ed Ruthinowski
Ford Division General Fleet Office, Emil Loeffler
Ford Division, Public Affairs, Della DiPietro
Ford, Mike, 1950 LAPD Ford
Gasperetti, David, 1975 Ford LTD
Hastings, Nebraska Police, Lieutenant Monty McCord
Honchell, Tim 1976 Starsky and Hutch Torino
Huntington County, Indiana Sheriff Rod Jackson, 1938 Ford
Indiana State Police, curator Jerry Federspiel
Indiana State Police, Sergeant Rick Hammer
Indiana State Police, Sergeant Dave Morrison
Johnson, Quay, 1969 SCHP Galaxie 500
Johnson, Charles, 1969 SCHP Galaxie
Kemp, Neal, New England photos
Kieffer, Mick "Barney," 1963 Mayberry Ford
Law and Order, Bruce Cameron, editorial director
Law and Order, Tom Yates, vehicle specialist
Law Enforcement Technology, Donna Rogers, editorial director
Law Enforcement Technology, Tricia Walsh McGlone, editor
Los Angeles Police Historical Society, Sergeant Chuck Shaw
Los Angeles County Sheriff Department, Sergeant Michael Borges
Los Angeles County Sheriff Department, Donald Sachs
Los Angeles County Sheriff Department, George Ducolumbier, public information

Los Angeles County Sheriff Department, Lieutenant Robert Sedita
Los Angeles Police Historical Society, Officer Karen Klobuchar
Madderom, Chuck, Edsel photos
Martin, John, 1951 Ford
McElhearn, Kirby, New England photos
Michigan State Police, Lieutenant Curt VanDenBerg, (retired)
Michigan State Police, Trooper Doug Lubahn
Michigan State Police, Trooper Mark Reaves
Michigan State Police, Trooper David Halliday
Michigan State Police, Sergeant Denny Steendam
Michigan State Police, Dawn Brinningstaull, timer
Michigan State Police, Shirley Goodson, photo technician
Michigan State Police, Sergeant Bob Ring
Michigan State Police, Sergeant Bill McFall
Michigan State Police, Trooper Scott Beard
Michigan State Police, Sergeant Dave Storer (retired)
Missouri State Highway Patrol, Captain Terry Moore
Morgan County, Missouri, Sheriff, Deputy Ray Miller, 1989, 1990, and 1993 Mustang
Murphy, Marvin, 1961 Mayberry Ford
Murrell, Ed, 1991 OSHP Crown Victoria
Muscle Mustangs and Fast Fords, Jim Campisano, editor
North Carolina Highway Patrol, Sergeant M. K. Holcomb
Oklahoma Highway Patrol, Lieutenant Roy Brown
Old Cars, John Gunnell, editor
Old Cars, Phil Skinner
Pinellas County, Florida, Sheriff, Sergeant Robert Helmick
Post, Jim, PCOOA president and founder
Rice, Bob, New England photos
River Oaks, Texas, Police Chief Terry Fiene
Russell, Paul, New York photos
Seymour, Thomas, 1989 Attica, Indiana, LTD Crown Victoria
Stiegelmaier, Douglas, New England photos
Sokolofsky, Glenn, WSP photos
Taylor, Chris, RCMP-GRC photo
Washington State Patrol, Chief Annette Sandberg
Washington State Patrol, Trooper Jim Jordan
Washington State Patrol, Trooper Larry McKissick
Washington State Patrol, Trooper Don Ginter
Washington State Patrol, Sergeant Ed McCullar
Washington State Patrol, Trooper Jack Sareault
Watson, Chris, 1970 CHP Mercury
West Virginia State Police, Corporal. A. W. Robinson
Yeaw, John, California Highway Patrol (retired)

Appendix B
Sources for Cars & Parts

A. Other Police Car Books

Cars of the State Police and Highway Patrol by Lieutenant Monty McCord

Chevrolet Police Cars, 1955–1996 by Corporal Ed Sanow

Dodge, Plymouth & Chrysler Police Cars, 1956–1978 by Corporal Ed Sanow and Corporal John Bellah

Dodge, Plymouth & Chrysler Police Cars, 1979–1994 by Corporal Ed Sanow and Corporal John Bellah with Galen Govier

Modern Police Cars by Robert Genat

Police Cars, A Graphic History by Bruce Cameron

Police Cars, A Photographic History by Lieutenant Monty McCord

Vintage Police Cars by Corporal Ed Sanow

All books are available from Classic Motorbooks, P.O. Box 1, Osceola, WI 54020; 800-826-6600, or Krause Publications, 700 E. State Street, Iola, WI 54990; 800-258-0929.

B. Police and Car Clubs

The Andy Griffith Show (TAGS) Rerun Watchers Club
Jim Clark, Editor
9 Music Square South, #146
Nashville, TN 37203-3203
Newsletter: *The Bullet* (quarterly) $10

Emergency Vehicle Owners and Operators Association (EVOOA)
John Bujosa, President
West 14311 Lincoln Road
Olympia, WA 99204-9398
Newsletter: *Code-4* (bi-monthly) $30

Police Car Owners of America (PCOOA)
c/o Jim Post, President
Route 6, Box 345B
Eureka Springs, AR 72632
Newsletter: *Rapsheet* (quarterly) $20

C. Police Badge, Patch, and Memorabilia Shows

Police Collectors News
Mike Bondarenko, Editor
R.R. #1, Box 14
Baldwin, WI 54002
Newsletter: *PCNews* (monthly) $22

D. Vintage Police Car Literature

Ed Faxon's Auto Literature
1655 East 6th Street
Corona, CA 91719

Darryl Lindsay
Code 3 Collectibles
P.O. Box 412
San Carlos, CA 94070
(also photos, equipment)

Walter Miller
6710 Brooklawn
Syracuse, NY 13211

E. New/Used/Rebuilt Emergency Equipment

Jack Attig
P.O. Box 407
Meriden, KS 66512
(used police gear)

Charles Brooks
Chanute Radar Service
15 South Highland
Chanute, KS 66720
(new and used radar)

John Dorgan
The Engine House
7381 E. Stella Road
Tuscon, AZ 85730
(used police gear)

Dave Dotson
501 North Vine Street
Sparta, IL 62286
(new and used gear)

Gall's Inc.
2470 Palumbo Drive
Lexington, KY 40555
(new police gear)

Rick Osbon
P.O. Box 782
Elmhurst, IL 60126
(used police gear)

Jim Post
Police Collectibles
Route 6, Box 345B
Eureka Springs, AR 72632
(new and used gear)

Darren Pupo
Emergency Equipment Systems
1429 Maplegrove Drive
Fairborn, OH 45324
(vintage radar)

Dennis Sanchez
1205 W. Main Street
Festus, MO 63028
(used police gear)

F. Used Police Car Dealers

Blue Streak Motors
1703 Cannonsburg Road
Ashland, KY 41102

Cruisers Unlimited
1108 Malvern Street
Middletown, OH 45042

Day Ford
3696 William Penn Highway
Monroeville, PA 15146

Diversifleet
7150 Kaw Drive
Kansas City, KS 66111

Donna Motors
15 Roosevelt Avenue
Bellville, NJ 07109

Excellent Auto Sales
269 Page Boulevard
Springfield, MA 01104

Live Oak Auto Center
34906 Louisana Highway 1019
Denham Springs, LA 70726

Mossberg Specialty Cars
Route 48
Wall, PA 15148

Pursuit Unlimited
1329 N. Harrison
Shawnee, OK 74801

Rinto Enterprises
2077 W. Roosevelt Road
Wheaton, IL 60187

Sun Chevrolet
104-108 W. Genesee
Chittenango, NY 13037

Veto Enterprises
212 W. Exchange Street
Sycamore, IL 60178

Woodside Motors
43-29 Crescent Street
Long Island City, NY 11101

Appendix C
Ford V-8 Engine Families, 1955-1997

Y-block
272 ci, 292 ci, 312 ci

Small-block 90-degree V-8 Windsor
221 ci, 260 ci, 289 ci, 289 horsepower, 302 ci, Boss 302, 351W

FE-series Big-block
332 ci, 352 ci, 360 ci, 361 ci, 390 ci, 391 ci, 406 ci, 410 ci, 427 ci, 428 ci

335-series Cleveland Big-block
351C, 351M, Boss 351, 400 ci

385-series Big-block
429 ci, Boss 429, 429 CJ, 460 ci

Modular SOHC V-8
4.6L, 5.4L (proposed)

Author Biography

About the Author: Edwin J. Sanow

Ed Sanow received his bachelor of science degree from Purdue University. Sanow raced cars before he got his driver's license. He oval raced a 1963 Galaxie stock car on dirt tracks, drag-raced a 1962 tri-power Catalina, and ran collegiate go-karts. Sanow raced a 1967 SCCA Mustang on road courses in the Midwest for seven years. He is a graduate of the Bob Bondurant School of High Performance Driving, Summit Point's BSR, Inc. Tactical Driving School, and SkidCar USA's Vehicle Control Course. Sanow currently serves as the pursuit driving advisor for the Benton County, Indiana, Sheriff's Office. He has been a sheriff's deputy with the BCSO since 1986 and also serves as their firearms, chemical agents, and in-service police instructor. Sanow is the senior reserve officer, holds the rank of corporal, and is one of the most active traffic officers in the county. Sanow's articles on muscle cars and police cars have appeared in *AutoWeek*, *Old Cars Weekly*, *Chrysler Power*, *Muscle Mustangs*, *High Performance Mopar*, *Chevy High Performance*, *Super Chevy*, *Super Ford*, *Mopar Muscle*, *MorPerformance*, *Muscle Cars of the 60s/70s*, *Chevy Truck*, *Law and Order*, *Police*, *Law Enforcement Technology*, *Kansas Trooper*, and *Chevrolet Motor Division's Professionals*.

Sanow is the lead co-author of the books *Dodge, Plymouth & Chrysler Police Cars, 1956–1978* and *Dodge, Plymouth & Chrysler Police Cars, 1979–1994* and the author of *Vintage Police Cars* and *Chevrolet Police Cars*. Sanow makes the police car circuit with his 1972 police package, Frohna, Missouri Police 402-ci-big-block Chevrolet Bel

Cpl. Ed Sanow with a 1997 Ford Crown Victoria Police Interceptor.

Air and his 1987 police package, Oxford, Indiana Police 318-ci small-block Dodge Diplomat. Sanow attends the annual police vehicle tests conducted by the Michigan State Police and the Los Angeles County Sheriff. He is the Indiana state representative for the Police Car Owners of America (PCOOA) and the Emergency Vehicle Owners and Operators Association (EVOOA).

About the Author: Matt Campbell

Matt Campbell is a 27-year-old photojournalist who lives in Saginaw, Michigan. He is a graduate of the University of Missouri School of Journalism and is currently employed as the sole contract photographer in the state of Michigan for the international wire service Agence France-Presse. Campbell is also a part-time staff photographer for the *Saginaw News* and the *Bay City Times* and is a stringer for the *Flint Journal*. Matt has worked for eight newspapers in Michigan, Missouri, and Massachusetts over the past eight years and has had photographs published in many of the country's major newspapers including *The New York Times*, *L.A. Times*, *The Washington Post*, *USA Today*, *Boston Globe,* and many others. His photographs and writing have also appeared in several books both related and unrelated to police cars.

Campbell has been a member of the Police Car Owners of America since 1993 and his collection of retired police cars has included a 1988 Ford Crown Victoria, a 1990 Ford Special Service Mustang, a 1992 Ford Crown Victoria, and a 1994 Chevy Caprice. He became interested in police vehicles while working as a reporter for the Columbia, Missouri, *Missourian* as a police reporter covering the Missouri State Highway Patrol. Several photos in the Mustang chapter of this book are from that time period.

Campbell lives with his wife, Kim Chapin, the design editor of the *Saginaw News* and also a graduate of the University of Missouri School of Journalism, and their two cats, Murphy and Aikiko.

About the Author: Bill Hattersley

Bill Hattersley, a southern California native, has lived in the Seattle, Washington, area since 1976. A history major in college, Hattersley minored in Traffic Safety Education. He spent 10 years teaching behind-the-wheel and classroom driver's education. A fire engine and police car buff, Hattersley turned his hobby into a business. He currently writes articles and shoots photos for *Fire Apparatus Journal*, takes calendar and advertising photos of fire rigs, and sells police car and fire engine photos by mail order. Hattersley currently owns a 1990 ex-Washington State Patrol 350-ci Caprice that he uses as a daily driver. (He wishes he bought the ex-WSP 1989 5.8L Crown Vic instead of the Caprice, when both were at the same state police auction!) He lives with wife, Carol, and their cat, Libby, in Seattle. He enjoys collecting and shooting .22-caliber rifles, collects model vehicles, and follows NASCAR racing on television.

Index